LIBERTY, DESERT AND THE MARKET
A Philosophical Study

Are inequalities of income created by the free market just? In this book Serena Olsaretti examines two main arguments that justify those inequalities: the first claims that they are just because they are deserved, and the second claims that they are just because they are what free individuals are entitled to. Both these arguments purport to show, in different ways, that giving responsible individuals their due requires that free market inequalities in incomes be allowed. Olsaretti argues, however, that neither argument is successful, and shows that when we examine closely the principle of desert and the notions of liberty and choice invoked by defenders of the free market, it appears that a conception of justice that would accommodate these notions, far from supporting free market inequalities, calls for their elimination. Her book will be of interest to a wide range of readers in political philosophy, political theory and normative economics.

SERENA OLSARETTI is Lecturer at the Faculty of Philosophy, University of Cambridge and Fellow of St John's College, Cambridge. She is the editor of *Desert and Justice* (2003) and has also published in the *Journal of Political Philosophy* and *Utilitas*.

LIBERTY, DESERT AND THE MARKET

A Philosophical Study

SERENA OLSARETTI
University of Cambridge

CAMBRIDGE
UNIVERSITY PRESS

PUBLISHED BY THE PRESS SYNDICATE OF THE UNIVERSITY OF CAMBRIDGE
The Pitt Building, Trumpington Street, Cambridge, United Kingdom

CAMBRIDGE UNIVERSITY PRESS
The Edinburgh Building, Cambridge, CB2 2RU, UK
40 West 20th Street, New York, NY 10011–4211, USA
477 Williamstown Road, Port Melbourne, VIC 3207, Australia
Ruiz de Alarcón 13, 28014 Madrid, Spain
Dock House, The Waterfront, Cape Town 8001, South Africa

http://www.cambridge.org

First published 2004

Printed in the United Kingdom at the University Press, Cambridge

Typeface Adobe Garamond 11/12.5 pt.   *System* LATEX 2$_\varepsilon$ [TB]

A catalogue record for this book is available from the British Library

ISBN 0 521 83635 2 hardback

To my father, Antonio Olsaretti (1936–2004),
with gratitude and love

Contents

Acknowledgements

This book is based on my D. Phil. dissertation, which I undertook under the supervision of G. A. Cohen. I am very grateful to him for his unwaveringly probing comments as a supervisor, and to Alan Ryan and Hillel Steiner, who examined the dissertation and offered both insightful critical feedback and supportive guidance over how to revise the material into a book. I am also indebted to Raymond Geuss and Peter Vallentyne, who have read a draft of the whole book and provided me with invaluable constructive criticism.

Over the last few years I have received comments on various parts of the manuscript from various other people, and I would like to thank, in particular, Ian Carter, Matt Kramer, Ingrid Robeyns and Andrew Williams. Special thanks go to Paul Bou-Habib for his comments on various versions of various chapters. I have also benefited from the input of audiences to which I have presented material from this book, including audiences at the conference on 'Freedom and Choice: Theory and Applications' at the University of Pavia, the Political Studies Association Conference in Manchester, the Philosophy Seminar in Manchester, the 'Desert and Justice' Conference in Cambridge, the Philosophy Seminar in Sheffield and the Political Theory Seminar at the London School of Economics. I should also like to thank Hilary Gaskin and Hilary Hammond of Cambridge University Press.

Finally, many thanks to Emmanuel College, Cambridge, for a research fellowship that enabled me to complete work on this book, and to St John's College for providing an ideal setting for bringing it to completion.

Chapter 2 is a revised version of 'Distributive Justice and Compensatory Desert', in S. Olsaretti (ed.), *Desert and Justice* (Oxford University Press, 2003); chapter 3 is a revised and expanded version of 'Desert and Luck', in D. Bell and A. de Shalit (eds.), *Forms of Justice* (Rowman & Littlefield, 2002); chapters 5 and 6 draw and expand on 'Freedom, Force and Choice: Against the Rights-Based Definition of Voluntariness', *Journal of Political Philosophy* 6 (1998). I thank Oxford University Press, Rowman & Littlefield and Blackwell for allowing me to republish this material.

Introduction

'The time when "we are all socialists"', H. B. Acton said in 1971, 'is the very time to reconsider the morality of the free market.'[1] Three decades later, this dictum may, as it were, be reversed. The time when the market is, in its different variants, unanimously taken as a given across the political spectrum, is the very time to subject the morality of the market to critical scrutiny.

The question 'Should we have a market?' is now, and for an indefinite time, off the agenda. As is now nearly universally acknowledged, there are overwhelming arguments in favour of market-based economies. One such argument is the informational or epistemic one: the market, as a process whereby property rights are exchanged and decisions by suppliers of goods and services made and adjusted in light of prices, is a discovery procedure that allows valuable information dispersed throughout society to be transmitted.[2] Furthermore, as the incentive argument for the market emphasises, the price mechanism acts as a signalling device for what demand there is for what goods and services, and, by so doing, it offers suppliers an incentive to supply what is in demand by way of prospects of increased profits. Arguments of this sort are amongst the reasons that have lead even those who have been traditionally suspicious about the market's justification, such as socialists, to recast their views in a way that makes room for some role for it.[3]

Whilst these efficiency-based justifications of the market are well known and rarely contested today, the question is still open as to whether the

---

[1] H. B. Acton, *The Morals of Markets: An Ethical Exploration* (Harlow: Longman, 1971), p. 2.

[2] F. A. Hayek, *Individualism and Economic Order* (London: Routledge & Kegan Paul, 1949).

[3] See A. Nove, *The Economics of Feasible Socialism* (London: HarperCollins, 1991); D. Miller, *Market, State and Community. Theoretical Foundations of Market Socialism* (Oxford: Clarendon Press, 1989); C. Pierson, *Socialism after Communism. The New Market Socialism* (Cambridge: Polity, 1995); J. Roemer, *A Future for Socialism* (Harvard University Press, 1994), among others. Socialists also appeal to other considerations as relevant for their support of the market, but efficiency is certainly a central one.

defender of the market can seize the 'moral high ground' thus far occupied by its critics.[4] Attempts at seizing such grounds are made especially arduous by problems regarding the justice of distributions of benefits and burdens generated by the free market. By 'free market' I refer to the free or unregulated process whereby full private property rights are exchanged, so that goods and services over which people have rights are transferred and exchanged at whatever conditions the individuals whose rights these are choose. That the distributional consequences of free market choices raise serious concerns for justice seems so undeniable to some commentators that they find that arguments which try to establish otherwise merit relatively little attention.[5] Yet, for defenders of the free market to be able to occupy the moral high ground, showing that the distributional consequences of free market choices are compatible with justice is a central objective. If it could be shown that the free market produces distributively just outcomes, then the case for the free market would altogether be very strong indeed.

This book is concerned with those attempts at trying to show that the free market can, its critics notwithstanding, produce outcomes that are just. In particular, I examine two of the most important lines of justification that have been offered in defence of unregulated market outcomes.[6] The first appeals to a substantive principle of distributive justice, namely the principle of desert. Market rewards are here viewed as deserved either as compensation for the non-monetary costs attached to different occupations, or as remuneration for one's productive contribution. As I will show, these justifications of free market inequalities enjoy some support among political philosophers, and they constitute the seemingly most promising, though ultimately unsuccessful, ways of showing that the unregulated market can be substantively just.

The second line of justification appeals to individual rights of self-ownership and of private property over external resources, together with

[4] J. Gray, *The Moral Foundations of Market Institutions* (London: IEA Health and Welfare Unit, 1992), see pp. 16–17 in particular.

[5] C. R. Sunstein, *Free Markets and Social Justice* (Oxford University Press, 1997), p. 386; J. O'Neill, *The Market. Ethics, Knowledge, and Politics* (London and New York: Routledge, 1998), p. 3.

[6] Throughout, by 'market' I refer to 'unregulated market' or 'free market'. By talking of the 'free' or 'unregulated' market I by no means want to imply that no institutional regulations and norms are needed to sustain the market. Institutions of private property and of contract, together with a host of social norms and psychological dispositions, are constitutive of a free market, but I do not explore these much discussed issues here. For discussions of these issues, see, for example, K. Polany, *Origins of our Time. The Great Transformation* (London: Victor Gollancz, 1945); R. M. Titmuss, *The Gift Relationship* (New York: Pantheon, 1971); B. Barber, 'Absolutization of the Market: Some Notes on How we Got from There to Here', in G. Dworkin, G. Bermant and P. G. Brown (eds.), *Markets and Morals* (New York: Halsted Press, 1977). Note also that I leave aside problems to do with market imperfections, and assume a competitive free market.

related notions of liberty, choice and of procedural justice. Unregulated market outcomes, in this view, are just insofar as they are the result of the exchange of legitimately acquired and transferred private property rights individuals have over themselves and worldly resources. Whatever distributions of rewards result from such exchanges are just so long as they respect certain constraints on just appropriation and transfer.

For the sake of exposition, I will refer to these two main arguments as *desert-based* and *entitlement-based* justifications of the free market respectively. By this I mean that both desert-based and entitlement-based arguments aim to justify the distributional consequences of market choices. Whilst both defend unregulated market outcomes, they clearly do this in different ways, however, and it may be helpful to note at the outset three salient differences between them.

First, the primary subject of justice is different in the two justifications. With desert-based arguments, the primary subjective of justice are outcomes, patterns or distributions of burdens and benefits, whereas with entitlement-based arguments individual acts are the primary subject of justice, and distributions are only derivatively just.[7] When we ask whether everyone in a society has what he *deserves*, we are asking whether a given distribution of resources matches a certain pattern. When we ask whether everyone in society has what he or she is *entitled* to, by contrast, we are asking whether a given distribution has come about through rights-respecting steps, and whether or not such a distribution reflects any pattern is irrelevant for its justice.

A second difference between desert-based and entitlement-based arguments is as follows. Whilst both can be seen to be defences of the 'unregulated market', what the latter comprises is different in the two cases. With the desert-based arguments I examine here, the 'unregulated market' refers only to the labour market, so that the incomes people reap is the market price for their labour. The free labour market, according to defenders of the market who appeal to desert, is part of a market economy in which intervention in other spheres may well be allowed.[8] However, what

---

[7] See H. A. Bedau, 'Social Justice and Social Institutions', *Midwest Studies in Philosophy*, vol. III (University of Minnesota Press, 1978).

[8] One area in which such interference is typically allowed is in the enforcement of meritocratic, or equality of opportunity, policies. But this interference does not, it is assumed, affect labour prices. Note that the appeal to desert in justifications of meritocracy is not something I examine here. There is a distinction between the question of whether the differential rewards of different activities is justified on grounds of desert, on the one hand, and the question of how particular individuals should be recruited for differentially remunerated jobs, on the other. In this book I am concerned with the first, not the second, question.

is crucial for our purposes is that, while such intervention may or may not affect other benefits people receive, it is supposed that it will not affect the 'earned' incomes they reap, which are said to be deserved. This is important because, if income inequalities are deserved, then the burden of justification on those who defend redistributive measures in the name of other principles of justice, such as need, is very great. With entitlement-based defences of the unregulated market, by contrast, the 'unregulated market' refers to the unfettered exercise of all private property rights, including the right to one's labour. Individuals are seen to have full private property rights over their mind and body, as well as over any worldly resources they acquire in line with the principle of justice in acquisition and transfer. Consequently, what entitlement-based arguments provide, standardly, is a justification of a full market society in which everything is owned by individuals or by voluntary associations of individuals.

Finally, a third difference between desert-based and entitlement-based arguments concerns the sense in which they provide a 'justification' of the market. With entitlement-based arguments, an endorsement of certain fundamental individual rights – rights of self-ownership and, possibly, of ownership of worldly resources – is argued to yield a justification of the unbridled market: the market is not valued derivatively, but is seen as 'part and parcel' of the exercise of those pregiven rights.[9] Desert-based arguments, by contrast, provide 'justifications' of the market in a weaker sense: some desert theorists do not deny that a desert-based distribution of incomes may, in principle, be achieved in a non-market economy, but they insist that market-generated incomes, too, are rewards that reflect individuals' deserts.

Despite these differences, both desert-based and entitlement-based arguments are, for present purposes, viewed as attempts to provide justifications of the free market. Although desert-based arguments focus primarily on the justice of distributions of earned incomes while entitlement-based ones emphasise the justice of outcomes produced by individual acts involving the exchange of private property rights, both converge in claiming that the free market is a just distributive mechanism, and that free market-generated income inequalities are just.[10]

[9] See A. Sen, 'The Moral Standing of the Market', in E. F. Paul, F. D. Miller and J. Paul (eds.), *Ethics and Economics* (Oxford: Blackwell, 1985), pp. 1–19.

[10] The focus on *income* inequalities, in particular, should not be taken to reflect a conviction that income is itself of fundamental moral significance, or that it is the only thing that has significance. Income inequalities matter insofar as income is an all-purpose means that enables individuals to pursue their conception of the good life and contributes to securing the conditions in which to achieve well-being.

This book, then, examines in depth these two main attempts at showing that the free market can occupy the 'moral high ground'. In so doing, it leaves a host of related issues concerning the justice and ethics of markets to one side. One such issue concerns the scope of the market. Even if a society commits itself to economic liberalism, as I have suggested earlier it is widely thought any society must do, there is room and, indeed, urgent need for a critical discussion about the justifiable extent of the market domain.[11] Other issues that will not be explicitly addressed in what follows include general questions of whether social justice requires markets,[12] of whether and how the market can be regulated in order to reach justice, of whether some other moral value justifies the free market,[13] and the issue of the moral status of welfare-based arguments for the market.[14]

These questions are certainly of great significance for the ethics of markets, and some of the ground covered in what follows does have implications for some of them. The entitlement-based defence of the free market, for example, is an argument for the unfettered exercise of private property rights, and for the unlimited extension of the market domain, in that it holds that everything can be legitimately owned and exchanged by individuals. To the extent that individuals have rights of full self-ownership, they may justifiably alienate or transfer for money any bodily or mental powers and resources. Entitlement-based defences of the free market, then, have clear implications for the scope of the market domain, as do some of the claims I make in analysing such defences. Yet while this and other questions are obviously important, and while the views developed in this book are by no means neutral *vis-à-vis* them, I have decided to deal with them only tangentially, so as to make room for my central objective, that of subjecting to scrutiny desert-based and entitlement-based justifications of the free market.

Pursuing this objective, as will appear in what follows, requires an in-depth examination of some of the central notions utilised by defenders of the market, which have so far, in my view, not been subjected to sufficiently close scrutiny. The ensuing analysis is fruitful both insofar as it reveals fatal

---

[11] See E. Anderson, *Value in Ethics and Economics* (Harvard University Press, 1993); M. J. Radin, *Contested Commodities* (Harvard University Press, 1996).

[12] See R. Dworkin, *Sovereign Virtue* (Harvard University Press, 2000), chapter 2.

[13] See Gray, *Moral Foundations of Market Institutions*. For a critique of arguments for the market that appeal to neutrality, human welfare, autonomy, epistemic considerations and self-interest, see J. O'Neill, *The Market. Ethics, Knowledge, and Politics* (London and New York: Routledge, 1998).

[14] See A. M. Okun, *Equality and Efficiency: The Big Trade-Off* (Washington, DC: Brookings Institution, 1975), and D. Hausman and M. S. McPherson, *Economic Analysis and Moral Philosophy* (Cambridge University Press, 1996), especially pp. 43–4.

weaknesses of these arguments and insofar as it casts light on notions which these arguments utilise and which, I believe, a defensible conception of distributive justice should accommodate. The investigation I undertake in this book, then, while primarily focusing on a critical examination of desert-based and entitlement-based defences of the free market, also generates insights into the principle of desert, the notion of voluntariness and the theory of personal responsibility which, I argue, we must adopt and which, rather than sanctioning free market outcomes, provide a justification for regulating the market.

To see why an in-depth examination of desert-based and entitlement-based arguments for the free market is needed, consider, first, desert-based justifications. An analysis of the role of desert in justifying market outcomes seems particularly timely. In discussions about welfare and the need for its reform, desert has been appealed to as a principle for guiding social policy. Some welfare policies, it is claimed, have failed to recognise that we must refrain from rewarding the undeserving poor.[15] At the same time, the principle of desert has been attracting growing attention among political philosophers, some of whom claim to find support for their adoption of desert as a principle of justice in the fact that so doing squares up nicely with ordinary attitudes toward desert and distributive justice.[16] The desert debate has been intermittent, however, and mostly dominated by defenders of desert, with sceptics of desert mostly relinquishing discussion of it. The result is a fairly eclectic collection of contributions by desert theorists whose views differ widely, and a careful analysis of the role of desert in justifying market-generated inequalities is, I believe, seriously wanted.

The motivation for examining entitlement-based defences of the unbridled market is somewhat different. The debate following and around Robert Nozick's *Anarchy, State, and Utopia* – which to date remains the most significant contribution to right-libertarianism – has been considerably more sustained and richer than the desert debate.[17] My view, however, is that some central concepts employed in both the defence and critique of libertarianism have not been fully brought out and analysed. In particular, the extent to which freedom and voluntariness, as a notion distinct from that of freedom, play a role in the libertarian argument for the free

---

[15] See R. J. Arneson, 'Egalitarianism and the Undeserving Poor', *Journal of Political Philosophy* 5 (1997), pp. 327–50.

[16] D. Miller, 'Distributive Justice: What the People Think', *Ethics* 102 (1992), pp. 555–93 and reprinted in his *Principles of Social Justice* (Harvard University Press, 1999).

[17] R. Nozick, *Anarchy, State, and Utopia* (Oxford: Blackwell, 1974). From now on I will refer to right-libertarianism as 'libertarianism' *simpliciter*.

market has not been sufficiently appreciated. Nozick's own analysis of the notions he employs is altogether disappointing, and the contributions of other right-libertarians are not more enlightening in this respect. Those critiques of libertarianism that have focused on Nozick's appeal to freedom have also failed to distinguish between voluntariness and freedom, and to provide a satisfactory account of the way in which freedom, voluntariness and related notions of coercion and responsibility are related, and of how an analysis of them bears on the libertarian defence of the free market. Finally, in recent discussions about libertarianism, and left-libertarianism in particular, the focus has been mostly on original rights and the principle of just acquisition. Whilst not denying the salience of questions regarding original rights and appropriation, my own view is that we can gain greater insight than has so far been achieved into the libertarian justification for the free market by examining the notions of freedom and voluntariness which are crucial to the principle of justice in transfer.

To each of the desert-based and the entitlement-based arguments I dedicate three chapters: chapters 1 to 3 deal with desert and desert-based justifications of the market, chapters 4 to 6 with the libertarian argument. Given the different state of the debates on desert and on libertarianism, it is unsurprising that my approach in examining them is also different. As far as the analysis of desert is concerned, one great difficulty here consists in the variety and diversity of the uses of the notion of desert, with intuitions and ordinary language not providing any solid guidance for straightforwardly favouring one or some of these uses over others. In this context, desert theorists may broadly be divided into those who analyse and defend all existing uses of 'desert', on the one hand, and, on the other, those who choose to focus on, and to adopt, one particular interpretation of desert. Neither of these approaches, I believe, is wholly satisfactory. The former tends to overlook the fact that, while several interpretations of desert may be appropriate in different contexts, not all uses of 'desert' are relevant for distributive justice; the latter, by contrast, mistakenly proceeds as if there were a principle of desert sufficiently determinate to be adopted and put to the task of justifying market outcomes. I try to steer away from both these tendencies, and suggest that we proceed by laying down some constraints on what an eligible principle of desert must look like for it to lend itself to the task at hand and in order for it to overcome some objections that have been levelled against it. My main conclusion here is that desert as a principle of distributive justice is a notion of *active*, or *responsibility-sensitive* desert, that is, desert on the grounds of choices individuals make and activities they undertake, and that inequalities are just because deserved when individuals have a fair opportunity to acquire differential deserts. When we consider some of the main desert-based arguments for free market inequalities with this notion of desert in mind, we find that none of them is successful.

My analysis of the libertarian justification of the unbridled market proceeds differently. Here, and unlike with desert, it unfolds mostly through an in-depth examination of a particular argument – that of Nozick – and my first task is to expound the main steps of that argument, in the course of which I characterise it as one in which freedom and voluntariness play a salient justificatory role. In particular, I argue that a treatment of the conditions under which the transfer of rights is carried out and choices are made is crucial for analysing the libertarian justification of the free market, and that an attempt to circumvent the appeal to voluntariness would render libertarianism unappealing and, ultimately, incoherent. I then develop my critique of the libertarian argument for the free market, where the main contention of that argument is that a free market society is one in which freedom and justice are realised because all (supposed) limitations of freedom derive from specific voluntary undertakings.

My arguments against the libertarian justification of the free market unfold against the background of a number of assumptions. First, I assume that self-ownership is a defensible thesis, and that there is a principle of just acquisition which yields a justification of full private property rights over external resources. Second, I assume that the endorsement of self-ownership justifies positing a requirement of voluntariness for the legitimacy of all obligations and interferences with individuals, with the exception of those obligations that are the correlative of (other) individuals' (libertarian) rights. Finally, the definition of freedom I use is a negative definition, on which an individual is unfree to do x if and only if his doing x is prevented by another agent.

I make these assumptions with the aim of developing a critique of the libertarian argument that proceeds within shared premises. My main contention is that the libertarian defence of the free market relies on a flawed rights-definition of voluntariness, as well as a rights-definition of freedom, and an incorrect understanding of the relationship between freedom and voluntariness. If voluntariness is a necessary condition for holding individuals responsible, then the question of what counts as voluntary choice merits careful analysis, and an account of voluntariness must be formulated that squares up with a defensible view of personal responsibility.

The examination and defence of the conditions for the attribution of responsibility is an appropriate point at which to conclude an analysis and critique of two principal attempts at showing that the market is just.

The theme of responsibility runs throughout the book. In different ways, defenders of desert as much as libertarians view their theories as founded upon a recognition that individuals should be treated as free and responsible agents. And the concern with making room for individual responsibility within theories of justice opens up the possibility of a crossing point between theories of justice and defences of the market: the appeal to freedom, choice, and responsibility has often been associated with a eulogy of the market, as the realm of choice *par excellence*, where free individuals have both the burden and the benefit of choice.

An analysis of the relationships between responsibility, desert, voluntariness and freedom, is, then, of crucial importance for assessing the justice of markets. The conclusions of this book are that entitlement-based arguments do not successfully establish that treating individuals as responsible agents requires that they be left to enjoy both the burdens and the benefits of their choices on a free market, and that desert-based arguments are no more convincing in establishing that rewards generated by a free labour market are what responsible individuals are due. The recognition of the importance of giving responsible individuals their due, in fact, far from justifying the unbridled market, supports its regulation. This is true whether a commitment to voluntariness and freedom or the endorsement of desert is defended as the most attractive interpretation of the requirement that we treat individuals as freely choosing and responsible agents.

CHAPTER I

Desert and justifications of the market

I. INTRODUCTION

The idea that people deserve to be paid for the work they do is a familiar one in common thinking about justice, and finds support in various arguments put forward by political philosophers who endorse desert.[1] Some argue that entrepreneurs deserve their profits as prizes for their alertness to the misallocation of resources. Others suggest that workers engaged in hazardous and unpleasant jobs deserve their wages as compensation, or as rewards for the effort they have made. Yet others claim that productive contribution makes people deserving of the incomes they earn. These and other claims are offered in defence of the view that at least some incomes are deserved, and that *economic desert* – namely, desert of monetary benefits – is a principle of distributive justice. That is, the justice of a distribution of incomes among individuals is thought to be at least in part a function of those individuals' deserts.

Different claims of economic desert have different implications concerning the moral status of the market. Some support viewing free market income inequalities as unjust. In this book I leave these claims aside. I am concerned with arguments that purport to show that the distribution of monetary rewards or incomes (where these are taken to refer, broadly, to profits, wages and other earnings) generated by a free market is just because deserved. Broadly speaking, these arguments unfold by defending two main contentions. The first is that one particular interpretation of the principle of desert – for example, desert as a principle of contribution, requiring that people be rewarded in proportion to the valuable

---

[1] I will consider several such views in the course of what follows. But for a few classic examples, see J. Feinberg, 'Justice and Personal Desert', in *Doing and Deserving* (Princeton University Press, 1970); D. Miller, *Social Justice* (Oxford: Clarendon Press, 1976); D. Miller, *Market, State and Community. Theoretical Foundations of Market Socialism* (Oxford: Clarendon Press, 1989); G. Sher, *Desert* (Princeton University Press, 1987); W. Sadurski, *Giving Desert its Due. Social Justice and Legal Theory* (Dordrecht: D. Reidel, 1985).

contribution they make, or desert as a compensation principle – is attractive as a principle of justice.[2] The second is the claim that free market rewards reflect desert so understood. Desert-based justifications of the free market, then, can be assessed by reference to either or both of these two main contentions. A critique of such justifications could question the proposed principle of desert or could challenge the contention that that principle of desert is respected by free market income inequalities.

My analysis of desert-based justifications of the free market mostly focuses on the first of these two contentions, since the merits of the second largely depend on empirical facts about the workings of the market and are of less direct interest for a philosophical investigation of desert and the market. Furthermore, ascertaining whether or not a particular interpretation of the principle of desert is attractive is of central importance *whatever* the merits of contention that the free market meets that principle. In the case in which the free market does meet desert, the analysis of that principle is clearly crucial, in that it will determine whether or not the justification of the free market is successful. It is also of great relevance, however, in those cases where the free market does *not* satisfy desert. In these cases, assessing the principle of desert in question, besides casting further light on the attempted justification of the free market, is necessary to determine whether there are reasons to favour the regulatory measures that may ensure that the market satisfies desert.

As my examination of desert-based arguments focuses primarily on whether the interpretations of the principle of desert they rely on is defensible, my first task, which I undertake in this chapter, is that of providing an outline of what a defensible principle of desert is. This task may seem an arduous one, in light of the fact that the concept of desert is used in a great variety of contexts, and desert theorists offer a number of diverging and sometimes conflicting conceptions of desert.[3] In the face of this, as I have already suggested in the Introduction above, I do not think we should accept that all these uses of desert are equally relevant for justice, nor try to show that some seemingly meaningful uses of desert do not make sense. Instead, I suggest that we gradually delimit the notion of desert that we are interested in, by identifying some *desiderata* or constraints that the

---

[2] By 'principle of desert' I refer to a prescriptive statement of the demands of desert, of which different (but not necessarily mutually exclusive) interpretations are available. For example, we may believe that the principle of effort is a principle of desert, so that the latter prescribes that individuals be rewarded in proportion to the effort they make.

[3] Throughout, by 'desert theorist' I refer to anyone who discusses desert, and not only to someone who defends it.

principle of desert must meet in order to be defensible, that is, in order to be a candidate principle of justice that could justify market inequalities. Besides enabling us to formulate, at least in broad outline, what a defensible principle of desert must look like, this exercise of delimitation and focusing provides us with a vantage point from which to conduct our analysis of desert-based arguments for the free market in the chapters that follow.

The present chapter, then, identifies and justifies the main constraints which a defensible principle of desert must meet. I will argue that there are five such constraints. I will refer to the first three as 'formal', insofar as they are not informed by any particular substantive view of what justice requires, but only by a concern with ensuring that the principle in question is *eligible* as a justificatory principle. The remaining two constraints I refer to as 'substantive', in that they are indeed informed by a particular view concerning what convictions an attractive principle of justice should accommodate. Only when an eligible principle of desert satisfies these two further substantive constraints can we say that *a distribution justified by desert is just*. Whilst the substantive constraints on desert are more controversial than the formal ones, I will argue that we have good reasons to endorse them. They are supported by some convictions we readily associate with a commitment to desert-based justice, and they allow a desert-based theory to overcome some otherwise potentially fatal objections that have been levelled against it.

The chapter proceeds as follows. Section 2 introduces the concept of desert and the three formal constraints. Section 3 draws some implications of the adoption of these constraints, and argues that it justifies sidelining some attempted desert-based defences of the market. Sections 4 and 5 introduce the two substantive constraints on the principle of desert, by showing how they can be seen to be generated as responses to some plausible objections that have been moved against desert-based justice.

2. THREE FORMAL CONSTRAINTS ON THE PRINCIPLE DESERT

Before I can begin to identify the *desiderata* a defensible principle of desert must meet, I should say something about the concept of desert in general. Desert is generally characterised as a three-place relation between a person,[4] P, the thing that is deserved *x*, and the grounds or bases B on which P is

---

[4] Throughout, by 'desert' I refer to *personal* desert, that is, desert for which the subjects are persons. We may and do use the notion of desert to refer to things other than persons, but those uses are not relevant here.

said to deserve *x*. Three main points about desert so defined are often made, which are derived from the analysis of the concept itself.

The first is that desert bases must be a fact about the supposedly deserving person, whether something she is or has done, in virtue of which she can be said to deserve *x*.[5] So, for example, we can assert that Audrey deserves to do well in her exams because she has worked hard for them, but it is simply misplaced to say that she deserves to do well in her exams because her parents have invested a lot in her training. Secondly, desert is a sort of 'fittingness' between certain features and actions of one person on the one hand, and another's responsive or evaluative attitudes on the other.[6] Claims of desert have an appraising character. It is because we take up evaluative attitudes towards other people's features and actions that they deserve some response, good, or treatment. Finally, desert claims have, or are supposed to have, moral or normative force. To ascribe desert to someone is to claim that, other things being equal,[7] she ought to receive something, advantageous or disadvantageous, in virtue of either some feature of hers or some action or some result she has brought about, or that it would be a morally good thing if she did.[8] To say that desert claims have moral force is not to say that they all ground obligations, or that they do so in the same way. A desert claim may be such that someone – whether a specific individual or society – has an obligation to provide the deserving party with what she deserves. But it is also possible to think that the moral force of some desert claims is a matter of value, not of right. An example is the judgement that saints deserve to be happy and sinners to pay for their sins. One could then hold that someone deserves something regardless of whether anything could and should be done to ensure that this person gets

---

[5] See Feinberg, 'Justice and Personal Desert'.

[6] Feinberg, 'Justice and Personal Desert'; Miller, *Social Justice*; G. Cupit, *Justice as Fittingness* (Oxford University Press, 1996).

[7] In my view, desert claims are *prima facie* claims, that is, they are not conclusive, and may be weighed against claims based on other, moral and non-moral, considerations. Some theorists suggest that there are 'all-in' as well as *prima facie* desert claims. See O. McLeod, 'Desert and Institutions', in L. P. Pojman and O. McLeod (eds.), *What Do We Deserve? A Reader on Justice and Desert* (Oxford University Press, 1999), pp. 186–95, at p. 193. Since 'all-in' desert claims are presumably those cases where the *prima facie* desert claim has been weighed against other, non-desert-based considerations, I prefer to refer to these cases simply as cases where the person should, all things considered, get what she deserves. This is one of those points where we can helpfully economise on the use of 'desert'.

[8] Not all claims that invoke the term 'desert' have moral force. Sometimes, as with the claim that 'political candidates of different views deserve to be heard', the desert claim is a shorthand to suggest that 'it would be desirable if *x* happened', without this having any moral force. Those sorts of desert claims are not relevant here, however. I here follow George Sher. Sher talks of desert as having 'normative force', where the latter is actually broader than the one of 'moral force', since it also includes non-moral value. See Sher, *Desert*, p. xi.

what she deserves.[9] Since in what follows I am concerned with desert as a principle of justice, I assume that the relevant desert claims are capable of grounding obligations, whether directly or indirectly.

Apart from agreeing on these very general contentions about the concept of desert, desert theorists tend to agree on little else, if anything, that may be said about desert in the abstract. We could say that, while they endorse the by now well-established contentions about the *concept* of desert I have just listed, desert theorists disagree on a number of crucial points regarding how to flesh out the concept of desert, and thus adopt different *conceptions* of desert.[10] In particular, they develop different conceptions of desert depending on what view they adopt on several crucial issues, such as what constitutes an appropriate desert basis, what the relation between desert and responsibility is, what status virtue-based desert has, and so on. So, for example, some desert theorists hold that genuine desert requires that individuals be responsible for their deserts, while others deny this and suggest that there are many different claims of desert, only some of which involve the ascription of responsibility.[11] Relatedly, some hold that only what people *do* can ground their deserts, while other desert theorists claim that people's features, too, can be grounds of desert, among a plurality of desert bases that include people's needs, natural talents and even rights.

---

[9] Desert theorists adopt different views regarding whether desert claims of this sort ground obligations. David Miller refers to desert that does not have a correlative obligation as 'cosmic desert', and holds that cosmic desert has no prescriptive implications. Kristján Kristjánsson takes issue with this claim, and holds that the endorsement of cosmic desert *can* be a guide for action. See Miller, *Social Justice*, pp. 114–15, and K. Kristjánsson, 'Justice, Desert, and Virtue Revisited', *Social Theory and Practice* 29 (2003), pp. 39–63, at p. 47. I agree with Kristjánsson, and believe that the endorsement of cosmic desert could be conjoined with other principles to ground obligations.

[10] The distinction between 'concept' and 'conception' is drawn by J. Rawls, *A Theory of Justice* (Oxford University Press, 1972), p. 5. A 'concept' refers to the general structure of the term, whereas a 'conception' is a specification of that concept once a few details have been fleshed out. Different conceptions of desert support different interpretations of the principle. For example, a conception of desert which takes a lenient view concerning what counts as a desert basis will hold that various interpretations of desert (effort-based desert, needs-based desert, etc.) are equally legitimate.

[11] See, for example, B. Barry, *Political Argument* (London: Routledge & Kegan Paul, 1965). Barry claims that 'a person's having been able to have done otherwise is a *necessary condition* of ascribing desert' (p. 108). Along similar lines, Sadurski holds that the idea of desert is 'to screen out all those factors that are "unearned", that are beyond human control, that are dictated by dumb luck, and for which a person cannot claim any credit'. Sadurski, *Giving Desert its Due*, p. 134. This view is contested by other desert theorists who think that, although *some* desert is related to responsibility, not all of it is. See, for example, Sher, *Desert*; Cupit, *Justice as Fittingness*; and F. Feldman, 'Desert: Reconsideration of Some Received Wisdom', *Mind*, 104 (1995), pp. 63–77. I discuss this and other points on which various desert theories differ at greater length in 'Debating Desert and Justice', in S. Olsaretti (ed.), *Desert and Justice* (Oxford University Press, 2003). I return to the question concerning the relation between responsibility and desert in section 4 below.

In the face of these conflicting conceptions, my view is that, rather than attempting to formulate a general theory of desert, we proceed by delimiting the kind of desert that is relevant for current purposes. Whilst not denying that the notion of 'desert' can be used intelligibly in many different ways, I suggest that our goal should be that of identifying a principle of desert that can lend itself to be a defensible principle of justice that can justify market outcomes. In the rest of this section I argue that such a principle must meet the following three formal constraints: (i) it must not be a principle of moral or virtue-based desert; (ii) it must be a pre-institutional principle; and (iii) it must be independent, that is, it should not be parasitic on an independently defined principle of justice. Let me now illustrate these constraints and say something in support of their adoption.

(i) *The relevant principle of desert must not be moral or virtue-based desert.*[12] The first constraint on the notion of desert that can serve as a principle of justice is that it should not be a principle of moral desert. By 'moral desert' I refer to something quite specific, namely, desert on the basis of morally appraisable characteristics, so that to ascribe moral desert to someone is to judge that person as a moral agent, or from a moral perspective. Moral desert is what we invoke when we say that someone who benefits needy persons deserves moral praise, or that good persons deserve to do well in life. Non-moral desert claims, by contrast, are grounded in features of an agent *other than* her morally appraisable characteristics, such as, for instance, the purposeful effort she exerts, or her having incurred certain costs, or the fact that she has made a prudentially unwise choice and now deserves the outcome.[13] Whilst the moral quality of motives may be relevant to moral desert, it is not relevant to non-moral desert. So, in order to deserve the reward for having captured the criminal, the deserving person need not have acted out of a sense of justice, though she may well have needed to be thus motivated in order for her to deserve moral praise.[14]

---

[12] I use these two terms interchangeably here. Neither is entirely satisfactory, but I use them for want of a better alternative.

[13] The notion of prudential desert is illustrated by Peter Vallentyne, who says: 'Moral desert is a matter of how deserving one is from the perspective of morality (for example, the extent to which one has helped others). Prudential desert is a matter of how deserving one is from the perspective of prudence (for example, how wisely one looked after one's own interests).' P. Vallentyne, 'Brute Luck Equality and Desert', in Olsaretti (ed.), *Desert and Justice*.

[14] D. Miller, *Principles of Social Justice* (Harvard University Press, 1999), pp. 133–4. Of course, moral considerations about the deserving agents, actions, or goods may be relevant in assessing the moral force of certain desert claims. This is where the problem of 'evil institutions' is relevant. See Sher, *Desert*, chapter 3; McLeod, 'Desert and Institutions'.

The suggestion that the relevant principle of desert must be non-moral desert should not be confused with the claim, which I made at the beginning of this section, that desert has moral force. Non-moral desert (such as, for example, desert on the basis of the purposeful effort one makes) still has moral force.

If all desert were moral or virtue-based desert, there would be little hope for the claim that the market rewards in accordance with it. Even if we think that people have moral deserts, and that it is a good thing if more virtuous people fare better than less virtuous people, we need not believe that moral desert is relevant to economic desert. It seems implausible to hold that what virtuous people deserve is to be monetarily rewarded for their good motives. As Thomas Hurka suggests, we should not confuse different types of value: 'What people deserve on the basis of virtue is not money but happiness. What makes them deserve money is not virtue but the instrumental qualities of contribution and effort.'[15] Indeed, the receipt of monetary benefits is arguably an *inappropriate* reward for virtue. Economic desert not only may not be required by, but may actually be in tension with, moral desert.[16] In any event, even if people deserved to be monetarily rewarded for being morally praiseworthy agents, it would be implausible to suggest that the market rewards in accordance with moral desert. Market incomes can hardly be seen to track goodness of motives or to register individuals' worth from a moral perspective.

(ii) *The relevant principle of desert must be pre-institutional.* The second constraint on the notion of desert that can serve as a principle of justice is that it should not be an institutional principle of desert. Desert is an institutional principle if its demands are wholly determined by the rules

---

[15] T. Hurka, 'Desert: Individualistic and Holistic', in Olsaretti (ed.), *Desert and Justice*, p. 59. See also Miller, *Social Justice*, p. 87, and *Market, State and Community*, pp. 158–9. Kristjánsson contests this view, in my view unsuccessfully, but I cannot discuss this disagreement here. This should not be a problem for present purposes, since, even if Kristjánsson were right, he would not necessarily disagree with the substantive conclusions we reach as a result of imposing this constraint on desert. His main claim is that defensible desert claims can, when scrutinised, be revealed to be a virtue-based desert claim, and it would be open to Kristjánsson to show that the principle of desert that is defensible as a principle of justice ultimately rests on a virtue-based account of desert, without this undermining the main thrust of my discussion. See Kristjánsson, 'Justice, Desert, and Virtue Revisited'.

[16] We could draw here on Thomas Nagel's contention that income cannot be construed as a 'natural reward': 'The concept of a natural reward should be restricted to those advantages that are strictly inseparable from the recognition and appreciation of a quality by others, and I doubt that this is ever true of money. People's willingness to pay for something is a direct manifestation of their valuing it. But it needn't take the form of payment to the producer.' T. Nagel, *Equality and Partiality* (Oxford University Press, 1991), p. 113, n. 35.

and purposes of institutions within which desert claims arise. By contrast, desert is a pre-institutional (or natural) notion if its demands are not wholly reducible to those created by the rules and purposes of the institutions within which desert claims arise.

Desert claims we ordinarily make seem to appeal to both pre-institutional and institutional desert. For example, pre-institutional desert is what we invoke when we hold that two equally productive people deserve the same rewards, even if one is willing to work for less than the other, and quite independently of what the institutional rules are.[17] Other desert claims that use a pre-institutional notion include judgements such as 'hard-working people deserve rewards for their efforts', 'beautiful individuals deserve praise', and the claims of moral desert I have already cited, such as 'she consciously and deliberately hurt you and deserves to be blamed for what she did'. Many other familiar usages of the notion of desert, however, seem to appeal to one or other version of institutional desert.[18] For example, we may say that a runner deserves the prize, in the sense that she has met some qualifying rule for receiving the prize, such as having run the fastest time. This claim rests on a view of institutional desert *as rule-based*. On such a view, to say that someone deserves a given good on the basis of a given feature is to say that a rule of an institution establishes that someone with that feature should get that good. On a second interpretation of institutional desert, the latter is *goal-based*. On this view, to say that someone deserves a given good on the basis of a given feature is to say that a goal of an institution is achieved when those with that feature get that good. Assuming that the goal of the institution of the running race is to single out the best runner, and that the best runner is deemed to be the one who can run the fastest, then the fastest runner deserves the prize insofar as her getting the prize promotes the goal of the race. A well-known version of goal-based institutional desert is the one defended by Rawls, according to whom individuals 'deserve' the share that just institutions assign to them, the receiving of which promotes justice.[19]

Unless we assume that there is such a thing as pre-institutional desert, an attempt at justifying the market by appeal to desert would be a non-starter.

---

[17] Although we may well believe that the requirement to honour the desert claim is outweighed by the individual's choice not to get what they deserve. The role of consent and desert is discussed by M. A. Slote, 'Desert, Consent, and Justice', *Philosophy and Public Affairs* 2 (1973), pp. 323–47, and C. Ake, 'Justice as Equality', *Philosophy and Public Affairs* 4 (1975), pp. 69–89, at pp. 82–4.

[18] For a thorough discussion of institutional desert, see McLeod, 'Desert and Institutions'.

[19] Rawls, *Theory of Justice*, p. 103 and pp. 313–14.

Institutional desert has no substantial justificatory force.[20] The moral force of desert, on any institutional account, is derivative, and will crucially depend on the independent and non-desert-based justifications of the existing or just institutions by reference to which desert claims would be defined. To deserve, on any institutional account, is to have *legitimate expectations*, where those expectations are legitimate as a result of the institutional rule or purpose which justifies them. On this view of desert, it would not make sense to suggest that some institutions are unjust because they do not reward in accordance with desert, nor to suggest that some people's deserts call for the establishment of institutions which would reward them. Justifications of the market that use institutional notions of desert are only very weak ones, parasitic on the non-desert-based justification of market institutions. Desert as a candidate principle of justice that could justify the market, then, must be a principle of pre-institutional desert, in the sense that its demands are not wholly determined by the rules and purposes of the institutions within which desert claims arise.

(iii) *The relevant principle of desert must be an independent, distinctive principle.* A third assumption of the analysis I will embark on is this. The notion of desert that can serve as a principle of justice must be an *independent* notion, that is, it should not be parasitic on an independently formulated conception of justice.[21] Only when desert is independent or non-parasitic in this sense does it express a *distinctive* demand of justice. Desert of the kind we are interested in, in other words, should not be dependent on values which are defined independently of desert, and which *wholly* define justice. If it is upheld that justice consists in promoting value V, where V is defined independently of desert, and claims of desert are used to

---

[20] Note, moreover, that rule-based institutional desert (but not goal-based institutional desert) conflates the notions of desert and of entitlement, where a person is entitled to something if she satisfies some qualifying condition for getting it. Since claims of desert and of entitlement often do come apart (we say that someone who is entitled to the inheritance did not deserve it, and that someone who deserves it is not entitled to it), a defensible conception of desert should reflect this distinction. Indeed, the distinction between desert and entitlement is by now part of the received wisdom about desert, endorsed by almost all desert theorists. See Feinberg, 'Justice and Personal Desert', p. 64. Rawls, too, recognises this distinction, and accommodates it in his institutional account of desert. See Rawls, *Theory of Justice*, pp. 313–14.

[21] The independence criterion is also endorsed by Samuel Scheffler, who refers to it as the requirement that desert be prejudicial. See S. Scheffler, 'Distributive Justice and Economic Desert', in Olsaretti (ed.), *Desert and Justice*. The issue of whether or not desert is independent should not be confused with the issue of whether desert is *fundamental*, where this is taken to denote the fact that no other value underpins desert. I tend to agree with Sher here, who denies that desert is fundamental in this sense. See Sher, *Desert*. So, for instance, I think it is plausible that the value of freedom is what confers normative force on desert claims to the effect that people ought to enjoy or suffer the predictable consequences of their acts.

convey the fact that V should be promoted in particular cases, then value V wholly defines what justice requires, desert is not independent, and claims made in its name are not distinctive. For example, suppose we believe that justice requires equality of outcome. Then, whenever a person is above or below equality, we would say that she 'deserves' to have less or more than what she has. That desert claim is parasitic on our conception of justice as equality of outcome. Or, imagine we believe that justice requires providing for people's basic needs, so that whenever a person has less or more than her basic needs, we would say that she 'deserves' to have more or less than what she currently has. In this case the desert claim is parasitic on our conception of justice as basic needs satisfaction. In neither of these cases is desert doing any work in setting the criteria of relevance for knowing what justice is, and in neither of them do claims of desert identify a distinctive demand of justice (as opposed to, say, demands of equality or demands of need).

The motivation for insisting that desert is independent is similar to that which underlies our insistence on a pre-institutional notion of desert. If the notion of desert one adopts is parasitic on an independently given conception of justice, claims of desert are rubber stamp claims. Rather than expressing the demands of the principle of desert as a distinctive principle of justice, claims of desert only serve as the expression of one or more principles of justice other than desert. Consequently, subscribing to the view that justice requires giving people what they deserve may be true but vacuous if what one has in mind is a parasitic notion of desert. We could easily say that justice requires giving people what they deserve, but 'what people deserve' just means 'what they ought to get according to various other principles'. If desert is parasitic on justice-defining values, it cannot be used to formulate what justice requires.

The assumption that there is an independent principle of desert, like the assumptions that there is non-moral desert and that some desert is pre-institutional, is adopted so as to make room for the possibility that there is such a thing as desert-based justice. A principle of desert that fails to meet any of the three constraints is not a candidate principle of justice and cannot ground a justification of the free market.

3. ENTREPRENEURIAL PROFITS AND DESERT

In the light of what I have said in the previous section alone, we are already in a position to consider, and discard, some desert-based arguments for some free market rewards, namely, entrepreneurial profits. These arguments, which have been offered by N. Scott Arnold and Jan Narveson, rest on conceptions of desert that do not meet one or more of the three constraints I have identified as relevant.

Consider, first, Scott Arnold's defence of profits.[22] Scott Arnold argues that entrepreneurs deserve their profits, where the latter are conceived as the gains that result from entrepreneurs' decisions over how to organise production, over and above any interest they may receive as owners of capital. Profits, according to him, are deserved not as compensation for bearing uncertainty, as is sometimes supposed, but as rewards for entrepreneurs' alertness to a sub-optimal allocation of resources.[23] This account of why profits are deserved, we are told, plausibly makes room for the widely held idea that desert involves a proportionality requirement, so that, the greater the extent to which a person displays the relevant desert basis, the greater the reward she deserves.[24] Entrepreneurs do reap greater profits, the greater their alertness to a misallocation of resources. Insofar as the latter is the relevant desert basis, then, we can affirm that the required proportionality is preserved between the desert basis and the deserved good.

But why exactly is alertness to the misallocation of resources the relevant desert basis here? Scott Arnold states explicitly his commitment to an institutional conception of desert: his view is that what grounds people deserve on are determined by the goal of the institution within which desert claims arise.[25] Since the essential goal of the market, he claims, is that of meeting the wants of consumers by allocating rights over scarce resources, and since this goal is promoted by entrepreneurs' keeping of the gains that result from their choices aimed at allocating resources efficiently, the basis on which entrepreneurs allegedly deserve their profits is their alertness to the sub-optimal allocation of resources.

Now, insofar as this defence of profits rests on an institutional conception of desert, it is not one that can provide a justification of the market. Scott Arnold himself, while aware of this, suggests that this fact is not as relevant as we may think.[26] To suggest otherwise, he insists, is to endorse the 'revolutionary' project of questioning wholesale, and of abolishing, the

---

[22] N. Scott Arnold, 'Why Profits are Deserved', *Ethics* 97 (1987), pp. 387–402.

[23] I examine the idea of compensatory desert in chapter 2 below.

[24] The proportionality principle is discussed again in chapter 3 below.

[25] For other accounts of institutional desert, see J. Lamont, 'The Concept of Desert in Distributive Justice', *Philosophical Quarterly* 44 (1994), pp. 45–64; D. Cummiskey, 'Desert and Entitlement: A Rawlsian Consequentialist Account', *Analysis* 47 (1987), pp. 15–19. This understanding of desert, it has been suggested, involves viewing it as a consequentialist notion. See Feinberg, 'Justice and Personal Desert', and Scott Arnold, 'Why Profits are Deserved'.

[26] Scott Arnold observes that his argument does not justify the social institutions themselves: 'institutional desert claims are not justified at this fundamental level . . . I shall make no attempt to justify "the market as such"'. Scott Arnold, 'Why Profits are Deserved', p. 394.

market. Since that project is indefensible, he argues, the consequences of not being able to provide a justification of the market as such must be of limited relevance. But this line of argument is, for our purposes, unsatisfactory. As I mentioned in the Introduction, we are concerned here not with whether there are any conclusive arguments for the market, but with whether defenders of the market can come to occupy the moral high ground by showing, specifically, that the distributional consequences of market choices are just. In particular, we are now considering the possibility that an argument may be made to the effect that they are just *because deserved*. Any argument that rests on a conception of desert as 'legitimate expectations', or institutional desert, cannot provide that kind of justification.

Narveson's defence of entrepreneurial profits fares no better. His aim is to give support to the intuition that people deserve profits at least in those cases in which their profits are reaped as a result of their having been 'very, very acute, shrewd, persistent, imaginative, enterprising, even rather courageous, and so on'.[27] The conception of desert on which his argument rests is one that makes desert depend solely on whatever appraising attitudes people actually have: according to Narveson, the fact that certain features are appraised by at least someone is sufficient to ground desert. Unlike most other desert theorists, who suggest that only some appraising attitudes are relevant for desert, Narveson opposes the view that only some features ground desert. He states:

Of the qualities in persons that interest people, some consist outright of capacities to exert effort . . . That's a major part of it, certainly. But not all. Just as we admire the sunset . . . so we admire human qualities even if they are not ones that can respond to deliberate cultivation.[28]

According to Narveson, then, given that people admire certain things and desire to display that admiration by rewarding, praising and so on, the individuals who are identified as having the features that are admired are deserving of the treatment that those who appraise are ready to give them. There is no constraint on what can make one deserving: depending on what people decide to appraise, anything can count as a desert basis. It suffices that a group of people (or even a single person?) decide to elect something as a rewardable attribute, and that attribute thereby becomes a desert basis.

---

[27] J. Narveson, 'Deserving Profits', in R. Cowan and M. J. Rizzo (eds.), *Profits and Morality* (University of Chicago Press, 1995), pp. 48–87, at p. 74. For further discussion of the morality of profits and desert, see E. Nell, 'On Deserving Profits', *Ethics* 97 (1987), pp. 403–10, and J. Christman, 'Entrepreneurs, Profits, and Deserving Market Shares', *Social Philosophy and Policy* 6 (1988), pp. 1–16.

[28] Narveson, 'Deserving Profits', p. 65.

On this view, it does not make sense to say that an attribute is admired but that it is misguided to view that attribute as giving rise to desert claims. As Narveson himself points out, 'one could stretch things and regard luckiness as a rewardable attribute'.[29] If some admire the creativity or the luckiness of successful entrepreneurs, then, entrepreneurs deserve their profits.

Narveson's view accommodates well the fact that many different types of desert claims are commonly made, and explains the legitimacy of such diverse uses by focusing on the response of the appraisers rather than on the features of the appraised, and hence deserving, individuals themselves. Nonetheless it is clearly inadequate as an account of desert that could serve as a principle of justice, for the following reasons.

First, this view puts no limits to what sorts of appraisal can underpin desert claims, and thereby allows for forms of appraisal that have nothing to do with desert to give rise to supposed desert claims. As a result, desert claims are not distinctive and comprise all kinds of different claims, including claims based on other principles of justice, such as need or entitlement. It is conceivable, on Narveson's view, that so long as people are willing to consider neediness as a basis for rewards, needy people qualify as deserving their rewards.[30] As I suggested earlier, a notion of desert that lacks distinctiveness in this way, and that includes claims of desert that are parasitic on other, independent principles of justice, cannot be a principle of justice in any non-vacuous sense. To say that justice is to respect people's deserts would only mean that justice requires giving to people what they should get, where what they should get may be dictated by a principle of need, or by considerations of people's rights, or by anything else that the rewarders consider as appropriate grounds for the allocation of rewards.

Second, Narveson's view of desert is problematic insofar as by relying on whatever appraising attitudes happen to exist as the only ground for identifying desert, it either offers a notion of desert that lacks moral force, or it is best seen as an institutional, rather than as a pre-institutional, view of desert. Narveson's view fails to account for why (at least some) desert claims have any moral force, rather than being only descriptive claims about how people *in fact* respond to other people. If, however, Narveson insists that desert claims have moral force because the 'rewarders' or 'sponsors', as he

---

[29] *Ibid.*

[30] This is confirmed by Narveson's assertion that 'To say that A deserves x is to say that there is some person(s), B, such that something about A is such as to constitute a reason for A's getting or having x from B – in other words, it constitutes a reason for B to bestow x on A' (p. 64). Nothing on this definition characterises 'desert' in a distinctive way, and claims of need or rights are, on Narveson's definition, claims of desert.

calls them, have decided to treat certain features as the bases of reward, and consequently, those features constitute the grounds for desert claims, then the desert claims are institutional in nature. Indeed, Narveson does assert that 'it is the *rewarder* whose interests crucially determine the nature of the competition or other social undertaking that creates the context in which the notion of desert is applied'.[31] He thereby endorses an institutional view of desert, on which people acquire deserts on the basis of displaying certain features that have been singled out by the relevant social undertaking as being the appropriate grounds for desert claims.

Narveson's defence of profits as deserved, then, rests on a conception of desert that does not meet two of the constraints I identified earlier, and is therefore easily discarded. Desert, according to Narveson, can be parasitic on independently defined principles of justice; furthermore, the principle of desert as he characterises it only seems to have moral force as a principle of institutional desert, which, however, cannot serve as a principle of justice.

Narveson's and Scott Arnold's are only two views that attempt to justify some free market rewards by utilising indefensible principles of desert, and we can easily imagine a number of other arguments that appeal to institutional or parasitic conceptions of desert to defend free market rewards. If people's deserts are determined by the institutional context in which claims arise, and if employers' choices of desert grounds are thought to define people's institutional claims, then people can be said to deserve on the basis of their good luck in the market if the latter is declared by employers to be the relevant qualification for well-remunerated jobs. If anything that is conducive to efficiency and therefore thought admirable counts as a desert basis, then people's productivity is a desert basis, and less productive people deserve less than more productive ones, regardless of whether they are less productive as a result of their inferior efforts or their poor social connections. Defences of market rewards that appeal to these ecumenical conceptions of desert – to conceptions of desert on which there are very few limits, if any, on what can count as desert – are easily and commonly formulated, and seem to reach their target without difficulty, but do so at a serious cost. They may coherently affirm that free market rewards are deserved, but the principle of desert in question is not one which confers justification. Rewards could be 'deserved' in some sense, but it does not follow that they are *just insofar as they are deserved*, since the principle of desert in question is either parasitic on another, independently defined principle

---

[31] Narveson, *Deserving Profits*, p. 65.

of justice, or purely institutional, and therefore is incapable of justifying the institutions themselves.

4. RAWLS ON DESERT AND THE FAIR OPPORTUNITY CONSTRAINT

The formal constraints on the defensible principle of desert I have laid out so far are relatively uncontroversial. As I have said, they are constraints that most desert theorists would be ready to endorse. Furthermore, although they may well favour some such conception over others, as I have just shown, their adoption is motivated by a concern with identifying a principle that *could* lend itself to justifying free market outcomes. In the rest of this chapter I shall suggest that the candidate principle of desert must meet two further *desiderata* in order to be defensible. These are, first, a fair opportunity requirement, such that, for desert to be a defensible principle of distributive justice, it must also be a principle that does not give some people an unfair advantage to deserve rewards over others. Second, for desert to justify differential rewards, claims of desert must be congruent with the demands of comparative justice. That is, a distribution of differential rewards is just when all individuals are treated equally relative to their deserts. The fair opportunity requirement and the comparative justice requirement, as I will refer to them, are thus two more constraints that the relevant principle of desert must meet. We could say that, while an interpretation of desert that meets the formal constraints I outlined earlier is really a principle of desert, it is only when it meets these two further constraints that it is a principle that justifies distributions as just. Only when it meets all the constraints is the principle a defensible principle of justice, so that we could say that, if the free market respected it, then the free market would be just.

In this and the next section I outline and defend these two further constraints. They are generated through an examination of two potentially lethal objections to the view that justice is desert-based. The first is Rawls' well-known critique of desert, the second is Feinberg's suggestion that, while economic justice is comparative in kind, desert is a non-comparative principle. This has led some to suggest that the idea that there is such a thing as economic desert is indefensible.[32] I will try to show that neither of these challenges undermines the possibility that desert is a principle of economic

[32] Feinberg does allow for one exception, namely, some claims to compensation. I discuss this in chapter 2 below.

justice, and that, when properly understood, each tells us something about the conditions under which that possibility can be realised. That is, both these challenges support the positing of constraints that the principle of desert must meet in order to be defensible.

Let us start by considering Rawls' well-known critique of desert. Rawls observes:

> It seems to be one of the fixed points of our considered judgements that no one deserves his place in the distribution of native endowments, any more than one deserves one's initial place in society. The assertion that a man deserves the superior character that enables him to make the effort to cultivate his abilities is equally problematic; for his character depends in large part upon fortunate family and social circumstances for which he can claim no credit. The notion of desert seems not to apply to these cases.[33]

If it is true that natural endowments and efforts are undeserved, what follows from this? A common suggestion has been that Rawls provides here a general anti-desert argument. Rawls, it is said, holds that, in order to justifiably deserve something, it is necessary to deserve the grounds on which one (supposedly) deserves.[34] As a result, it is never possible for anyone to deserve anything at all, since, for any possible of desert, it must be deserved on the basis of some further ground, and the latter must also be deserved on the basis of yet another ground, and so on *ad infinitum*. No one ever deserves anything at all.[35] So, if Rawls is right, then desert has no role to play in distributive justice. I suggest, however, that, even if Rawls is right, the challenge is not one that supports jettisoning desert, but only constraining it. My response to Rawls' challenge unfolds in three main steps.

First, as George Sher has pointed out, Rawls' claim is best seen not as a general anti-desert argument, but only as an argument concerning the justifiability of *differential* or *unequal* deserts.[36] Rawls' concern in the passage I quoted above is not that of identifying the necessary conditions for desert in general. Rather, it is with casting doubt on the claim that the

---

[33] Rawls, *Theory of Justice*, p. 104.
[34] See, for instance, R. Nozick, *Anarchy, State, and Utopia* (Oxford: Blackwell, 1974), p. 224; A. Zaitchick, 'On Deserving to Deserve', *Philosophy and Public Affairs* 6 (1977), pp. 370–88.
[35] Zaitchick, 'On Deserving to Deserve'. For an analysis of the difficulties Rawls faces with his position on desert, see S. Scheffler, 'Responsibility, Reactive Attitudes, and Liberalism in Philosophy and Politics', *Philosophy and Public Affairs* 21 (1992), pp. 299–323, and 'Justice and Desert in Liberal Theory', *California Law Review* 88 (2000), pp. 965–90. Both essays are reprinted in his *Boundaries and Allegiances. Problems of Justice and Responsibility in Liberal Thought* (Oxford University Press, 2001).
[36] Sher, *Desert*. I discuss Sher's view in section 4, as I disagree with the conclusions he reaches.

unequal distribution of talents and effort-making capacity may justifiably give rise to *inequalities* in deserts. His aim is to reject the view that the morally arbitrary and differential possession of attributes may give rise to differential deserts.

Thus understood, Rawls' concern has a narrower focus and greater plausibility than if it were a general anti-desert argument. It does not result in the contention that no one ever deserves anything, for the claim is not that one must deserve the desert basis *in all cases*, but only in those cases in which the basis for deserving is unequally distributed, thereby giving some an unfair advantage over others. The concern at the basis of this requirement does capture an important point, which, as I see it, is as follows. There is an important difference between someone being able to claim credit for something in isolation on the one hand, and someone being able to claim credit for the fact that she should get *more* than someone else on the other. If you climb a high mountain, then, and so long as this is an achievement that is recognisably yours (you were not transported to the peak on mule back), you can claim credit for it, compatibly with the fact that it is an achievement made possible by your having certain skills and physical traits the possession of which is partly a matter of luck. But if we ask, instead, whether you can claim credit for your achievement *being greater* than mine (I only climb hills), then the answer to it will depend on why it is that I only climb hills, and here the fact that our respective achievements may be (in part) the result of factors that are a matter of luck no longer seems irrelevant. If we are roughly equally skilled and equally well endowed climbers and the reason I only climb hills is that I find the effort required to climb high mountains too great for what it's worth, or if I have simply declined to seize the opportunity to acquire the required skills, then you can indeed claim credit for your achievement being greater than mine. If, by contrast, the reason I only climb hills is that I have unavoidably deficient lungs, or a paralysing and ineradicable fear of heights, then the situation is different: much though you can pride yourself on your achievement, you cannot boast its being greater than mine.[37] Here, insofar as what we are called upon to justify is the *inequality* in the deserts of the two climbers, it matters that this inequality should arise against a background in which both had a fair opportunity to acquire the deserts they have.

---

[37] This is not to say that we cannot make comparisons between achievements for which individuals can claim credit in isolation. We certainly can: we can say that you can claim credit for A, that I can claim credit for B, and that A is better than B. But we still may not be able to claim that you can claim credit for your achievement A *being better* than my achievement B.

So, my first point is that Rawls' claim, properly understood, is a point about the justifiability of unequal deserts arising as a result of people possessing unequal morally arbitrary features. The concern at the basis of Rawls' anti-desert position, which, in my view, we have reasons to subscribe to, is that, for a differential distribution of benefits to be justified, it does not suffice that each one of us can claim credit for her achievements in isolation. Rather, we must be able to claim credit for our deserts being greater than others' for us to justifiably deserve more, that is, for us not to have an unfair advantage over them.

My second point is that, unlike what Rawls himself suggests, it is not the case that his worries about fair opportunity and desert necessarily support abandoning desert-based justice. This conclusion would be justified if it were true that (some) desert bases have to be deserved, for, since these are not deserved, the inequalities they give rise to are also undeserved. Indeed, this is what Rawls himself, and some who have concentrated on his anti-desert position, seem to believe.[38] But the concern he raises need not take the form of the requirement that any desert basis be deserved at all. We can endorse Rawls' worry about the justifiability of differential deserts, while doing away with his suggestion that unequally distributed desert bases should be deserved. Instead of insisting on this suggestion, we can defend the view that *only some desert* is relevant for justice, namely, that desert that meets the fair opportunity constraint. In particular, endorsing this constraint supports viewing only *responsibility-sensitive* desert as the relevant type of desert. For desert to be a principle of justice that can justify inequalities among people (so that a distribution of unequal deserts-reflecting rewards does not reflect unfair advantage of some over others), it is necessary that

---

[38] Rawls' endorsement of the view that desert bases have to be deserved was clear in the original version of *A Theory of Justice*, where he stated, in a passage which precedes the one I quoted earlier: 'Perhaps some will think that the person with greater natural endowments deserves those assets and the superior character that made their development possible. *Because he is more worthy in this sense, he deserves the greater advantage that he could achieve with them*' (pp. 103–4, emphasis mine). In the revised edition of *A Theory of Justice*, this passage has been replaced by the following: 'it is incorrect that individuals with greater natural endowments and the superior character that has made their development possible have a right to a cooperative scheme that enables them to obtain even further benefits in ways that do not contribute to the advantages of others.' He then continues, however, in a way that hardly departs from his earlier version, and says: 'We do not deserve our place in the distribution of natural talents, any more than we deserve our initial starting place in society. That we deserve the superior character that enables us to make the effort to cultivate our abilities is also problematic; for such character depends in good part upon fortunate family and social circumstances in early life for which we can claim no credit. The notion of desert does not apply here.' Rawls, *Theory of Justice*, p. 89. Although Rawls' opening sentence in the revised version no longer explicitly states, as the italicised passage of the original version did, that desert bases have to be deserved, his remarks about having to deserve effort and natural talents – desert bases – imply precisely that.

it be a principle that tracks or reflects people's exercise of responsibility. If the desert in question is such that people can be held responsible for being more or less deserving than others, then unequal deserts do not reflect the unfair advantage of some over others.[39]

To insist that the type of desert that can justify inequalities is responsibility-sensitive desert certainly means that the sheer possession of unchosen, and differentially distributed, natural talents, such as a particular IQ, is not an appropriate desert basis. A principle of desert that took IQ as the relevant desert basis does not meet the fair opportunity constraint. Desert as a candidate principle of justice, we could say, has to be *active desert*, that is, it is desert on the basis of the choices they make and the activities they undertake, rather than on the basis of the sheer possession of unequally distributed unchosen factors, or on the basis of certain things happening to people not as a result of their choices. More strongly, the fair opportunity constraint also implies that the defensible principle of desert is one which does not make the magnitude of people's unequal deserts depend on unchosen, and unequally distributed, factors. People may then deserve more or less than others on the basis of the choices they make or the effort they exert, given certain fair background conditions that enable them to make free or voluntary choices, including the choice to exert more or less effort than others. When these background conditions are in place, people have a fair opportunity to acquire deserts, and their becoming more or less deserving than others is just.

To sum up, my second point is that endorsing the concern with not giving some individuals an unfair opportunity over others need not, *pace* Rawls,

---

[39] I do not offer a fully-fledged statement of the relevant account of responsibility here and I remain neutral, for current purposes, between some of the competing views of responsibility that are offered in the literature on responsibility-sensitive egalitarianism. In particular, the view of desert I put forward is neutral between Ronald Dworkin's and G. A. Cohen's competing accounts of responsibility. See R. Dworkin, *Sovereign Virtue* (Harvard University Press, 2000) and G. A. Cohen, 'On the Currency of Egalitarian Justice', *Ethics* 99 (1989), pp. 906–44. The relevant notion of responsibility here is that of 'consequential responsibility', in Dworkin's terms. Dworkin illustrates the idea of consequential responsibility as referring to '[w]hen and how far [it is] right that individuals bear the disadvantages or misfortunes of their own situations themselves, and when is it right, on the contrary, that others – the other members of the community in which they live, for example – relieve them from or mitigate the consequences of these disadvantages': Dworkin, *Sovereign Virtue*, p. 287. Thomas Scanlon refers to the similar idea of 'substantive responsibility', and John Roemer to that of 'accountability'. See T. M. Scanlon, *What We Owe to Each Other* (Harvard University Press, 1998), chapter 6, and J. Roemer, *Equality of Opportunity* (Harvard University Press, 1998), pp. 16–21. Note, furthermore, that the present discussion also remains neutral over whether desert 'sanctions' responsibility-sensitive inequalities in the mandatory or permissive sense, that is, whether desert requires, or simply permits, responsibility-sensitive inequalities. I favour a choice-sensitive account of responsibility of the type Cohen endorses, and a permissive reading of the role of desert, but I need not defend this here. I briefly return to these points in chapter 6 below.

result in rejecting desert. We can endorse that concern but reject the claim that it justifies requiring that desert bases be deserved – a requirement that *cannot* be met by any desert bases – and formulate instead a fair opportunity constraint on the relevant principle of desert. I have suggested that the principle of desert that would satisfy that requirement is a principle of active desert that would sanction inequalities that individuals are responsible for, on a plausible account of responsibility. The fair opportunity constraint supports singling out, as a defensible principle of desert, desert that meets a responsibility requirement.

My third and final point about Rawls' challenge is as follows. Insisting on the fair opportunity constraint and the related responsibility requirement need not, unlike what some have implied, result in ultimately undermining desert. The worry some may express is that, if we insist on too strict a responsibility requirement, we will not be able to judge a person's deserts, since we will have to screen out that part of a person's achievements which she is not responsible for, and only deem her deserving for that part of her achievements which she *is* responsible for. Since doing this is impossible, we will never be able to judge how deserving people are, and the principle of desert will be discarded as impracticable.[40]

This worry can be defused, however. First of all, holding that the type of desert that meets a fair opportunity constraint is desert for which people are responsible need not always require that, for every desert judgement we make, we screen out that part of people's unequal achievements which is due to unchosen and differentially distributed factors. For we may go some way in realising the demands of desert so understood by operating on the background conditions against which desert claims arise. Ensuring free and equal high level primary and secondary education, for example, goes some way towards ensuring that making access to universities conditional upon desert (where desert is assessed by some appropriate entry test, say) is just. Such measures contribute to ensuring that all individuals have a fair opportunity to become deserving. Secondly, and more importantly, there may, despite what the objection suggests, be feasible ways of trying to form reliable judgements about responsibility-sensitive desert. One proposal here, as Jonathan Wolff has recently reminded us, is John Roemer's

---

[40] This objection is advanced by Rawls when he considers moral, or virtue-based, desert. See *Theory of Justice*, p. 312, where Rawls states: 'The precept which seems intuitively to come closest to rewarding moral desert is that of distribution according to effort, or perhaps better, conscientious effort . . . The idea of rewarding desert is impracticable.' David Miller worries that imposing too strict a requirement of responsibility will result in doing away with it altogether as a principle of justice. See Miller, *Principles of Social Justice*, p. 148.

equality of opportunity view.[41] Roemer's suggestion, in a nutshell, is that we form judgements about what part of individuals' achievements is due to the effort and choices of individuals by classifying individuals into groups, or 'types', identified by shared unchosen circumstances (such as genes, family background, and so on), and by considering variations in achievement *within* each type as the result of effort and choice. This proposal would, if successful, allow us to make some determinate judgements about what specific individuals deserve: we start with a view about what circumstances are beyond individuals' control, so that individuals cannot be held responsible for them, and view differences between individuals that share those circumstances as differences that they *can* be held responsible for.

Much more can be said about Roemer's proposal, of course, but my main concern at this point is not with providing a fully worked out account of the implementation of the principle of desert that meets the fair opportunity constraint, but rather with showing that we can meet Rawls' challenge to desert in a way that is more favourable to desert than Rawls himself allows for. Rawls' challenge, I have suggested, is best understood not as a general anti-desert argument, but as expressing a worry about the justifiability of unequal deserts arising as a result of people possessing unequal morally arbitrary features. That worry does not support Rawls' contention that people should deserve the desert bases in order for their greater or lesser deserts to be justified – a requirement which, if endorsed, would indeed lead us to abandon desert-based justice – but rather a fair opportunity constraint on the principle of desert that is defensible as a principle of justice.[42] That fair opportunity constraint, I have suggested, is met by responsibility-sensitive desert.

Before concluding this discussion, I should consider two possible objections to my suggestion that the endorsement of a fair opportunity constraint on desert in response to Rawls' challenge supports a responsibility-sensitive principle of desert. The first objection holds that the standard candidate desert-bases, including natural talents, do not, unlike what Rawls says, fall foul of the fair opportunity requirement, and that they can legitimately ground unequal deserts. The second objection contests the conclusion of

---

[41] Roemer, *Equality of Opportunity*; J. Wolff, 'The Dilemma of Desert' in Olsaretti (ed.), *Desert and Justice*. I thank Peter Vallentyne for suggesting that I consider Roemer's view.

[42] This may seem not to be in keeping with Rawls' suggestion that effort-making ability, just like natural talents, is unequally distributed, and that what effort one can exert is morally arbitrary. But even allowing that people's propensity to make effort is substantially affected by factors they have no control over, I think that a solution to this problem may be found. We may identify, and try to neutralise, those factors that are likely to affect this propensity.

my argument on the grounds that not all desert claims involve responsibility. Let me reply to each of these objections in turn.

The first objection is Sher's reply to Rawls. Sher, as I mentioned earlier, is one philosopher who has clearly recognised that Rawls' observations on desert raise a problem for the justifiability of unequal deserts based on unequally distributed, unchosen features.[43] As Sher sees it, Rawls is best understood as suggesting that not all desert bases, but only those that are unequally distributed, must be deserved. He then argues that neither effort-making ability nor natural talents fall within the class of desert bases that should be deserved, since the fact that they are unequally distributed does not mean that those who are at the short end of the inequality are unfairly disadvantaged. Sher claims:

Even if M is initially stronger or more intelligent than N, this difference will only entail that M does not deserve what he has achieved relative to N if the difference between them has made it impossible for N to achieve as much as M. However, differences in strength, intelligence, and other native gifts are rarely so pronounced as to have this effect.[44]

We may, however, contest this claim on two grounds. First, the suggestion that the fair opportunity constraint is only violated when the inequality in putative desert bases renders it *impossible* for those at the short end of the inequality to achieve as much as those who are better placed unduly weakens that constraint.[45] For even if it were *possible*, in some scenario, for N to achieve as much as M, N would have to work more, apply himself harder, and overcome considerably more obstacles than M in order to try and achieve what comes easy to M. *That* is precisely where M's unfair advantage over N lies.

Second, even if Sher were right in suggesting that differences in natural talents *by themselves* are rarely so pronounced as to make it impossible for those with less natural talents to achieve as much as those with more talents, those differences, when conjoined with different social and economic circumstances and external brute luck, are indeed likely to result

---

[43] Sher suggests that Rawls' point is best seen as being as follows: 'If one person does not deserve to have X while another does not [have X], and if having X enables the first person to . . . do Y while the second does not, then the first person does not deserve to have or do Y while the second does not.' Sher, *Desert*, p. 26. Sher makes here the same mistake as Rawls, endorsing the latter's claim that – at least in some cases – desert bases would have to be deserved in order for them to ground just inequalities.

[44] Sher, *Desert*, pp. 31–2.

[45] I assume well-being is indeed what Sher refers to. We have in mind here some *global*, rather than *specific*, assessment of the individual's situation: N may not have as much success at activity A as M, but may have as much or more success in other activities, and thereby achieve as much well-being as M.

in inequalities that it would be extremely difficult and unlikely, or indeed impossible, for the less well off to overcome. Insofar as typical desert claims based on natural talents arise in contexts in which differences in those talents *are* accompanied by unequal opportunities to develop and apply those talents (and hence, by unequal opportunities to be deserving), these desert claims do reflect unfair advantage. Sher's argument, then, does not show that *these* desert claims justify inequalities. It is not, therefore, an objection against typical desert claims based in natural talents. That argument may at most show that inequalities in natural talents *alone* do not violate a fair opportunity constraint, since they do not make it impossible for those who are less talented to overcome their disadvantage in natural talents and achieve as much as the more talented, *given the appropriate circumstances.*

If Sher were right that inequalities in natural talents are of this kind, then his conclusion is congruent with the line of argument I have sketched, rather than constituting an objection to it. We would still exclude the sheer possession of natural talents to count as a desert basis, but would allow for individuals to acquire active deserts that are in part acquired as a result of having certain natural talents, so long as those deserts arise against the appropriate background conditions. If it were true that most individuals can, if placed in the right circumstances, choose to develop whatever unequal natural talents they have so as to achieve as much well-being as all others, then this is a reason to ensure that those circumstances are secured for them. So, for example, if N lacks the musical talents M has, but can, given the adequate educational resources, achieve as much well-being as M can by pursuing a career as a teacher, then N should be given the opportunity to achieve as much well-being as M by having access to the required educational resources. Sher's argument, then, does not weaken my suggestion that the endorsement of a fair opportunity constraint on desert supports a responsibility-sensitive principle of desert.

Let me now consider the second objection to my suggestion that the defensible principle of desert is responsibility-sensitive desert. The objection proceeds quite simply. It points to the fact that some common desert claims do *not* involve responsibility, and insists that we accommodate these, too, as desert claims that justify inequalities. My main reply to this objection unfolds in two steps.

First, as I have already remarked earlier in this chapter, the notion of desert is used in diverse contexts, with different and sometimes conflicting meanings. Whilst all or most of these diverse usages of desert may make sense, not all of them are relevant for justice. There is no reason why all usages of 'desert' should be relevant to justice, just as there is no reason why all usages of 'need' should be relevant when one sets out to defend need as a principle of justice. To say this does not commit us to the claim, disputed by many desert theorists, that only some usages of desert are correct or genuine.[46] This claim, and the objection to it, both rest on the view that the choice of the relevant type of desert must proceed by analysis of the concept alone. But this, I submit, is not the case. We may legitimately select, among the various desert claims, only those that square up with certain convictions about what justice requires. So, the mere fact that there are some usages of desert that do not involve responsibility does not suffice to cast doubt on the contention that the type of desert that is relevant for justice is responsibility-sensitive desert.

Second, as I have argued, there are good reasons to select responsibility-sensitive desert as the principle of desert that is relevant for justice. That principle is not liable to the Rawlsian challenge against desert, which, when properly understood, does raise a legitimate concern about fair opportunity to deserve. Moreover, responsibility-sensitive desert is a principle that clearly meets the three formal constraints outlined in the previous section. It is a pre-institutional and independent notion which, while not appealing to virtue as a basis of desert, accounts for the latter's normative force, reflecting the conviction that people are responsible for the results of their choices and should be treated accordingly. We want our conception of justice to make room for notions of responsibility and autonomy, and in the light of that we single out, as a candidate principle of justice, only that desert which is linked with these notions in the requisite way. Since responsibility-sensitive desert is one legitimate interpretation of desert, and one that meets some plausible constraints better than competing interpretations of this principle, we have reasons to endorse it as a defensible principle of desert.

5. DESERT AND THE COMPARATIVE JUSTICE CONSTRAINT

The view that desert can be adopted as a principle of distributive justice is also liable to another weighty challenge besides the Rawlsian argument we

---

[46] Miller is one desert theorist who proceeds by identifying only some desert as genuine. Miller, *Principles of Social Justice*, pp. 137–8. Although I do not think that trying to accommodate all usages of desert should be our aim, I should note that there is one particular type of desert claim that does not seem to be related to responsibility in the requisite way, and yet to constitute a demand of justice, namely, desert claims to compensation. A plausible account of desert as a principle of justice, it would seem, must make room for compensatory claims. I defer discussion of this until the next chapter, where I undertake an analysis of compensation, desert and the market.

have just considered. That challenge, in a nutshell, is as follows. Distributive justice is comparative in nature, requiring that what each person is due should be ascertained by comparing her to others. But desert is a non-comparative principle, requiring that what each person is due is determined by facts about her alone. If we accept that distributive justice is comparative in kind, then, how can we retain desert, and insist that it is a principle of distributive justice?[47] As with the Rawlsian challenge, I now argue that, once it is subjected to scrutiny, the present challenge, too, can be shown not to pose a threat to the view that justice is desert-based. It does, however, point to another – a fifth and last – constraint on the defensible principle of desert, namely, the comparative justice constraint. For desert to justify differential rewards, claims of desert must be congruent with the demands of comparative justice.

Answering the comparative justice challenge is especially important for my purposes. In the course of what I have said so far, in fact, I have implicitly subscribed to both the claims that are now said to be tension. In the last section I endorsed the view that comparative considerations matter for distributive justice by insisting that individuals' claims must be justified relative to others' for any ensuing inequalities to be just. And in the Introduction I have taken on board the claim that desert is a non-comparative principle, suggesting that desert-based justice, like entitlement-based justice, requires that each person be given her due. Showing that these two seemingly contradictory convictions can fit together is then a pressing task. My main claim is as follows. The contention that justice is comparative and desert non-comparative needs to be formulated more carefully than it has been. In particular, it is helpful to distinguish between two different ways in which justice may be said to be comparative, neither of which points to an irresolvable tension between the comparative demands of justice and the demands of desert.

Let us first consider the distinction between comparative and non-comparative principles. To think of a principle of justice as non-comparative amounts to holding, as Feinberg has pointed out, that, once we have formed a judgement of what a person is due, 'that judgement cannot be logically

---

[47] For a discussion of the difference between the demands of desert as a non-comparative principle and the demands of comparative justice, see J. Feinberg, 'Social Justice', in his *Social Philosophy* (Englewood Cliffs, N.J.: Prentice-Hall, 1973), and 'Noncomparative Justice', in his *Rights, Justice, and the Bounds of Liberty* (Princeton University Press, 1980); S. Kagan, 'Equality and Desert', in L. P. Pojman and O. McLeod (eds.), *What Do We Deserve? A Reader on Justice and Desert* (Oxford University Press, 1999), pp. 298–314. See also Scheffler, 'Justice and Desert in Liberal Theory'; Scheffler, 'Distributive Justice and Economic Desert'; and D. Miller, 'Comparative and Non-Comparative Desert', in Olsaretti (ed.), *Desert and Justice*.

affected by subsequent knowledge of the conditions of other parties'.[48] By contrast, justice is comparative when our judgement about what an individual should get is affected by how much others get, so that we should treat them all equally relative to their respective dues.[49] This statement of the distinction, however, does not in my view distinguish sufficiently between two different ways in which comparisons matter for justice. They may, first, be relevant for determining whether individuals should get exactly what each is due, and second, they may be relevant for determining what each person's due is in the first place.[50]

Consider, first, the latter sense in which comparisons can be relevant for justice. In this sense, comparisons do clearly and without any problems affect judgements about what a person deserves. Considerations about other parties may be relevant for determining what a person's due is both insofar as they enter judgements about desert bases (how deserving she is, we could say) and judgements about the deserved treatment or good (what and how much she deserves). So, for example, comparisons can be relevant in the context of co-operative enterprises, in which how deserving a person is is determined by reference to the extent to which she displays a certain feature relative to others, as when we talk about someone's relative contribution. They can also be relevant in those cases where the basis for coming to have a claim is the pre-eminent possession of a feature (as with prizes). Comparative considerations can also matter for determining what or how much one deserves, as when we determine what sort of reward, say, is appropriate for a given amount of effort by reference, in part, to how much of that reward is likely to be available.

That someone's deserts should be affected by comparative considerations in these ways seems perfectly acceptable. Surely how much one deserves is not a wholly context-free matter that can be settled without any information about the world. How much an hour of hard work deserves will depend, among other things, on how much there is of the relevant deserved good: we cannot just settle arbitrarily on a given quantity of it.[51] To recognise that comparisons can matter for determining what one's due is, that is, how much one deserves, then, is both unavoidable and unobjectionable.

---

[48] Feinberg, 'Social Justice', p. 98.
[49] Feinberg suggests that comparative justice requires equality of ratios between people's claims and the treatment they receive.
[50] Phrasing the distinction in a satisfactory way is difficult. Since in both cases what we are asking is what justice requires that individuals should get, and since 'what an individual should get as a matter of justice' can be referred to as that individual's 'due', it seems that in both cases what we are asking is what an individual is due. But the distinction I want to highlight will become clear presently.
[51] See Miller, 'Comparative and Non-Comparative Desert'.

The view that desert is a non-comparative principle may, and sometimes is, wrongly taken to amount to an implausible view about comparisons being wholly and thoroughly irrelevant in judgements about what one deserves, as if we could arbitrarily determine what exactly one deserves by looking at the deserving individual alone.[52]

What about the other way in which comparisons are relevant for justice? Once we know what an individual's due is, we may ask whether comparisons with others matter for determining how much she should get relative to what she is due. Now, this way in which comparisons are relevant, rather than the one we have discussed so far, seems potentially to conflict with desert. For once we have formed a judgement of what each person deserves, knowledge of the situation of other parties surely does not affect *that* judgement. If Audrey and Burt are equally deserving but Audrey gets less than she deserves, comparative justice may require that Burt get proportionally less than he deserves, but it seems strange to say that Burt is *less* deserving, or deserves less, as a result. Comparisons between what people get relative to their deserts do not, then, affect how much people deserve.

Asserting this, however, does not amount to showing that a desert-based view of justice cannot make room for comparative considerations even in this sense. For desert-based justice itself requires that *everyone* gets what she deserves, so that, when someone has less than she deserves while others have all they deserve, desert itself recommends that she be given more of what she deserves. Indeed, when all individuals get what they deserve, the resulting distribution is comparatively just. If each person is given her due, then it is necessarily true that all are treated equally relative to their respective dues, which, as we saw earlier, is demanded by comparative justice. Furthermore, an independent presumption in favour of equal treatment, or comparative fairness, may be endorsed alongside desert. It is possible, in other words, that the conception of justice of which desert is part is a pluralist one, making room for both desert as a non-comparative principle and for considerations of comparative fairness that apply when the demands of desert cannot be respected. When, for example, one of two people gets less than she deserves while the other gets exactly what she deserves, and if it were impossible to give the former more, there may be at least *a* reason of comparative justice

---

[52] Matt Cavanagh insists that desert is not to be thought of as 'context-free', and uses this to support the claim that what an individual deserves can very well be affected, or determined, by factors that may seem 'external' to him, including others' responses to him and how much they want what he has to offer. See M. Cavanagh, *Against Equality of Opportunity* (Oxford: Clarendon Press, 2002), p. 41. But acknowledging that desert is not context-free does not commit us to the view that we cannot discriminate between factors that do and factors that do not legitimately affect individuals' deserts.

why the latter should be given less than she deserves. Similarly, if two people both get what they deserve but one gets more than he deserves, then considerations of comparative justice will demand that the other person, too, get more than she deserves.[53]

So, endorsing the view that desert is a non-comparative principle of justice, such that desert-based justice enjoins that each individual get what she deserves, is compatible with the injunction that, either where people cannot get what they deserve or where all have what they deserve, comparative, desert-based justice requires that all be treated equally in the sense that their position relative to their respective deserts be the same.[54] Short of everyone getting what they deserve, recognition of the importance of the comparative element in justice requires that all be treated equally *relative to their deserts*. We can then posit a comparative justice constraint on the principle of desert as a defensible principle of distributive justice. The constraint is, strictly speaking, a constraint on what a distribution of deserved goods must be like in order to be (comparatively) just, so that what each gets is justified given what others get.

6. SUMMARY

Attempts at justifying the free market by appeal to desert must, in order to be successful, defend two main contentions. First, they must show that the principle of desert is a defensible principle of justice. Second, they must show that the free market respects desert. The task of this chapter has been that of outlining what desert as a defensible principle of justice (or, in short, a defensible principle of desert) looks like. I have suggested that we go about the task at hand by laying down some constraints that the relevant principle – one which can lend itself to justifying market outcomes as just – must meet. I have then identified five such constraints, which are as follows: (i) desert must be a non-virtue-based principle, that is, it must not involve judging agents in light of whether their motives are virtuous;

---

[53] The fact that comparative justice will require, in some cases, that someone be given less of the deserved good than she deserves, seems to suggest that comparative justice supports levelling down. This may seem to cast doubt on the demands of comparative justice. I do not consider this objection here, since I believe that we may say that a scenario in which comparative justice is done is in one respect better than one where it is not.

[54] Some desert theorists would express some of what I have said in terms of comparative *desert*. Two philosophers who do suggest that there is such a thing as comparative desert are Shelly Kagan and Thomas Hurka. See Kagan, 'Equality and Desert', pp. 298–314; Kagan, 'Comparative Desert'; Hurka, 'Desert: Individualistic and Holistic'. I prefer to avoid talk of 'comparative desert' as a separate principle, as 'comparative desert' so understood is not, in my view, a distinctive principle, but just an implication of an endorsement of comparative justice and of desert as a non-comparative principle.

(ii) it must be pre-institutional, that is, its demands must not be wholly determined by the rules and purposes of institutions within which desert claims arise; (iii) it must be independent, that is, it must not be parasitic on some other value which wholly defines justice; (iv) it must meet a fair opportunity constraint, so that inequalities in desert do not reflect unfair advantage, and are therefore just; (v) it must be congruent with the demands of comparative justice, so that everyone must be treated equally relative to their deserts. The first three constraints identify the features a principle must have in order to be eligible as a principle of desert; that is, to be a distinctive principle of desert that could have independent justificatory force. The last two constraints identify the conditions under which a distribution justified by desert is just.

Besides identifying and motivating the adoption of these constraints, in this chapter I have also begun putting these constraints to some use. I have shown that some arguments for the justice of entrepreneurial profits rely on interpretations of desert that do not have justificatory force, and I have argued that the defensible notion of desert is responsibility-sensitive or active desert. A distribution of unequal rewards is just because deserved when individuals can be held responsible for being more or less deserving than others, so that some having greater deserts than others does not reflect unfair advantage. Active desert is a principle of desert with moral force that is pre-institutional and independent, and a distribution that respects this principle is a just one.

With these points in mind, I now turn to examine arguments to the effect that the distribution of rewards achieved by a free market can indeed be justified by desert. In the next two chapters I analyse two main ways in which incomes are argued to be deserved, the first regarding them as deserved compensation for job-related costs, the second as deserved reward for productive contribution. Each of these two arguments, which I will refer to as the compensatory desert argument and the contribution argument respectively, will be assessed by reference to, first, the principle of desert which they employ, and, second, the contention that a distribution of rewards produced by the free market meets that principle. On neither of these counts, as I will show, are the arguments under consideration satisfactory.

CHAPTER 2

Incentive payments and compensatory desert

The idea that inequalities in earned incomes can be deserved as compensation enjoys some currency even among theorists who are otherwise sceptical about justifying economic rewards by appeal to desert. Joel Feinberg, for instance, holds that although we frequently make claims of economic desert, such claims cannot be defended insofar as they appeal to ideas of reward for moral worthiness or ability, or to the idea of deserving prizes for displaying special skills. The only way in which earned incomes may be seen as deserved, Feinberg continues, is by viewing them as *compensatory* payments for exceptionally costly or hazardous work.[1] Other desert theorists are sympathetic to the ideal of compensatory desert and to giving it some role in justifying economic rewards, claiming that at least some such rewards are deserved compensation for the costs people incur in their occupations.[2]

That compensation is a defensible principle of desert, and that this principle may be used to justify some economic rewards, are then deemed relatively uncontroversial claims. More controversial is the contention that compensatory desert may be used to justify at least some *free* market rewards, in particular. Common compensatory desert claims, such as the claim that those who undertake hazardous jobs deserve extra monetary rewards as compensation for the unusually high costs associated with their occupations, seem to be more apt as grounds for arguments against, rather than for, the free market. Yet the principle of compensation has been appealed to in order to justify at least some free market inequalities, and in this chapter I will focus mostly on a particular version of the argument that justifies free-market-generated incentive payments. I will refer to the argument that purports to justify some inequalities generated by a free labour

---

[1] J. Feinberg, 'Justice and Personal Desert', in *Doing and Deserving* (Princeton University Press, 1970).
[2] See, for instance, C. Ake, 'Justice as Equality', *Philosophy and Public Affairs* 4 (1975), pp. 69–89; G. Sher, *Desert* (Princeton University Press, 1987); W. Sadurski, *Giving Desert its Due. Social Justice and Legal Theory* (Dordrecht: D. Reidel, 1985).

market by viewing them as deserved compensation for job-related costs as 'the compensatory desert argument'.

The compensatory desert argument holds, first, that the principle of compensation is a principle of desert (that is, it is eligible as a candidate principle of justice); second, that a distribution justified by the principle of compensation is just;[3] and third, that (some) rewards people reap on a free labour market are compensation for the costs they incur. It concludes that, therefore, a distribution of (some) rewards generated by a free labour market is just. In what follows I argue that we have reasons to reject all three premises of this argument. After introducing the compensatory desert argument and rejecting two, in my view unsuccessful, objections against the view that compensation is a principle of desert, I turn to develop my own critique of the compensatory desert argument. I show that the principle of compensation is not a principle of desert, since it does not meet the independence constraint I discussed in chapter 1. I also argue that the free market does not adequately register costs, and that a distribution justified by the principle of compensation as understood by the argument is unjust, in that it fails to meet the fair opportunity constraint, also discussed in chapter 1.

I. THE COMPENSATORY DESERT ARGUMENT

Let us start by taking a look at the main claims made by defenders of the view that some income inequalities are justified as deserved compensation, so as to introduce the compensatory desert argument for the free market. Defenders of compensatory desert as economic desert hold that at least certain monetary rewards people reap are deserved as compensation for job-related costs. Wages, profits and other market earnings are the deserved compensation for the costs people incur when they engage in socially useful activities.

Typical compensatory desert claims are claims to the effect that people deserve compensation for the suffering of costs or harm that they are not responsible for, as when we say that someone deserves to be compensated for an injury caused by someone else. The compensatory claims we are interested in include those in which individuals suffer job-related costs they could not have predicted, such as accidents in the workplace. Importantly, however, they also include claims made in cases where individuals undergo

---

[3] So long as no other principles of justice are violated, if one endorses a pluralist theory of justice.

costs that attend the activity they perform, and which were predictable, but for which the individuals in question are not *held responsible*.[4] We can follow Feinberg in viewing job-related costs as the 'inevitably ubiquitous consequences of the specialization of labor in a technologically complex society', so that, although such costs can be predicted, it is not the case that they can be altogether avoided, even if we assume that individuals can choose what job to take. *Someone* must bear those costs, and the person who does is not held responsible for them, in the sense that it is not deemed justifiable to leave her to bear (all) those costs alone.[5]

Compensatory desert arguments, then, need not limit their claims to those cases in which individuals suffer costs that they could not have predicted, and the range of compensatory desert claims can, in principle, be rather wide. There are in fact different views supporting the claim that economic rewards are deserved as compensation, and it is useful to briefly characterise them before concentrating on one of them in particular. Such views vary in accordance with how they treat three main issues: first, what the notion of costs is seen to include; second, and relatedly, what type of earnings qualify as compensation; and finally, how broadly the notion of compensation is seen.

First, then, let us consider the issue of what is seen to count as a cost in the relevant sense, that is, a cost for which compensation is said to be deserved. We can identify three main positions here, where the notion of cost is increasingly broader. First, some compensatory arguments only view one particular feature of certain occupations as being the relevant sort of cost. An example is George Sher's account, where the subordination of one's purposes to someone else's, which is involved in the role as someone's employee, is what underpins compensatory claims.[6] Second, costs may be viewed to include a number of specific burdens involved with various types of jobs, ranging from physical hazard and unpleasantness to risk and responsibility. And finally, costs may be understood more broadly, being

---

[4] See Feinberg, 'Justice and Personal Desert'. Feinberg thinks that people also deserve compensation, of course, for injuries that are tortiously inflicted and simply unavoidable accidents. I here treat together all job-related costs individuals are not (held) responsible for, without distinguishing them according to whether someone else is responsible for those costs being suffered, or whether those costs are due to bad brute luck. This distinction is relevant for determining who should bear the burden of compensating the individuals who have suffered the costs, which is not what I focus on in what follows. See, however, H. Steiner, 'Choice and Circumstance', in A. Mason (ed.), *Ideals of Equality* (Oxford: Blackwell, 1998).

[5] This only holds true if one assumes that the jobs in question are jobs that must be performed. One could challenge this claim, and insist that compensation is only deserved for unchosen costs. This would support viewing only very few job-related costs as the appropriate object of compensation.

[6] Sher, *Desert*.

viewed to include effort itself as well as the particular burdens accompanying various types of jobs.

A second feature of compensatory desert arguments regards which economic rewards count as compensation. Some arguments view only wages as deserved compensation, whereas others focus more generally on earned or occupational incomes. Wages are the economic rewards of employees, and the view that only wages are deserved compensation is tied to the contention that there are particular costs involved in the relationship of dependence on employers. Most compensatory desert arguments, however, take a fairly broad view of what rewards qualify as compensation, including all occupational incomes (including wages). The crucial distinction in this case is between earned incomes (including self-employment fees) on the one hand, and unearned incomes on the other, such as capital gains. Thus understood, earned incomes also comprise entrepreneurial profits. Clearly, the first and second features of compensatory desert arguments are closely related: the broader the definition of costs, the greater the range of the types of incomes that are viewed as deserved compensation.

And finally, a distinguishing feature of compensatory desert arguments is the way in which compensation is characterised. Compensatory desert may be viewed as either one of many principles of desert or as the only defensible principle of desert. The first view is defended, for instance, by Feinberg, who considers compensation as just one mode of treatment among others, such as rewarding and punishing, the assignment of grades, and so on.[7] Similarly, Sher thinks that the notion of diachronic fairness that justifies compensatory desert claims is only one of various notions that justify other types of desert claims.[8] More generally, those commentators on desert who adhere to the view that there is a plurality of desert bases often consider burdens as one of them, and, consequently, conceive of compensatory desert as a specific type of desert. But there are also defenders of the view that claims of desert are generally and as such best understood as claims of compensation.[9] This is either because contending interpretations of the principle desert are rejected as inappropriate[10] or because it is suggested that we are only interested in considering desert as part of a conception of justice insofar as it expresses an actual burden.[11]

As I briefly mentioned earlier, different views of incomes as deserved compensation have varying implications for the moral standing of the market.

---

[7] Feinberg, 'Justice and Personal Desert'.   [8] Sher, *Desert*.
[9] See, for instance, Ake, 'Justice as Equality'; J. Dick, 'How to Justify a Distribution of Earnings', *Philosophy and Public Affairs* 4 (1975), pp. 248–72; and Sadurski, *Giving Desert its Due*.
[10] See Dick, 'How to Justify'.   [11] Sadurski, *Giving Desert its Due*.

Not all defenders of compensatory desert are defenders of the unregulated market, and, in fact, most compensatory desert theorists imply that an endorsement of compensatory desert justifies regulating the market in order to match incomes to people's deserts. I will focus, then, only on one particular version of the compensatory desert argument, which has been recently offered by Julian Lamont.[12] According to Lamont, the earned incomes people reap on an unregulated labour market (that is, the free market price of their labour) are deserved as compensation. More specifically, Lamont's claim is that incentive payments – which are defined as the amount necessary to attract a person to a job or keep her in her present employment – are compensatory payments. Lamont, I should emphasise at this stage, does not at all set out to provide a defence of *laissez faire* capitalism, and indeed, on this view, government intervention may affect other benefits individuals receive, including some incomes that are not 'earned'. However, he does hold that individuals deserve as compensation the earned income they reap on a market where the price for labour is not regulated. If Lamont is right, then one of the effects of market mechanisms themselves (the existence of incentive payments), the importance of which theorists of justice are often accused of ignoring, has an independent justification by appeal to desert. In the rest of this section I illustrate Lamont's argument, before turning, in the next few sections, to examine it.

We must note first of all that a number of assumptions underpin the argument. First, it is assumed that, although the government could interfere in the market to correct whatever deficiencies it deems necessary, it would *not* control or interfere with labour price (p. 27). Second, it is also assumed that certain just background conditions are in place. Lamont does not elaborate much on what such conditions are, but they certainly include equality of opportunity and, crucially, full employment (p. 28). Finally, individuals are assumed not to engage in strategic behaviour (p. 28).

According to Lamont, when these assumptions are respected, the incentive payments individuals reap, which are the amount of financial rewards that is just necessary to induce a person to take a job or maintain her in her present job compared with some specified alternative, are compensatory payments.[13] The alternative in question is 'the job and duration of work

---

[12] J. Lamont, 'Incentive Income, Deserved Income and Economic Rents', *Journal of Political Philosophy* 5 (1997), pp. 26–45. All parenthetical page references in what follows are to this article.

[13] It is, of course, an interesting, and difficult, question what the relevance of Lamont's argument is, given the likelihood that some or all of the background assumptions will not apply. I do not pursue this point here. For a general critique of the practicability of the compensatory model, see Dick, 'How to Justify'.

which an individual would choose if all jobs were paid the same base wage rate' (p. 29).[14] Whatever amount above that base wage rate that is necessary to induce a person to take a different job than the one she would have chosen at the base wage rate is compensation for the non-monetary costs attached to that job. The idea seems appealingly simple. Lamont explains:

[I]f a job requires an incentive payment to induce people to work in it, then that means that it has burdens (or disutility) over and above some (arbitrary) base level. Under the desert theory being used here, the payment will be justified because it compensates for this burden (or disutility) – not because it would increase the social product (although it will normally also do that). (p. 35)

Compensatory desert, then, provides an independent justification for incentive payments, where the latter are distinguished from economic rents. Economic rents, as Lamont defines them, are payments earned by, in this case, labour, over and above the amount necessary to keep it in its present employment (p. 28). Economic rents are reaped as a result of natural and institutional barriers making the increase in supply of a factor input – in this case, labour – impossible. They are thus the result of a factor input being scarce, and not of the activity being costly. Economic rents, unlike incentive payments, are thus *not* compensatory payments. Now, according to Lamont, it is because we fail to distinguish clearly between economic rents and incentive payments that we are generally unwilling or unable to see that, although some payments people reap on the market – economic rents – are (generally) undeserved, incentive payments are deserved payments.[15] Incentive payments, unlike economic rents, are equalising differences in pay. That is, they are monetary differences that compensate for non-monetary differences in jobs, and are therefore deserved compensation for the costs incurred in various occupations.

Lamont's is a well-worked out account of what sort of economic rewards would be justified by compensatory desert. If it were successful, it would give strong support to the view that the distribution of a substantial class

---

[14] The base wage rate is determined by factors that have nothing to do with desert, such as technological development, the desired level of public goods, and so on. See Lamont, 'Incentive Income', p. 33. Note that, in Lamont's view, there are negative incentives as well as positive ones: some jobs may be paid less than the base wage rate. Lamont would say, about cases of individuals occupying such jobs, that the non-monetary benefits of the jobs in question (more than) offset the negative monetary incentives. Since it seems to me that negative incentive payments are not 'compensatory' in the sense we are interested in here, I leave discussion of such incentives aside.

[15] It should be noted that Lamont's notion of economic rents is not uncontroversial. For some discussion of economic rents and their relations to incentives, see J. Carens, 'Compensatory Justice and Social Institutions', *Economics and Philosophy* 1 (1985), pp. 36–67; see also G. A. Cohen, *Self-Ownership, Freedom, and Equality* (Cambridge University Press, 1995), pp. 217–19. I return to this point in section 4 below.

of free market rewards is just. Before turning, in the next sections, to consider some serious difficulties the compensatory desert argument faces, it is worth pointing now to the implications that argument would have if it were successful. As I have suggested, Lamont's argument unfolds against a number of assumptions, some of which imply that the government may have a role in securing that certain appropriate background conditions obtain. Furthermore, we should also observe that the role for government intervention may be even greater than what is necessary in order to secure those background conditions. This is because, on a free market, substantial economic rents would obtain *within* each occupation: market-generated rewards do not adequately reflect intra-occupational differences in the costliness of an activity; and yet these variations are likely to be substantial.

To see this, we must take into account that different individuals experience certain features of jobs differently: whilst some experience them as costly, others find them pleasant. Decision-making is a pertinent example here, being something that some individuals find stimulating and pleasantly challenging while others experience as mostly burdensome. Moreover, even when something is generally experienced as a cost, its magnitude varies greatly for different individuals. This is partly because of the interdependence between costs and difficulties. The distinction between cost and difficulty has been drawn by G. A. Cohen, who suggests that '[t]he cost of an action for me is what I lose (but would have preferred to keep) as a result of performing it, and also whatever pain or other unpleasantness attends the act of performing it, whereas its difficulty for me is a function of how my capacities measure up to the challenge it poses'.[16] Since people differ in the way their capacities measure up to a given activity, different individuals will find the same activity to be more or less difficult; and since greater difficulty may give rise to additional costs, individuals who find a given activity more difficult may also incur greater costs when engaging in it than others who are better equipped with the relevant capacities. Consider again decision-making, which may be particularly difficult for some individuals who, say, lack or score badly on the relevant capacities, such as resoluteness, assertiveness and so on. For these individuals, making decisions is going to be more costly.

Costs, then, are not fixed magnitudes attached to particular activities, and we cannot identify job-related costs that do not make reference to variations

---

[16] G. A. Cohen, 'Political Philosophy and Personal Behaviour', in *If You're an Egalitarian, How Come You're So Rich?* (Harvard University Press, 2000), p. 171.

in how costly a given job is for different individuals. But the market is indifferent to these differences. As a result, there is always going to be a great deal of economic rent in most people's income, since rewards for a given job will be at a level that is necessary to compensate the person who most hates that job and will overcompensate all others. Lamont explicitly sets this issue aside, and states that his focus is on inter-occupational incentives only. Whilst this is not in itself problematic, what I have said suggests that the implications of Lamont's justification of incentive payments for the justification of the market mechanism are considerably narrower than we may think at first, and they must be so by Lamont's own lights.[17]

So, even if Lamont's argument were successful, its implications for the moral legitimacy of the free market would be relatively limited, and more would need to be said by anyone who would like to use this argument to confer that legitimacy on the free market. In the rest of this chapter, in any case, I turn to consider the difficulties Lamont's argument faces, in the light of which, as I will show, we have reasons to contest even the contention that inter-occupational incentive payments are just because deserved.

2. TWO (INCONCLUSIVE) OBJECTIONS TO COMPENSATORY DESERT

One line of critique of the compensatory desert argument concerns the notion of desert it employs, and holds that compensation is not a principle of desert. As I anticipated earlier, I myself defend an argument along these lines in what follows. Before doing so, however, I would like to consider two other objections that may be moved against the ideal of compensatory desert. Neither of them, in my view, is successful, but examining them helps to shed light on some salient questions about desert.

The first objection I would like to consider has been formulated by David Miller. According to Miller, to suggest that someone could deserve compensation mistakenly suggests that something that is the object of negative appraisal – namely, *costs* such as unpleasantness, deprivation and so on – could ground desert claims to favourable treatment, that is, the conferral of benefits by way of compensation. Compensatory 'desert', then, does not display what Miller claims is a fundamental feature of desert, that is, a direct and positive correlation between the evaluation of the grounds of

---

[17] Lamont says: 'To make the discussion more focussed and accessible, I will assume throughout that everyone within a job gets the same pay and that the preferences of those within a job are similar. This will allow us to focus on interoccupational incentives, while leaving open the question of what to do about intraoccupational ones' (p. 33).

deservingness and the nature of the deserved good or treatment. Positively appraised features ground desert claims to favourable treatment, as when an individual engaging in some admired performance deserves rewards, and negatively appraised features ground desert claims to unfavourable treatment, as in the case of the criminal who deserves punishment.[18]

I do not think that this argument successfully establishes that compensatory desert is not an appropriate principle of desert, *even if* we grant that desert bases and deserved treatment must be correlated in the way I have just outlined. This is so for two reasons.

First, note that effort can, and often is, viewed as a basis for compensatory desert claims.[19] Since we do generally admire effort-making, it would seem that it could legitimately ground claims to favourable treatment. Admittedly, since effort *as such* is not a cost, we should distinguish between effort that is experienced as a cost on the one hand, and effort that is enjoyed on the other, and only view the former as a desert basis for compensation. But it does seem that it is true of cost-incurring effort, that, like other effort, it is the object of positive appraisal, and therefore that it can be the basis for deserving favourable treatment. This means that Miller's insistence on the requirement that desert bases for the conferral of benefits be the object of positive appraisal would only limit the range of compensatory desert claims, but would not result in an argument against compensatory desert as such. We would, at most, have to refer to only cost-incurring effort, rather than to the incurring of any costs, as the appropriate basis for compensatory claims.

Secondly, and more generally, with compensatory desert claims of the sort we are considering, which involve compensation for job-related costs, it is indeed the case that there is something we positively appraise about the deserving agent. This is the fact that she bears such costs while undertaking some socially valuable activity, as we are assuming (most) jobs are.[20] The positively evaluated activity undertaken by the deserving individual provides the context in which the suffering of costs is adequately met by favourable treatment. This view seems attractive, and it supports the plausible claim that, if someone suffered costs as a result of undertaking an activity that is negatively appraised, or simply not appraised at all, he would not be

---

[18] See D. Miller, *Social Justice* (Oxford: Clarendon Press, 1976), p. 112.

[19] See Sadurski, *Giving Desert its Due*.

[20] A different way of proceeding from here is to formulate such compensatory desert claims as having, as their desert basis, the *voluntary incurring* of socially useful costs, and then to suggest that, insofar as individuals are deserving for the voluntary incurring of socially useful costs, they are deserving of being *rewarded*, not of being compensated.

said to deserve compensation. Just as we think that it is *purposeful* effort, rather than misguided or useful effort, that grounds desert, so we could think that people are deserving for the purposeful incurring of costs, rather than cost-incurring as such, regardless of the context in which it takes place. So, it seems, we cannot reject compensatory desert on the grounds Miller proposes.

There is a second challenge that could be moved against the ideal of compensatory desert, which concerns the relation between desert and responsibility. The principle of compensatory desert does not seem to accommodate the conviction that the ascription of desert involves responsibility. This is a conviction a number of desert theorists subscribe to and which I, too, have endorsed in the context of considering which principle of desert can serve as a principle of justice. As I argued in chapter 1, the defensible principle of desert is one of active desert that would sanction inequalities that individuals are responsible for, on a plausible account of responsibility. Desert that meets a responsibility requirement, or responsibility-sensitive desert, would sanction inequalities that do not reflect unfair advantage of some over others. But typical compensatory desert claims are claims to the effect that individuals deserve compensation for costs they are not responsible for (or are not held responsible for). It may be objected, then, that if we insist on the responsibility requirement and on the claim that only 'active desert' is a defensible principle, then we should reject compensatory desert, because it is not related to responsibility in the requisite way.[21]

I do not think this objection is successful. Even if we hold, as I think we should, that desert is related to responsibility, this does not, by itself, support the contention that compensatory desert is an indefensible interpretation of desert. Although compensatory desert is desert for suffering certain costs and harm one is not (held) responsible for, it seems that the very same concern that motivates respecting people's 'active deserts' also underpins those desert claims where people are deserving on the grounds of having suffered harm they are not (held) responsible for. A concern with respecting individuals as freely choosing and responsible can underpin both the claim that, where people undertake activities and apply themselves, they deserve the outcome of their activities insofar as they are responsible for it, *and* the

---

[21] The supposed tension between the responsibility requirement, on the one hand, and compensatory desert claims, on the other, may be adduced as a reason to reject the responsibility requirement, if we are convinced that an account of desert should make room for compensatory claims. I raise this possibility in chapter 1, in the context of my discussion of fair opportunity and responsibility. Since I now argue that the tension in question is not real, what I say in what follows is an answer to both someone who points to the supposed tension to raise an objection to compensatory desert, and to someone who thinks it should motivate us to forgo the responsibility requirement.

claim that, where people suffer harm, the fact that they are not responsible for it gives rise to claims to the effect that they be compensated. The same rationale that underlies making room for the responsibility requirement, one could suggest, also grounds claims to the effect that compensation is deserved for costs one is not (held) responsible for.

Although to my knowledge no one has articulated this objection to compensatory desert, it is clear from the desert literature that the endorsement of compensatory desert and the contention that desert involves responsibility are viewed as conflicting positions, so that we are forced to give up one if we endorse the other.[22] This, as I have suggested, is not the case. We are able, then, to make room for compensatory desert claims in an account of desert as responsibility-sensitive.

Neither of the above two objections to compensatory desert, then, is successful, but, as I will argue, the conclusion they support, namely, that compensation is not a principle of desert, is one we do have reason to endorse.

3. COMPENSATORY DESERT IS NOT A PRINCIPLE OF DESERT

In this section I develop the first part of my critique of the compensatory desert argument, to the effect that the principle of compensation is not an independent principle of desert that can inform what justice requires. My main claim, in a nutshell, is as follows. When we ask what justifies compensatory claims, we find that the desert claim to compensation is either illicitly derived from a *negative* desert claim – the claim that someone does not deserve to suffer a cost – or premised on a tacit endorsement of an independent demand of justice, to the effect that justice requires that non-deserved costs be relieved.[23]

---

[22] Fred Feldman, for example, rejects the link between desert and responsibility on the grounds that we do often make compensatory desert claims: 'There are countless perfectly ordinary cases in which we deserve things in virtue of facts for which we bear no responsibility. A familiar sort of case involves compensation for injury.' Further: 'There are familiar cases in which *no one* is responsible for a certain misfortune, and yet the person who suffers the misfortune deserves something in virtue of the fact that he has suffered.' See F. Feldman, 'Desert: Reconsideration of Some Received Wisdom', *Mind* 104 (1995), pp. 63–77, at pp. 68 and 69, emphasis mine. Saul Smilansky replies to Feldman in a way that is in some ways similar to the one I am proposing here. See S. Smilansky, 'Responsibility and Desert: Defending the Connection', *Mind* 105 (1996), pp. 157–63.

[23] In this section I use the term 'non-deserved' rather than 'undeserved', which I have used in a previous formulation of this argument, because it has been pointed out to me that the latter is ambiguous between two readings, one of which expresses the fact that something is *not* deserved (someone deserves *not* to have something), and the other of which expresses the fact that something is *neither deserved nor not deserved* (someone has not acquired a desert claim relative to that thing). By 'non-deserved', I refer to this second sense of 'undeserved'.

Recall that compensatory are claims to the effect that individuals should be compensated for certain costs, namely, those for which they are not responsible (whether because the costs were unpredictable, or whether because, while predictable, they are costs for which specific individuals should not be held responsible). In the context we are interested in, compensatory claims include, for example, cases in which individuals suffer accidents in the workplace, but also costs that are integral to the performance of the jobs themselves, such as the costs resulting from the job being physically strenuous, dirty, stressful and so on. In both these kinds of cases in which job-related costs are said to call for compensation, the defender of the compensatory desert claim deems that the costs themselves are not deserved, that is, the person has done nothing to deserve them. If they *were* deserved, no compensatory claim would ensue. The reasoning underlying the compensatory desert claim, then, is:

(1)   P does not deserve to bear certain costs (e.g. costs that result from brute luck, or predictable but necessary job-related costs);

therefore,

(2)   P, who has suffered those costs, now deserves to be compensated.

Is the move from the contention that a cost is non-deserved to the conclusion that the person who bears it deserves compensation that offsets that cost justified? It seems to me that it is not. Just pointing to the fact that some costs are non-deserved, as (1) does, is not sufficient to ground a claim to compensation, which (2) expresses. This is because, while the desert claim in (1) is 'negative', the desert claim expressed by (2) is 'positive', and we cannot extract positive desert claims from negative desert claims alone. Positive desert claims are those claims that assert that an agent deserves *x* (or deserves not *x*), whereas negative desert claims are weaker, asserting only that an agent does *not* deserve *x*. So, when we state that John deserves to be helped, or *deserves not* to be helped, we are making a positive desert claim. John ought, other things being equal, to get or be given what he deserves. The assertion that John *does not* deserve to be helped, by contrast, is a negative desert claim. All this states is that no desert claim to the help is in the offing, a claim that is different from, and weaker than, the claim that John *deserves not* to get the help.[24]

A negative desert claim does not, by itself, suffice to support a positive desert claim. We may say, for example, that a baby does not deserve

---

[24] On the notion of negative desert, see R. Goodin, 'Negating Positive Desert Claims', *Political Theory* 13 (1985), pp. 575–98.

exceptionally beautiful toys, in the sense that he has done nothing to deserve them, but this does not entail that he deserves not to have them. Or we may say, with John Rawls, that we do not deserve our native talents, without this implying that we deserve not to have them. Now, the compensatory desert claim expressed in (2) is a claim to the effect that someone (positively) deserves something; that claim cannot, then, be derived *only* from the contention that there are certain costs that are non-deserved, in the sense that people do not deserve to bear them, in the negative sense (that is, they have done nothing to deserve bearing those costs). Something else, together with the contention that some costs are non-deserved, then, is needed to support compensatory desert claims. If nothing else were in the offing, then compensatory desert would remain unsupported.

In fact, an additional claim that serves to support (2) is indeed endorsed, whether implicitly or explicitly, by defenders of compensatory desert. This is a claim to the effect that justice requires the rectification of the non-deserved inequalities that would result from people suffering non-deserved costs.[25] The reasoning then runs:

(1)   P does not deserve to bear certain costs (e.g. costs that result from brute luck, or predictable but necessary job-related costs);

(1a) Justice requires that people not suffer non-deserved costs;

therefore,

(2)   P, who has suffered those costs, now deserves to be compensated.

But notice that now all the compensatory desert claim formulated in (2) does is to express the demand of justice as laid out in (1a), where what justice requires is determined independently of considerations of compensatory desert. Different conceptions of justice may endorse (1a), and I will consider some below. What I want to emphasise here is that it is the endorsement of an independent conception of justice (one, that is, that is formulated independently of compensatory desert), together with some negative desert claim, that supports the claims to compensation. The compensatory measures called for by (2) are required so as to restore the just state of affairs from which P has been removed as a result of suffering non-deserved costs, and compensatory desert claims are not distinctive: they do not express demands of an independent principle of desert, desert as compensation.

---

[25] Recall that I am here considering desert as a principle of justice. Those who believe that desert is a moral value but not a principle of justice will ground compensatory claims in some non-justice-based moral value.

So, it seems, demands of compensatory desert either remain unsupported, being implausibly grounded in negative desert claims, or they are supported by a commitment to an independent notion of justice, so that the notion of compensatory desert does not meet one of the constraints I identified in chapter 1 as necessary for any notion of desert to qualify as a principle of justice, namely, the independence constraint. Theorists who defend 'compensatory desert', then, face a dilemma. Either they mistakenly try to extract positive desert claims from negative desert claims, or they rely on an independently defined notion of justice as a basis of compensatory claims.

To illustrate this point, let us consider further the suggestion that an independently formulated conception of justice underpins compensatory desert claims. Defenders of compensatory desert themselves often suggest as much, and often the ideal of justice in question is an egalitarian one. Feinberg, for example, emphasises overall equality or equality of burdens and benefits as the standard of justice that underpins compensatory desert, stating that 'to say that income ideally ought to be distributed only according to desert is to say that, in respect to all social benefits, all men should ideally be equal'.[26] Along similar lines, Heather Milne emphasises the rectificatory and, consequently, historical character of her well-being desert theory, where desert claims are viewed as expressing the need for rectification, to restore a situation of natural justice. Equality plays a role here insofar as it is taken to be 'a naturally just benchmark for a principle of rectification'.[27] As these remarks suggest, compensatory desert is nothing but the expression of an independently formulated conception of justice as restricted equality, which requires that inequalities be eliminated, with the exception of those inequalities that individuals are responsible for.[28]

Compensatory desert of the sort we are considering need not be tied to a notion of justice as equality, in particular. So, Sadurski views an equilibrium of burdens and benefits (which may but need not itself be egalitarian) as the

[26] Feinberg, 'Justice and Personal Desert', p. 93.
[27] H. Milne, 'Desert, Effort and Equality', *Journal of Applied Philosophy* 3 (1986), pp. 235–43. See also H. Spiegelberg, 'An Argument for Equality from Compensatory Desert', in L. P. Pojman and O. McLeod (eds.), *What Do We Deserve? A Reader on Justice and Desert* (Oxford University Press, 1999), pp. 149–56.
[28] Different versions of this restricted egalitarian ideal seem to be endorsed by a number of contemporary egalitarians, including Larry Temkin, Richard Arneson, G. A. Cohen, Ronald Dworkin and Eric Rakowski. See L. S. Temkin, *Inequality*, Oxford, 1993; R. Arneson, 'Egalitarianism and the Undeserving Poor', *Journal of Political Philosophy* 4 (1997), pp. 327–50; G. A. Cohen, 'On the Currency of Egalitarian Justice', *Ethics* 99 (1989), pp. 906–44; R. Dworkin, *Sovereign Virtue* (Harvard University Press, 2000), chapter 2; E. Rakowski, *Equal Justice*, Oxford, 1991.

substantive principle of the conception of social justice he elaborates.[29] This conception is compensatory in as far as justice is seen to require restoring that initial equilibrium, and burdens that give rise to departures from it are viewed to underpin desert claims. And with his notion of diachronic fairness, which I have already mentioned, Sher stresses the 'trans-temporal balancing of burdens and benefits'. As he himself suggests, this diachronic principle of fairness requires the offsetting of some past benefits as well as burdens, that is, those benefits and burdens the receipt of which has resulted in a violation of independent standards.[30] Along similar lines, a libertarian could hold the view that individuals deserve compensation for violations of their private property rights, even while not endorsing desert as an independent principle of justice. Here, too, compensatory desert is not an independent and distinctive principle of desert that informs what justice requires. Rather, it is an independent, non-desert-based conception of justice that determines what people 'deserve' by way of compensation.

Insofar as the notion of compensatory desert expresses the demand that individuals be given what justice requires (where what justice requires is defined independently of compensatory desert), that notion of desert at issue is not an independent one. Claims of compensatory desert are then non-distinctive. For this reason, nothing goes lost, and greater clarity is achieved, if, instead of talking about desert, we talk about people being entitled, as a matter of justice, to compensation, and if we talk of compensatory justice without making any mention of deserving compensation at all.

Furthermore – and more worryingly for the defender of the compensatory desert argument – the fact that compensatory desert is not an independent principle of desert means that it cannot be used to provide a justification of the free market. If anything does justify the market, it is the underlying principles of justice on which compensatory claims are parasitic. Any attempt at defending the market must show that *those* principles are attractive, rather than just pointing to the fact that the compensatory claims those principles support are satisfied by the market. As should be clear from these last remarks, to suggest that we forgo the notion of compensatory desert is not to deny that justice may require that individuals should in certain cases receive compensation. Rather, it is to insist on the

---

[29] Sadurski, *Giving Desert its Due.*

[30] Sher, *Desert*, chapter 6. Sher states: 'For every good *G*, every person *M*, and every period of time *P*, if *M* has less (more) of *G* than he should during *P*, then *M* should have correspondingly more (less) of *G* or some related good than he otherwise should during some later period *P¹*' (p. 94).

need to reveal, and assess the merits of, the independent view of justice that underpins compensatory claims when these are defended.

Before I conclude, I should consider a reply the defender of the compensatory desert argument may offer at this point. I have argued that compensatory desert is not an independent principle of justice, and that the compensatory arguments that have been offered typically rely on the endorsement of an independent, non-desert-based conception, of what justice requires. But someone could now suggest that versions of compensatory desert that *are* desert-based can be defended. For the conception of justice that requires the rectification of the inequalities that result from people bearing job-related costs could, after all, be itself based in desert, although not in compensatory desert. In the context we are interested in – that of compensation for job-related costs – the conception in question could, for example, be one based in desert as productive contribution.

The argument would then be this: justice requires that individuals be rewarded in proportion to the value of their productive contribution; when individuals bear job-related costs, these costs negatively affect their rewards, and the individuals involved get less than they deserve. Since they *deserve* the cost-free remuneration, which, we are assuming, is the deserved reward for their productive contribution, the compensation for the costs is itself deserved: the demand for compensation is nothing but an implication of the desert claim for productive contribution. In cases of this kind, it does seem as though we can say that compensation *is* a demand of desert, and that the compensatory claim *is* grounded in a desert-based ideal of justice.[31]

I do not contest this claim. It is certainly possible to argue that justice requires that people get what they deserve on the basis of their contribution, for example, and then to hold that a concern with respecting their deserts recommends that they receive compensation in certain cases. There is certainly a sense, then, in which we could say that compensatory claims of this sort *are* grounded in desert. However, this point does not seem to rescue the *compensatory desert* argument. For even in the cases we have just discussed, compensatory desert is not an independent principle of desert, but rather is parasitic on another interpretation of desert. So my claim still stands: compensatory desert is not a distinctive principle of desert that

---

[31] I thank Peter Vallentyne for pressing this point. The argument I have sketched is similar to the one Miller offers, although Miller does not quite put it in the same terms. Whilst he rejects the possibility that costs ground deserts, he allows for the possibility that compensation be owed to individuals whose contribution-based deserts are, in the absence of that compensation, not respected. See Miller, *Social Justice*.

informs what justice requires, and it cannot, therefore, be used to justify the market. If anything justifies the market, it is the principle of desert as productive contribution, for example, that underpins the compensatory claims. But that is another possibility altogether, and one that merits discussion in its own right. In the next chapter I turn to consider that possibility. As far as the principle of compensation itself is concerned, however, we can conclude here that it is not an independent principle of desert, and therefore not eligible as a principle of justice.

4. FAIR OPPORTUNITY, COMPARATIVE JUSTICE AND INCENTIVE PAYMENTS

The compensatory desert argument, I have suggested so far, is unsatisfactory because it uses a notion of desert that is parasitic upon an independently defined notion of what constitutes a just state of affairs. The first premise of the compensatory desert argument, then, which holds that the principle of compensation is a principle of desert, can be rejected. I now turn to argue that, even if compensatory desert were a defensible principle of desert, the compensatory desert argument would still be unsuccessful, because we have reasons to reject the other two premises of that argument – namely, the contention that a distribution justified by the principle of compensation is just, and that the incentive payments people reap on a free labour market are compensation for the costs they incur.

Let me briefly anticipate what the argument will be in very broad outline. Incentive payments, as Lamont defines them, are those payments that are necessary to attract a person to a job or to keep her in one, and which, he claims, offset the non-monetary costs attached to the job. In order to determine what counts as such payments, we must have in mind an alternative, or a baseline, relative to which the person is said to prefer the combination of monetary and non-monetary costs and benefits associated with a particular job – what I will refer to as the particular 'job bundle'. Lamont, as I have already mentioned, suggests that this baseline is 'the job which one would choose if all jobs were paid the same base wage rate' (p. 29). But this formulation, I now suggest, is ambiguous between two different interpretations of what the baseline is. On the first of these interpretations, I argue, it is true that an unequal distribution of compensatory rewards would be just, but it is not true that the free market would generate it. Free-market-generated incentives only count as compensatory payments on a second interpretation of the baseline. But it is not true that an unequal distribution of rewards that are compensatory in this second sense would be just. Lamont's attempted reconciliation of free market efficiency and justice, then, fails.

Consider, then, Lamont's suggestion that the alternative compared to which the payment a person reaps is an incentive payment is the job one would choose if all jobs were paid at the same rate. On the first interpretation, this refers to the job a person would choose *among all jobs that are available to anyone* (and regardless of whether or not they are jobs *she*, in particular, could get). In other words, we imagine here each person facing the same counterfactual jobs option set (that is, the set of jobs that are available in that individual's economy), and ask what amount would be necessary to attract a person to a particular job other than the job she would choose if all jobs were paid the same. The incentive payment, so understood, would compensate her for all the non-monetary costs associated with that particular job, compared to her preferred alternative.

If the baseline were understood in this way, and if people reaped incentive payments relative to *this* baseline, then a distribution of incentive payments – payments necessary to induce various individuals to occupy a job other than the one they would prefer to occupy in the counterfactual scenario – would, indeed, reflect their assessments of job-related costs, and would be just. Suppose, for example, that Audrey and Burt would both choose to be orchestra clarinettists if all jobs were paid the same. Suppose further that both think that, if cab-drivers were paid considerably more than clarinettists, they would both be cab-drivers, and if bankers were paid more than both clarinettists and cab-drivers, they would choose to be bankers. Both Audrey and Burt, then, would require some incentive payments to be attracted to being cab-drivers, and even greater ones to be attracted to being bankers. If, in this scenario, and once the required incentive payments are made available, Audrey chooses to be a banker and Burt a clarinettist, and Audrey is paid considerably more than Burt, the resulting inequality between them seems justified. It reflects their choices of what both deem to be equally good job bundles.[32] The greater income Audrey reaps would not reflect an unfair advantage. Although Audrey gets (and supposedly deserves) more income, this is to offset the greater non-monetary costs she

---

[32] Here I have assumed, for simplicity, that Audrey and Burt choose the same job and have the same preferences. But my argument does not hinge on these assumptions. If Audrey and Burt had different preferences, things would get slightly more complex, and we would have to allow for intra-occupational pay differentials. If, for example, Burt finds being a banker *less* costly than what Audrey does, then the incentive payments Burt reaps should be less than the ones Audrey reaps. He should be given what is individually, for him, an incentive payment, since if he reaped what Audrey reaps, he would be getting *an economic rent*. Recall that Lamont sidelines the question of intra-occupational pay differentials.

incurs as a result of being a banker rather than a clarinettist. She has no advantage over Burt by virtue of receiving more income, since the difference between their incomes is, indeed, an equalising difference in pay.

Note that these considerations would hold true even if Burt ended up being a cab-driver, rather than a banker, through no choice of his own. For even if Burt were barred from becoming a banker as a result of lacking the relevant skills or natural talents, or because of institutional barriers to too many people accessing bankers' jobs, it would still be the case that the greater payment Audrey reaps is compensatory, so that, overall, Audrey's job bundle is not better than Burt's.[33] So, even if we had a merit-based recruiting of individuals to different jobs, as we should have in order to ensure that people's talents are used efficiently and people are productive in their respective occupations, so long as the payments people are given are the incentive payments they would require *relative* to the job each person would choose *among all jobs that are available to anyone*, these payments are compensatory, and a distribution of them is just.

Incentive payments relative to the baseline so defined, however, are not co-extensive with the incentive payments generated by a free market. On a free labour market, where the price of labour is unregulated, the incentive payments available for attracting people to various jobs depend on the supply of, and demand for, labour of a particular sort. How much is available, by way of incentive payment for any occupation, depends crucially on how much demand and supply of labour there are for that particular occupation. As a result, the incentive payments generated by the free market will not coincide with the incentive payments we have considered so far. If, for example, most people own private cars and cab-drivers are consequently not in high demand in Audrey's and Burt's society, and/or there are more people able to be cab-drivers than there are to be either bankers or clarinettists, for which there is a high relative demand, it is likely that market-generated rewards for cab-drivers will be considerably lower than those for both clarinettists and bankers. The structure of payments now in the offing does not reflect Audrey's and Burt's relative assessments of the non-monetary costs associated with the three available occupations.

What the free market generates *are* incentive payments, but they are payments that count as incentives relative to a different baseline than the one we have considered so far. On the second interpretation of Lamont's

---

[33] Strictly speaking, it may be *slightly* better than Burt's. For the payment to give Audrey an incentive, rather than leave her indifferent between being a banker and other jobs, it must more than *just* compensate her. But the additional monetary benefit required would be minimal (assuming, that is, that Audrey and Burt are receiving individualised incentive payments).

suggested baseline, the latter refers to the job a person would choose among the jobs *that are actually available to her* (rather than the job she would choose among all jobs that are available to anyone). We now imagine each person facing mostly different (although sometimes overlapping, and sometimes co-extensive) option sets, and ask what amount is necessary to attract a person to a particular job *in that set* other than the job, still within that set, she would choose if all jobs were paid the same. Suppose that Burt's option set now comprises the following two options: being a cab-driver and being a supermarket assistant. Suppose further that, were these two jobs paid the same, he would be a supermarket assistant (he finds it would be comparatively less stressful) but would be willing to be a cab-driver if there were monetary incentives to offset the additional costs involved. Here it seems plausible that, if he chooses to be a cab-driver instead of a supermarket assistant, this reflects his favourable assessment of the relative costs and benefits associated with those two jobs. Since, *ex hypothesi*, he *could* choose either one of them, his choice of one must reflect his judgement that the job bundle associated with being a cab-driver is better than that associated with being a supermarket assistant. That part of his income he reaps as a cab-driver, over the base wage rate, is an incentive payment relative to the baseline. It is a payment that is necessary to induce him to be a cab-driver rather than a supermarket assistant. It is also a compensatory payment, relative to the alternative options within Burt's option set: it is a payment that offsets the extra costs associated with being a cab-driver *rather than* a supermarket assistant.

When we take the baseline for each person to refer to the option set *actually available* to each person, the incentive payments relative to *this* baseline are indeed market-generated incentive payments. We could also say, about these payments, that they are 'compensatory' payments: they are compensatory payments relative to the actually available alternative. But it is no longer true that a distribution of these payments is just, since it is not true that the income differences between individuals facing different option sets are equalising differences in pay. For what determines each person's actual jobs option set – the set of differently rewarded jobs actually available to her that she can choose from – is a function of her talents and personal attributes, and the extent to which these are demanded and supplied in her economy. The payments available to Burt, given his restricted option set and the fact that there is a relative oversupply of labour for the occupations he is qualified for within that set, only reflect the relative costliness of any one occupation within that option set, not the relative costliness of those occupations relative to others not actually available to Burt.

It may be true, then, that what extra payments cab-drivers get over the base wage rate is, for Burt, an incentive payment to switch from his preferred base wage job – supermarket assistant – to being a cab-driver, and one that compensates for the extra costs attached to this option. It may also be true that what Audrey gets as a banker, over and above the base wage rate, is an incentive payment that compensates for the extra costs she incurs by turning to banking rather than undertaking a clarinettist's profession. But what is *not* true is that the income inequality between Audrey and Burt reflects, and compensates for, a difference in the costliness between being a banker and being a cab-driver. Unlike Burt, Audrey, we are assuming, faces a much larger option set (she can probably choose the jobs Burt can choose, but also has access to others that are unavailable to Burt). Furthermore, what she can reap by way of incentive payment for the various occupations is affected by what talents she has. Since bankers are in demand and (let us assume) the required talents and skills are rare, the incentive payments that will be available to potential bankers like Audrey are much greater than *any* incentive payments that are available to someone like Burt. Whilst it may *very* costly, for Audrey, to be a banker rather than a clarinettist, it may be equally *very* costly, or more costly, for Burt to be a cab-driver rather than a supermarket assistant. But what Audrey can reap, as either a clarinettist or a banker, is much higher than what Burt can reap as either a cab-driver or a supermarket assistant. The only comparisons we can now make are between individuals who face the same option set. But across option sets, it is not the case that the *inequalities* in incomes that arise among individuals are compensatory and therefore deserved. The fair opportunity requirement here is violated, because some individuals do now have an unfair advantage over others.

So, the compensatory desert argument does not show that the incentive payments people get on the free market are just because deserved. A defensible principle of desert, that is, one that satisfies the fair opportunity requirement, demands that inequalities across individuals be shown to not reflect unfair advantage. I have suggested that this requirement would be satisfied if the unequal payments different individuals get were incentive payments relative to a shared counterfactual baseline, or the same jobs option set. In that case, incentive payments would really be compensatory payments, and we could say, of different occupations, that the fact that they reap more or less monetary rewards than others is a reflection of their relative costliness. But the incentive payments generated by a free market are not of this sort: what incentive payments different individuals can reap on the market depends on their talents and the extent to which these talents are in demand and supply. These payments are compensatory, but only relative to a baseline constituted by each individual's actual option set. An unequal distribution of payments that are compensatory in this sense is not just.

We can put the same point in a different way. The notion of economic rent that Lamont utilises conflates two magnitudes which, as Cohen has argued in a different context, must be distinguished, namely, factor rent and producer surplus.[34] Factor rent is the difference between the price of a factor and the lower price at which it would sell if it were possible, contrary to fact, to increase its supply.[35] A scarce talent that is in demand is a case in point. Producer surplus, by contrast, is the difference between the price at which a factor is supplied and the minimum price its supplier would accept to supply that factor. When he insists that economic rents are not incentive payments, Lamont has in mind producer surplus, of which it is true *by definition* that eliminating it would not affect supply. However, in illustrating the notion of economic rent he uses, Lamont makes reference to the fact of scarcity, which is characteristic not of producer surplus as such but of factor rent, where the latter may, or may not, be co-extensive with producer surplus (p. 29). If someone with a scarce talent that is in demand hates putting that talent to use, the factor rent he receives is an incentive payment, not producer surplus.

When factor rent and producer surplus are distinguished, the problem with Lamont's argument becomes apparent. The crucial distinction on which that argument rests must be the one between producer surplus on the one hand and incentive payment on the other, where the latter could, sometimes, include factor rent. But then the argument justifies inequalities that, although compensatory in the sense at issue, are factor rents and, hence, commanded by virtue of possessing scarce talents. Lamont overlooks the fact that what people can claim, and supposedly deserve, as compensatory payments is a function of their talents and of external luck as much as it is a function of their preferences.

This result should not surprise us. The suggestion that market-generated incentive payments can be an adequate indicator of costs in the general case seems implausible, since the magnitude of incentive payments is a function of existing levels of supply and demand. In two separate economies, for

---

[34] See Cohen, *Self-Ownership, Freedom, and Equality*, pp. 217–19.
[35] We need a benchmark here, by reference to which we can specify by how much supply of the relevant factor – in this case, labour – would be increased. We can assume that the relevant counterfactual scenario is one in which supply of labour is increased up to the point at which it would be perfectly competitive.

instance, similar in every respect except for the availability of people trained for and willing to be teachers, the incentive payments accruing to teachers will be different, but it cannot be claimed that the costs or burdens of being a teacher are therefore different, even when the criterion for measuring job-related costs is, as is the case in Lamont's argument, a subjective standard of utility. The situation is similar, I have argued, with comparisons among persons in the same economy. Just as the unequal teacher salaries in the two-economies case does not reflect the fact that the costs of being a teacher are different in the two economies, so the unequal salaries accruing to bankers and cab-drivers in the same economy do not reflect the fact that the costs of being a banker are higher than those of being a cab-driver. All that the unequal salaries reflect, in the latter case, are the costs of these two occupations relative to the specific alternatives actually available to prospective bankers and cab-drivers. The inequalities between bankers and cab-drivers are not compensatory, remain non-deserved and are therefore unjust.

The appeal to compensatory desert, then, cannot ground a case for the free market. As the beginning of this chapter showed, the compensatory desert argument makes three claims. It holds, first, that the principle of compensation is a principle of desert; second, that a distribution justified by the principle of compensation is just; and third, that the incentive payments people reap on a free labour market are compensation for costs they incur. I have argued that we have reasons to dispute all three claims. I have suggested, against the first claim, that the principle of compensation is not an eligible principle of desert, in that it does not meet the independence constraint. And I have argued that the second and third claims cannot be true together. The second claim is only true on an interpretation of the demands of the compensation principle which it is impossible for market-generated incentive payments to realise; the third is only true on an interpretation of what counts as 'compensation' of which it is not true that, where individuals reap different amounts of it, the resulting inequalities are congruent with the demands of fair opportunity. Furthermore, we can add, on the market, only some individuals will get what they (supposedly) deserve by way of compensation. The distribution of incentive payments, therefore, also fails to satisfy a comparative justice constraint. The distribution of market generated incentive payments, then, while being a distribution of payments that are 'compensatory' in some sense, is not just.

CHAPTER 3

Productive contributions and deserved market rewards

In this chapter I turn to consider an alternative, and more familiar, desert-based defence of the market, which I will refer to as the contribution argument. This argument views differences in free market incomes as deserved rewards for people's productive contribution.[1] Like the compensatory desert argument, the contribution argument holds that the market is substantively just in as far as it respects people's deserts, basing this conclusion on the following three main premises. First, the principle of contribution is a plausible interpretation of desert; second, a distribution justified by the principle of contribution is just;[2] and third, the rewards people reap on the free market adequately reflect the productive contribution they make. Since David Miller's is the most sophisticated version of the contribution argument, the analysis that follows mostly concentrates on his claims.

The main claims of my analysis are as follows. Whilst I do not rebut the first main claim of the contribution argument, namely, that the contribution principle qualifies as a principle of desert, I suggest that, on scrutiny, this appears less evident than is generally believed. There are also reasons, which I briefly survey here, to doubt the third main claim, which holds that the rewards people reap on the free market adequately reflect their productive contribution. But my main reservations about the contribution argument concern the second claim it makes. Even if we concede that the principle of contribution is a plausible interpretation of desert, and even if equilibrium prices did reflect the value of individuals' productive contribution, the distribution of incomes produced by the market does not meet the conditions under which differential deserts would be justified.

---

[1] Like defenders of the compensatory desert argument, defenders of the contribution argument do not support *laissez faire* capitalism, and allow for regulation of the market as consistent with desert-based justice. In what follows, when referring to 'the market' I refer to a free labour market in which the price of labour is not regulated.

[2] So long as no other principles of justice are violated, if one endorses a pluralist theory of justice.

This is because the possession of natural talents and the role of luck are substantial determinants of productivity differentials among people; as a result, a distribution of unequal, productivity-based rewards does not satisfy the requirement of fair opportunity, nor are the demands of comparative justice likely to be respected by such a distribution. A commitment to respecting desert as a defensible principle of justice cannot serve as a basis for a justification of free market outcomes, in that it would require the elimination of precisely that sort of background luck which characterises the market and which the defender of the contribution argument tries to defend as reconcilable with desert.

I. THE PRINCIPLE OF CONTRIBUTION AND MARKET VALUE: SOME WORRIES

Let me start by looking in more detail at the first of the main claims the contribution argument makes. Following Joel Feinberg's distinction between different *modes of deserved treatment*, we could characterise this argument as committed to viewing incomes as being, distinctively, *rewards* for an outcome produced, rather than as compensation for costs (as in the compensatory desert argument) or as prizes for the possession of certain skills.[3] Unlike these other modes of deserved treatment, reward is thought to be fitting in response to an *activity* on the part of the supposedly deserving party, rather than in response to possession of a skill or the suffering of a cost. Miller emphasises that the contribution argument adopts a view of desert that requires voluntary performance, and which, therefore, views the ascription of desert as closely connected with the attribution of responsibility. Indeed, as I have mentioned before, Miller believes that only desert of this kind qualifies as 'genuine'. He says: 'Desert belongs together with "reactive attitudes" such as gratitude and resentment within what Strawson has called the "participant" perspective on human life, in which we regard others as freely choosing agents like ourselves, and respond to their actions accordingly'.[4] This conception of desert reflects the fact, which I mentioned in chapter 1, that desert is thought to have an appraising character. Miller's view delimits the kinds of appraisal that is relevant and holds that only a certain type of appraising attitude – reactive attitudes, specifically, which are attitudes that reflect appraisal of others *as agents* – characterises

[3] See J. Feinberg, 'Justice and Personal Desert', in *Doing and Deserving. Essays in the Theory of Responsibility* (Princeton University Press, 1970).
[4] D. Miller, *Principles of Social Justice* (Harvard University Press, 1999), p. 136.

desert.[5] Desert so understood, Miller insists, is a pre-institutional principle that defines what justice requires.[6] The principle of contribution is a particular interpretation of desert thus conceived. People undertake socially valuable activities and deserve to be rewarded for contributing to society in this way.

These contentions about the general characteristics of the principle of desert that is adopted by the contribution argument seem plausible, and square up with what I said in chapter 1 about the features an eligible principle of desert should have. In particular, an interpretation of the principle of desert that emphasises voluntary performance as a basis for desert accounts for the principle's moral force, its pre-institutional character and its being a principle that can inform what justice requires, rather than being parasitic on an independent, non-desert-based conception of justice. But the specific interpretation of desert the contribution argument relies on is also further characterised by the fact that the desert in question expresses a proportionality condition, so that people supposedly deserve *in proportion with the value of the productive contribution* they make. The contribution principle holds not just that individuals deserve to be rewarded for engaging in purposeful activities that make a positive contribution to society, but also that the rewards individuals engaged in productive activities reap should vary in accordance and proportionally with how valuable those activities are.[7]

It is a striking fact, in my view, that desert theorists, when they come to analyse and, in some cases, defend the contribution argument, assume that the contribution principle is a well-defined principle of desert, and consequently fail to formulate carefully what claim, exactly, the contribution

---

[5] Miller's view, like that of Jan Narveson which I examined in chapter 1 above, places emphasis on appraising attitudes. But unlike Narveson, Miller delimits the range of appraised features that can constitute desert bases. Whilst thinking that this delimitation is justified, and as I have mentioned earlier, I think that Miller's suggestion that only some desert is 'genuine' is misleading, since it wrongly suggests that the delimitation is operated by analysing the concept of desert itself. In fact, the delimitation is best seen as the result of the fact that the identified interpretation of desert squares up with our view about what justice should look like, and our conviction that it requires that we treat individuals as free and responsible agents.

[6] D. Miller, *Social Justice* (Oxford: Clarendon Press, 1976), p. 92. Miller says here that the appraisal precedes the establishment of the social undertaking, and that 'were we not to hold such attitudes, it is inconceivable that we should set up competitions and award prizes for athletic achievement. Here again the desert is prior to institutions and practices'. See also Miller, *Principles*, pp. 138–42.

[7] Hence Jonathan Riley upholds that 'individuals deserve rewards that are proportional to their productive labour'. J. Riley, 'Justice Under Capitalism', in J. W. Chapman and J. Roland Pennock (eds.), *Markets and Justice* (New York University Press, 1989), pp. 122–62, at p. 134. The proportionality requirement is also endorsed by Miller and, as I mentioned in chapter 1 above, by N. Scott Arnold, 'Why Profits are Deserved', *Ethics* 97 (1987), pp. 387–402.

argument involves. In particular, they conflate the two claims I have just distinguished. The first is the general contention that people deserve to be rewarded for their performance of productive activities, and that incomes, in particular, are to be viewed as rewards for the performance of productive, or socially useful, activities, rather than, say, as prizes or as compensation for unchosen costs. This first claim, it must be noted, does not say *how much* people are to be rewarded for the stated activities. The second claim is that the rewards people reap for their performance of certain activities should be apportioned in accordance with how valuable their contribution is. The second, and not the first claim, is what is really *distinctive* about the contribution argument, for the first claim captures other interpretations of desert, such as desert on the basis of purposeful effort, alongside that of desert as contribution.

I emphasise this because, when the contribution principle is thus charac-terised, its being an intuitive and compelling interpretation of the principle of desert appears less obvious than it does at first. In particular, I would like to raise two main worries that cast doubt on the contention that the contribution principle is an interpretation of desert, where the contribu-tion principle is a proportionality principle, stating that the size of one's rewards for the performance of socially productive activities should vary in accordance and proportionally with the value of one's activities.

The first worry is this: once we subject to scrutiny some of the claims adduced in favour of the contribution principle in light of the distinction I have just drawn, it appears that they do not support the contribution principle, in particular. One such claim is this: surely our appraisal of others' voluntary performance does not only focus on the intentions behind that performance – '[d]esert isn't *merely* a matter of good intentions'.[8] It matters, too, that those intentions result in socially valuable outcomes. But note, now, that this is not an argument for the contribution principle at all. Since all claims of economic desert are claims to the effect that individuals deserve to be rewarded for undertaking socially useful activities, the insistence on the importance of performance and the emphasis on the fact that '[d]esert isn't *merely* a matter of good intentions' do nothing to support the contribution principle over other interpretations of the concept of desert, such as desert as compensation or effort-based desert.

The same consideration applies to another argument that is offered in favour of the contribution argument by Miller, who states that '[d]esert does

---

[8] D. Miller, *Market, State and Community. Theoretical Foundations of Market Socialism* (Oxford: Clarendon Press, 1989), p. 166, emphasis mine.

not require that people should be paid for productive work, but if people *are* paid for work of this kind, then those whose productivity is higher deserve, *ceteribus paribus*, higher pay'.[9] I contest this claim. Even if we assume that people should be paid for productive work, it is not obvious that those whose productivity is higher deserve higher pay. Nothing in the concept of desert prescribes that, and there is no reason, dictated by desert, for why, even if we base people's deserts in their performance of productive activities, we should not, for instance, pay all those who do perform productive activities (as opposed to those who engage in non-productive ones) equal pay. The acceptance of the general principle that people deserve to be rewarded for productive work is compatible with a whole range of specifications of the principle of desert, as well as non-desert considerations, that may or may not justify differential rewards. It does not support the proportionality principle in particular.

Whilst so far we have seen that claims adduced in favour of the contribution principle do not actually seem to support that principle, we can also go further and question whether the proportionality principle is in fact a principle of desert at all. This is because – and this is the second worry I would like to raise about the contribution principle – in various cases in which that principle is said to be relevant, it seems that we may reduce its demands to those of some other principle or value. For example, it is said that it is because of our endorsement of the contribution principle that we condemn gender pay differentials.[10] However, it seems to me that we do not need to uphold a notion of desert to condemn those differentials. If we affirm that *how* productive individuals are is the relevant consideration for rewarding them differentially (and we could affirm this for reasons that have nothing to do with desert, but rather that appeal, for instance, to forward-looking, efficiency considerations), then we may uphold the proportionality principle not as a demand of desert but rather as a requirement of *non-discrimination*. Hence, we could suggest that, if people are paid for productive work, then gender pay differentials are unfair, because those differentials operate arbitrary discrimination against women, giving them unequal pay from their male counterparts although they do not differ in how productive their contribution is. The principle of non-discrimination is all we need here.

In other cases in which the contribution principle is adduced, moreover, it seems that we may be appealing to a notion of institutional, rather than

[9] Miller, *Principles*, p. 141.

[10] *Ibid.* Miller claims that Rawls' Difference Principle, by allowing only for a notion of institutional desert, would be unable to condemn gender pay differentials.

pre-institutional, desert. Indeed, the supposed desert basis with the principle of contribution that is invoked to justify the free market – namely, market value contributed – seems to be determined by reference to the goal of the institution in question – namely, the market – and the contribution principle looks like an interpretation of institutional desert.[11] A concept of legitimate expectations, then, rather than an independent principle of desert, is what seems to be at work in contribution-based arguments for the free market.

A further reason to doubt that the contribution principle is principle of desert is that the proportionality principle, stating as it does that each individual deserves the equivalent of the value he has contributed to society, is hardly distinguishable from a notion of commutative justice, where the latter is seen as requiring that each be *repaid* or given back the equivalent of what he has given. As Miller has himself acknowledged, viewing desert on the basis of contribution as a principle of commutative justice already assumes what we are meant to show, namely, that one has a right to the fruits of one's labour.[12] But construing contribution as a principle of desert, and hence as distinguishable from the affirmation of an individual's entitlement to her talents and what one can reap through them, is by no means easy. In the absence of convincing arguments that do just that – and I have said that such arguments are wanting – we should remain sceptical about the claim that the principle of contribution is a principle of desert.

By raising these worries, I am not here denying that people may, on a pre-institutional sense of desert, deserve to be rewarded on the basis of, among other things, the outcomes they bring about. Nor am I suggesting that the worries I have raised are unanswerable. But I do want to emphasise that when we talk about people deserving rewards for engaging in productive activities, there is nothing that supports the contention that individuals deserve to be rewarded the equivalent of what they produce. The first main premise of the contribution argument, namely, that the principle of contribution, as the latter is usually understood, is a principle of desert, then, remains unsupported.

In a similar way, more arguments than we can explore here would be needed to fully defend the third crucial premise of the contribution

---

[11] In chapter 1 above I discussed supposed defences of the market which clearly appeal to institutional desert.

[12] Miller, *Social Justice*, see especially pp. 104–6. James Dick characterises a principle of commutative justice as one requiring 'repayment of debts, return of borrowed items, or compensation for wrongly inflicted damages'. See J. Dick, 'How to Justify a Distribution of Earnings', *Philosophy and Public Affairs* 4 (1975), pp. 248–72, at, p. 261.

argument, that the market can adequately measure the value of people's productive contribution. Since the contribution argument aims at justifying market incomes as rewards for the value of people's productive contribution, it is essential that market prices be an adequate indicator of that value. The argument adduced in support of this last claim is as follows. The market, at least when it gravitates towards competitive equilibrium, is supposed to provide a standard by which to measure the value of people's contribution, where how valuable one's activity is is defined in terms of one's capacity to meet desires. Under ideal market conditions, the market pays each factor of production the equivalent of the value of its contribution to society, where what value that factor contributes to society is claimed to be reflected by the price that others are willing to pay for it.

As Miller readily concedes, since the market does not naturally tend to gravitate towards competitive equilibrium, a politically controlled agency would be necessary to set ground rules and intervene in *ad hoc* ways to prevent major inequalities.[13] This means that some constraints on the market, which are required in order for the latter to function as an appropriate standard to measure deserts, are allowed. Here too, however, just as with the compensatory desert argument we examined in the last chapter, it is assumed that those constraints will not affect labour price, which is left to the market, so that the incomes people reap on the free labour market are supposed to reflect the value of their productive contribution.

Even when it is accompanied by the suggestion that the government may intervene in specified ways to secure the appropriate background conditions, the claim that market prices reflect the value of one's contribution has been subjected to a number of objections. Although I will not pursue these points further, I should here mention three main such objections, some of which have been met with replies by Miller with a view to rescuing the contribution argument.

First, it has been suggested that it is misleading to take market prices to reflect the value of one's contribution to society, insofar as they at best reflect the value which certain goods and services have only for a particular section of the population that purchases those goods and services. Further, if there are marked inequalities in incomes, and there is only a small number of individuals with substantial disposable income who are willing to purchase a good a supplier provides, the latter may reap rewards for that good which allegedly misrepresent the welfare value of that same good.

---

[13] Miller, *Market, State and Community*, pp. 157 ff.

Miller has interpreted this objection as being fundamentally an expression of a scepticism about the possibility of interpersonal comparisons. As long as such comparisons are viewed to be possible, however, and as long as the underlying inequalities are not too great, then, so Miller suggests, what the market does is solve the problem of aggregating the value that things have for discrete individuals into a general measure of value.[14]

A second line of criticism goes deeper and questions the very link between prices, which supposedly measure want-satisfaction, and value. What people are prepared to buy, the objection goes, is not necessarily what they value. This point is strengthened by the observation that sometimes people demand things that are not in their best interest, and that demand itself, sometimes, is manufactured by those who then seek to meet it. This objection, however, so Miller thinks, is problematic, insofar as it rests on the idea that there is an intrinsic standard of value to which want-satisfaction is contrasted. Further, Miller has tried to argue that to distinguish between value and want-satisfaction leads to severing the link between what a person deserves and personal responsibility.[15] This, presumably, is because if 'value' refers to 'real value' as opposed to 'want-satisfaction', then people would not know how much real value they are contributing and they could not have control over how much value they contribute.

I do not think that Miller's reply to this second objection is a forceful one. Upholding that individuals' deserts are based on their success in creating 'real value' does not amount to stating that they would acquire deserts 'through processes lying beyond their conscious control'.[16] An objective standard of what counts as value-satisfaction may satisfy conditions of publicity, however difficult it would be to defend it. Even if we agree, then, with the claim that the notion of an intrinsic standard of value is problematic, this does not suffice to justify jettisoning it.

Finally, a third, and very commonly voiced, objection to the view that the market rewards individuals in accordance with the value they contribute, stresses that the size of each individual's contribution is impossible to ascertain.[17] More fundamentally, it is sometimes held that the very notion of individual contribution, within the context of co-operative production, is meaningless. The debate here has generally ended up focusing on the

---

[14] *Ibid.*, pp. 164–5. It has been suggested that the scepticism about interpersonal comparisons is ultimately a kind of solipsism. See I. M. D. Little, *A Critique of Welfare Economics* (Oxford University Press, 1960), p. 55.

[15] Miller, *Market, State and Community*, p. 160.   [16] *Ibid.*

[17] See Feinberg, 'Justice'; Dick, 'How to Justify'.

relative strengths and weaknesses of marginal productivity theory, the out-come of the debate being rather inconclusive.[18]

These and other criticisms cast serious doubts on the contribution argu-ment. I now leave these particular worries aside, however, to focus instead on a different sort of problem for the contribution argument, which concerns the justice of a differential distribution of deserts where people's differential deserts are based on producing market value.

2. THE PROBLEM OF LUCK, AND GOOD INTENTIONS

Insofar as the contribution argument aims to establish that the distribution of differential earnings achieved by the market is a just one by virtue of that distribution reflecting individuals' differential deserts, it encounters a series of difficulties that may be referred to as constituting the problem of contingency or of luck. In a nutshell, the problem is as follows. Both in the short term and the long term, various factors that are outside individuals' control, and which they cannot be held responsible for, so crucially affect what they can reap on the market that the ensuing distribution of rewards can hardly be claimed to reflect a pattern of differential deserts and, there-fore, be just. The second main contention of the contribution argument, then, is indefensible.

Contingent factors affect individuals' productive contribution in differ-ent ways. Fluctuations in market prices and changes in market conditions that are due to factors not under the relevant individuals' control sometimes have sudden and drastic effects on how great market rewards are going to be, so that these rewards would not seem to reflect people's deserts. Instances of short-term consequences of changes in market prices include, say, the case in which demand for the good I have been producing and quite suc-cessfully trading suddenly goes down, or the case in which the price of a good I produce and currently sell for a given price changes as a result of another supplier unexpectedly entering the market. In both cases, the

---

[18] On the possibility of using marginal productivity theory for the purpose of justifying market rewards, see Dick, 'How to Justify'. Miller is sceptical about resorting to marginal product as a solution for measuring individual contribution to a joint product. Miller, *Social Justice*, p. 108. It is worth noting that, insofar as one's contribution is viewed as part of a *joint* productive enterprise, desert on the basis of productive contribution is comparative in one way I identified in chapter 1 above. That is, comparisons would here be relevant for ascertaining how much each deserves, insofar as the desert basis makes reference to one's exhibiting a certain feature (broadly understood) *relative* to others, and insofar as *what* one deserves is affected by how much there is of the relevant deserved good. As chapter 1 has shown, to view desert as making reference to comparisons in this sense is compatible with holding the view that it is essentially a non-comparative principle of justice insofar as it holds that justice requires that each person get her due.

rewards I reap may diminish, and yet it would seem odd to say that I have become less deserving than I was prior to the change in demand or prior to the appearance of the new supplier. More generally, the contribution argument implies, oddly, that people's deserts may be affected by background contingencies, in that the size of one's market rewards will depend on consumers' tastes and on others' willingness to meet them, as well as on people's unchosen talents and attributes.

One response that defenders of the contribution argument have offered to the problem of contingency hinges on insisting that how deserving one is can indeed depend on external factors. Miller, for instance, has tried to show that in none of the cases I have mentioned is desert undermined by the fact that it depends on factors that are outside the agent's control. In this context, he makes the observation, already cited above, that desert is not only a matter of good intentions. Rather, he emphasises, '[desert] also has to do with how much benefit you create for the recipient of your services, and in nearly every case that depends on the configuration of the world outside'.[19] Since what value one creates is not independent of what others do, Miller claims, it is indeed the case that the service I provide is less valuable if someone else, too, provides it, and perhaps at a more competitive price. Odd as it may seem, then, it is actually true that my deserts diminish as a result of other suppliers entering the market and outbidding my prices. Similarly, Miller claims, the dependence of an individual's desert on background contingencies is not problematic. In the long term, when equilibrium is reached, an individual's deserts will depend on how she has responded to the various contingencies she has faced. So someone may choose to become skilled at a task she (rightly) foresees will be much in demand. In this case, Miller remarks, the person 'is surely properly rewarded for making that choice'.[20] Even in the face of pervasive contingencies, there is no gap between what a person deserves and what she gets through the market.

A response of this sort to the problem of contingency is not satisfactory. Its main weakness lies in the fact that it preserves the presumed correspondence of market value and desert even under conditions of contingency by making desert depend *solely* on the outcome produced and on the fact that the agent brought about that outcome. This makes the appeal of the contribution argument limited, ruling out an interpretation of it based on the contribution-mirrors-effort view of desert, and goes against the conviction that, for a distribution of differential rewards to be justified

---

[19] Miller, *Market, State and Community*, p. 166.   [20] *Ibid.*, p. 167.

by desert, people must have had a fair opportunity to acquire differential deserts.[21]

Consider, first, the cases in which the effect of contingencies is sudden and drastic. Whilst we may agree with Miller that even in these cases desert is not *merely* a matter of good intentions, the opposite does not follow, namely, that intentions, effort and commitment do not significantly count. And yet that is precisely what we need to accept in order to retain the link between market value and desert in the cases I have illustrated above, for it may well be that, as a result of someone else supplying the same good I have been successfully trading at much more competitive prices, I may not only sell somewhat less, but sell hardly anything at all and quickly go bankrupt. It is undeniable that the value of my goods has decreased, but not obvious that I suddenly become undeserving. Yet Miller insists that my deserts will have changed. He claims: 'If desert is based on value created, that value cannot be estimated without taking account of what others have produced; the notion that the service you render has the same value regardless of what others do is absurd.'[22] This observation seems plausible. It does not, however, rescue the contribution argument, and is both question-begging and mistargeted. It is question-begging because the question under consideration is whether a person's deserts can be based solely on the market value of her contribution, given that the market value of that contribution can change suddenly and substantially due to factors that are wholly outside of the person's control, whereas it seems that one's deserts do not vary in this way. But Miller assumes that 'desert is based on value created', which is precisely what is being questioned. Further, Miller's claim that 'the notion that the service you render has the same value regardless of what others do is absurd', which presumably characterises the position he is attacking, is mistargeted. We need not assert that 'the service you render has the same value regardless of what others do', where the 'value' of a service is its market value. But we may, and must, indeed, assert that, although the market value of a service I provide decreases, the performance of that service is still relevant for how deserving I am, insofar as it reflects my efforts or good intentions; since desert is also *partly* a matter of good intentions, this means that market value does not appropriately reflect my deserts.

---

[21] On the contribution mirrors effort argument, see Riley, 'Justice Under Capitalism'; J. Lamont, 'Problems for Effort-Based Distribution Principles', *Journal of Applied Philosophy* 12 (1995), pp. 215–29; W. Sadurski, *Giving Desert its Due. Social Justice and Legal Theory* (Dordrecht: D. Reidel, 1985), pp. 134–5.

[22] Miller, *Market, State and Community*, p. 166.

Miller's remarks about the long-term effects of market contingencies on one's deserts similarly imply that good intentions not only are not the only thing that matters, but also that they do not matter at all. The claim that someone who chooses to become skilled at those tasks which he rightly foresees will be in high demand 'is surely properly rewarded for making that choice' should not mislead us. The market is inattentive to how certain profitable skills have been acquired. It rewards individuals who have the appropriate skills, whether those skills are the result of deliberate and attentive cultivation, whether they have been stumbled upon, or whether they were forced on to some individual against his will. So, although we may say of Joseph that the high rewards he receives as an IT consultant are justified by the fact that he has decided to train in IT skills and forgo the pleasure he would have derived from doing philosophy,[23] that justification is not what accounts for Robert's supposed deserts, who was forced by his parents to go into IT, or for Anna's, who became an IT specialist because that was the only course on offer at her local university, without even realising it would be a potential source of high rewards.[24] Here, too, what the market registers does not seem to adequately reflect people's deserts.

To better see the limits of Miller's 'desert is not just a matter of good intentions' reply, consider the example he adduces in support of his claim that the presence of market contingencies does not constitute a problem for desert. Miller asks us to imagine that every month I clean the windows of my elderly neighbour's house, thus deserving 'considerable' gratitude. If one month, after I have been doing this for a while, the neighbour's grandson turns up and does the job before me, I cannot expect to be thanked as warmly as I would have been otherwise. This supposedly confirms that the usefulness of my service, and not my good intentions, is what grounds my deserts. I suggest, however, that this conclusion is drawn too swiftly. If my neighbour displays considerably less gratitude, I think I may justifiably be disappointed. His withdrawal of gratitude would show that he has been failing throughout to appreciate the significance of my willingness to take

[23] Notice that this justification of Joseph's rewards seems at odds with Miller's general contribution-based account, for it actually appears to rest either on a notion of compensatory desert, or a notion of desert as the legitimate expectation to reap the results of one's earlier choices, both of which interpretations of desert are discarded by Miller.

[24] This example introduces the issue of comparisons between individuals' deserts, to which I return below. Here I want only to underline that the market rewards the value one creates, for which certain skills are crucial. Why or how these skills have been acquired is utterly irrelevant so far as the market is concerned, so Miller's claim that one is properly rewarded for making the choice to acquire those skills is only going to justify some individuals' rewards and cannot be a general account of why market rewards reflect people's deserts.

time off and help him out. My disappointment would be especially justified if the neighbour's grandson turns up unexpectedly, and I carry on with my usual task unaware that I have been forestalled. It *may* be somewhat less justified if, after a while and despite knowing that my service is no longer needed, I keep performing it nonetheless. What this suggests is that, particularly in the short term, it seems odd to say that my deserts have changed, though my deserts may indeed change in the longer term. But at any rate, whether or not the neighbour may, in the short term, be justified in not thanking me as warmly as he would do when my service, besides displaying good intentions, was also very useful, he would not be justified in displaying very little or no gratitude at all. Yet this is precisely what may well happen on the market: my sales may go down drastically and suddenly. The market does not display any concern at all for my intentions; the usefulness of my service is all that matters. That is what market value, standardly, registers.[25]

The fact that the value of people's contribution, where the latter is measured by market prices, is substantially affected by various types of contingencies casts doubt on the contention that the principle of contribution is a principle of desert that can justify income differentials. A distribution of unequal rewards that satisfies the principle of contribution, that is, is not just, in that it meets neither the fair opportunity nor the comparative justice constraints I discussed in chapter 1. Before unfolding this point further by considering another possible line of defence of the contribution principle recently offered by Miller, let me remark on one possible reply Miller may make to what I have said so far. Recall my earlier discussion, in chapter 1, of the comparative aspects of desert claims.[26] When considering the way in which comparative considerations are relevant for justice, I suggested that they can enter the determination of how much one deserves, since that is not a wholly context-free matter that can be settled without any information about the world. How much, by way of reward, an hour of hard work deserves, for example, depends, among other things, on how much there is of the relevant deserved good: we cannot just settle arbitrarily on a given quantity of it as the appropriate deserved reward.

---

[25] The analogy of the neighbour's gratitude and market rewards is in my view untenable anyway. It stretches credulity to believe that incomes are rewards for 'gratitude universalised', as Miller, following Henry Sidgwick, suggests. See Miller, *Social Justice*, p. 118, and H. Sidgwick, *The Methods of Ethics*, 7th edn (London: Macmillan, 1963), Book III, chapter 5.

[26] Chapter 1, fifth section.

This is the view that Miller himself subscribes to, as is apparent from his recent work on comparative and non-comparative desert.[27] There he suggests that we can view desert of reward for a performance such as productive contribution as involving comparisons both about the desert basis and the deserved treatment: what someone who has performed in the relevant way deserves is not some given or 'natural' amount of the deserved good, Miller claims, but rather 'an amount that corresponds to the proportion between what she has done and what others have done'. And, he adds, '[t]he idea that there is some absolute amount of money that a person could deserve solely by virtue of the work that he has done and without regard to how others have performed makes no sense'.[28]

But note that this suggestion, which I endorse, fails to provide support for the view that market prices adequately reflect what one deserves even when contingency affects them. It is one thing to assert that just how much value to attach to my deserts – how much one deserves – is *made determinate* by comparative considerations about how much of the deserved good there is to go around and by the extent to which others display the desert basis. It is quite another, however, to state that how deserving one is is determined by external facts, and can change, therefore, as those facts change, *regardless* of why the change occurs and regardless of whether those facts affect others' deserts in the appropriate way, that is, so as to reflect people's comparative deservingness. If we were engaged in a co-operative venture that has to date been more or less successful but the fruits of which on one occasion turn out, through some unpredictable and very bad luck, to be nil, we could all deserve to receive less than we would if the venture were more fruitful, but it is not the case that we are all undeserving. That this is the case is shown by the fact that we could say, in these circumstances, that while there is no comparative injustice in this case, there is some non-comparative injustice we all suffer, in that we do not get what we deserve.

So, Miller's argument to the effect that a correspondence of market value and desert is preserved even under conditions of contingency hinges on making desert, implausibly, depend solely on the outcome produced by individuals. An interpretation of desert of this kind remains unargued for, does not sit well with Miller's own emphasis on the importance of treating individuals as responsible and freely choosing agents, and conflicts with a concern with fair opportunity to acquire differential deserts. I should

---

[27] D. Miller, 'Comparative and Non-Comparative Desert', in S. Olsaretti (ed.), *Desert and Justice* (Oxford University Press, 2003).
[28] *Ibid.*, p. 32.

now consider whether Miller's recent discussion of desert and luck serves to rescue the contribution argument.

3. DESERT AND TWO TYPES OF LUCK

Perhaps, while some sort of luck does disrupt desert, not all luck does. After all, the presence of luck is so pervasive that admitting that it constitutes a problem for the attribution of desert may seem to threaten the possibility of making any room for the latter. In his recent work, Miller has devoted more attention to the problem of luck, and it remains to be seen whether that treatment provides principled reasons for why certain types of luck do not disrupt desert.

There is, Miller claims, a relevant difference between two ways in which luck affects performance, where by luck he means any random events outside the agent's control.

On the one hand, the performance itself – what the agent actually achieves – may depend to a greater or lesser extent on his luck. I gave the example earlier of a poor archer who shoots three lucky arrows and wins the competition. I shall label luck of this kind 'integral luck'. On the other hand, luck may determine whether someone has the opportunity to perform in the first place. The car carrying the athlete to the track may break down so that she has no chance to run. One soldier may be given an opportunity to show courage in battle, while another never gets within the range of the enemy. Luck of this kind can be called 'circumstantial luck'.[29]

The effect of luck of these two different types on desert is, for Miller, different. Integral luck, claims Miller, does appear to nullify desert. The athlete who crosses the finish line first because her competitor, who was going to win, has a sudden appendicitis attack just before the end, did not deserve to win, a desert we do attribute to the unlucky athlete. When we assess people's deserts, we try to factor out the effects of good and bad integral luck. But circumstantial luck is different. If, for example, the athlete does not get to the race due to bad luck, then, though we may think that she would have won had she got there, we would still not claim that she deserves to win. 'Circumstantial luck always lies in the background of human performance', Miller remarks, and it does not normally nullify a person's deserts.[30]

[29] Miller, *Principles*, pp. 143–4.   [30] *Ibid.*, p. 146.

The distinction between integral and circumstantial luck can then be used in defence of the contribution argument as follows. Some market contingencies are instances of integral luck: as far as these are concerned, it is indeed the case that the affected person's deserts are nullified. So, for example, Miller states that an entrepreneur whose product turns out unexpectedly to be a great success does not deserve all his gains, however difficult it would be in this case to factor out the effect of luck from an inspired hunch.[31] However, most cases of market contingencies are not of this kind, but are to be seen, instead, as cases in which individuals enjoy, or suffer, circumstantial luck. Most cases in which as individual's performance is affected by underlying market contingencies, as well as by the differential distribution of natural talents, are supposedly cases of circumstantial luck; they are not, therefore, instances in which the agent's deserts are nullified. The claim that the market is just insofar as it (mostly) rewards in accordance with people's deserts as productive contribution, then, can be defended, despite the presence of contingency or luck.

What are we to make of this suggestion? My view is that we can endorse Miller's distinction between integral and circumstantial luck and his claim that we should avoid treating these two types of luck on a par, lest we implausibly sabotage desert altogether. Nonetheless, I will argue that endorsing these points does not lead to the conclusion Miller supports, namely, that circumstantial luck has no effect on the justice of a distribution of differential rewards. Instead, I suggest, we can and should take note of the distinctive way in which the presence of circumstantial luck, while not nullifying deserts, does undermine the justice of a distribution of differential rewards. Miller's failure to consider this results from his overlooking the possibility that different types of luck affect the justice of distributions in different ways; the nullification of deserts is not the only way in which luck may disrupt the justice of a distribution of rewards.

Let me then, first of all, say something more about the distinction between integral and circumstantial luck. As I see it, that distinction rests, quite simply, on the distinction between the conditions affecting the performance and the conditions affecting whether the performance can occur in the first place. In both cases, I take it that we are concerned only with

---

[31] *Ibid.*, p. 144. I am uncertain as to whether Miller thereby qualifies his earlier claim by conceding that cases of this sort may be cases of integral luck. If the appearance of another supplier of the good I have been selling occurs unexpectedly, I would seem to suffer bad integral luck, and the decreased rewards would not reflect my (not commensurately altered, in this case) deserts.

brute, rather than *option*, integral and circumstantial luck.[32] So long as the desert in question is desert for a given performance, circumstantial luck clearly cannot affect desert claims for which the presumed basis is that performance. If performance P is to be a desert basis for getting G, then, unless one engages in P, no desert in G can be acquired. An athlete who cannot get to the race because of bad luck can sensibly regret not having had the opportunity to participate in the race, and can sensibly suggest that she is the best runner and would have won had she taken part in the race. But it would be odd for her to claim that she deserved to win. For someone to make that type of desert claim she must have had an opportunity to display the grounds on which her presumed desert would rest. So, clearly, when we are ascertaining how deserving a particular person is of a particular good or treatment, only integral luck is relevant.

To grant this much to Miller, however, should not lead us to overlook that circumstantial luck, too, is relevant, if in a different way, to the role desert can play in justifying outcomes that are affected by luck. The intervention of circumstantial luck, in fact, becomes relevant when we assess people's *differential* claims. The question here is not one regarding whether someone who, due to bad circumstantial luck, fails to perform but would have been deserving had he been able to perform, is as deserving of the prize or of the reward as the person who has performed in the relevant way and has thereby become deserving. Rather, the question is whether, if burdens and benefits are distributed differentially on the basis of people's differential deserts, the fact that some people do not have a fair opportunity to acquire greater or lesser deserts (because those differential deserts are acquired on grounds that are wholly beyond their control) makes the resulting distribution unjust.

So, insofar as we are concerned with circumstantial luck, we are not concerned with its potential role in nullifying individuals' deserts, but in the justice of a distribution of unequal deserts that are acquired against differential circumstantial luck. Yet Miller's treatment of the question whether circumstantial luck has any effect on how much a person deserves compared with others proceeds as though we were asking the former, not the latter, question. And it is because Miller treats the question as one regarding

---

[32] Miller does not explicitly say as much, but it seems plausible to assume that brute luck is what he has in mind. That is, he is concerned here with events that were beyond individuals' control, and which those individuals could not have predicted, rather than with any deliberate gambles people make. Introducing option luck complicates the picture, since individuals are arguably made to bear the costs of their option luck, under appropriate circumstances, and this may hold true of both integral and circumstantial option luck. I leave option luck aside here. What is clear is that giving people a fair opportunity to deserve requires neutralising differential brute luck. For the distinction between brute luck and option luck, see R. Dworkin, *Sovereign Virtue* (Harvard University Press, 2000), p. 73.

the legitimacy of making isolated desert claims, rather than the justice of a distribution of differential deserts, that he states:

circumstantial luck may lead us to qualify our judgements about the deserts of those who are its beneficiaries. But if we want to keep the notion of desert and use it to make practical judgements, we cannot compensate completely for luck of the second kind . . . Circumstantial luck always lies in the background of human performances, and only when it intrudes in a fairly clear and direct way on what different people achieve relative to one another do we allow it to modify our judgements of desert.[33]

Now, it is true, I submit, that, if we claimed that circumstantial luck nullifies people's deserts in the same way that integral luck does, then it would be hard to retain the notion of desert. But that claim, which I do not need to make, is different from the one, which I do make, that if people's differential deserts depend on their differential circumstantial luck, then the distribution of those deserts is not just. Denying the first claim, which would result in sabotaging desert, need not commit us to denying the second, which does not lead to sabotaging desert but which casts doubt on whether the contribution principle is a principle of desert that can show the distribution of market outcomes to be substantively just.

Although circumstantial luck does not, in Miller's view, standardly affect the justice of a distribution of unequal rewards, he concedes that there are limited cases in which it may do just that. By way of conclusion, then, let me suggest that Miller's diagnosis of such cases is misjudged, and that, when properly analysed, these cases support the conclusions I have defended about circumstantial luck. Miller's suggestion is that whether circumstantial luck has any effect on how much someone deserves compared with others will vary according to whether the deserved good is more or less competitive, so that someone's receipt of that good occurs, in a sense, at the expense of others. He then envisages a case in which this happens. Suppose that a chemistry Nobel prize is given to someone for a path-breaking discovery; then imagine that we have good reasons to believe that that discovery could have easily been made by several other chemists had they been in the appropriate position. Is our judgement about the justifiability of the Nobel prize winner's getting the prize altered in light of our knowledge that there are others who would have been as deserving as the actual winner in the appropriate circumstances?

Miller thinks that in cases like this one, in which the deserved good in question is competitive – in the sense that a person's receiving it stands

[33] Miller, *Principles*, p. 146.

in the way of others getting it – the fact that others have not been given the opportunity to come to deserve the prize makes the actual winner less deserving.[34] But he also thinks that this case does not generalise to that of market rewards, since these are not, recall, to be seen as prizes, and the context in which they are reaped is not a competitive one in the sense in which the award of a Nobel prize is.

But, I submit, some of the same reasons that support the judgement that circumstantial luck disrupts justice in the Nobel prize case also support similar conclusions in the case of market-generated rewards for productive contribution. To see this, we need to distinguish three different claims that may be made about the Nobel prize case, which are conflated by Miller's presentation of this example.

First, there is the claim that, insofar as the assignment of the Nobel prize is an expression of exceptional achievement, the fact that, barring epistemic difficulties in ascertaining this, we know that others would have been as deserving of the Nobel prize, means that the actual winner is not really deserving of what the Nobel prize stands for, to wit, the expression of admiration for exceptional achievement. In this sense we would say, indeed, that the actual winner is 'less deserving'. If there is a competition for who is the best x, and all the potentially good contestants fail to make it to the town where the competition is taking place due to tornadoes except for one, who is local, then, though he may indeed be the best x, the prize he gets becomes less deserved: it fails to express the extent to which it is supposed to select the best x among an adequate pool of contestants.

Second, we may claim that since the deserved good in question is scarce, and since there are other potential prize winners who are, we are sure, potentially just as deserving as the actual one, the assignment of the prize to one only fails to realise the demands of comparative justice, in that it will not reflect the distribution of people's deserts.

Third and finally, we could claim that excluding some individuals from competing for the deserved good on grounds that they are not responsible for seems unjust.[35] Notice that this claim does not support the contention that the actual Nobel prize winner is made any less deserving by the existence of these others. Rather, it is fundamentally a claim about the unfairness of excluding others from being potential beneficiaries of a good on grounds that they are not responsible for. But the judgement that the actual prize winner is (non-comparatively) deserving is unaltered;

---

[34] *Ibid.*, pp. 144–6.

[35] Since the good is the chemistry Nobel prize, the relevant others are individuals who could compete with the individual for the Nobel prize, to wit, other chemists.

his deserts are unchanged: to suggest otherwise is to suggest, implausibly, that his deserts are affected by things that have nothing to do with what he or others have done, namely, the existence of others who are *potential* deservers.

Now note that only the first of these three claims is one the relevance of which does not extend to the case of market rewards in general. The pertinence of that claim is closely related to the fact that the deserved good is a prize that supposedly marks exceptional achievement. Both the second and the third claims, however, are relevant for an analysis of the justice of market rewards, even when we assume that the latter are not to be conceived of as prizes in the general case. The second claim is premised in the concern with comparative justice, which I discussed in chapter 1 above. Insofar as we are concerned with justifying a distribution of burdens and benefits across persons, and given that the deserved goods are scarce where economic justice is concerned, a distribution will be just as long as the distribution of economic rewards reflects deserts in a comparative way. A distribution of unequal desert-reflecting rewards must respect the demands of comparative justice, but a distribution of market-generated rewards will not respect these demands: not everyone will get what they deserve. And the third claim, as will be obvious at this point, is certainly one that has relevance for the justice of a distribution of free market rewards. Insofar as we are concerned with justifying a distribution of burdens and benefits by reference to an underlying distribution of differential deserts, we note that circumstantial luck undermines the justice of that distribution, as the fair opportunity constraint is not met by that distribution.

With these observations in mind, we can now conclude by providing an overall assessment of how the contribution argument fares in the light of the fact that various contingencies affect how productive individuals' contributions are. There are three respects in which the distribution of market outcomes fails to reach justice, so that, even if the contribution principle were a principle of desert, a distribution defended by the principle of contribution would not be just.

First, some individuals' performance is affected by integral luck, so their deserts are nullified or at least seriously modified, but the market does not register this. An entrepreneur may make a decision that turns out, by fluke, to be extremely profitable, while another may be outbid by the unpredictable successful marketing of imported goods at competitive prices he cannot afford to compete with. When integral luck nullifies some individuals' deserts, those individuals will fail to receive what they deserve. Some will reap rewards that are higher, and some lower, than what they deserve, where respecting desert requires that integral luck not affect what people deserve. This claim can be made without forgoing the contention that the contribution principle is a principle of desert, for the contribution principle itself *may* be so formulated as to capture this claim. It may be said that there are cases in which the link between a person's actions and the outcome those actions bring about (in this case, the value of the contribution made by those actions) is weakened to such an extent that she can no longer be deemed to deserve that outcome.[36]

Second, however, even where the market rewards some people get reflect what they should get on the principle of contribution, the overall distribution of market rewards will not be comparatively just. For, if what people deserve is not adequately measured by market value, then, while it may be true that everyone gets the equivalent of the (market) value they contribute, it is not true that everyone gets what they deserve. So long as integral luck affects what rewards people reap, people's deserts will not be equally respected.

But third, and more fundamentally, the differential market rewards people reap largely depend on differential circumstantial luck so that, even if one insisted that market prices do reflect differences in people's productive performance, the distribution of market rewards for deserts based on productive performance is unjust. Suppose that someone suggests that the inequality in market incomes reaped by doctors and nurses is *just*, since they must reflect the unequal value of their productive contribution, and people deserve to be rewarded in accordance with the value of their productive contribution. Surely, it may be added, the fact that doctors regularly reap greater monetary rewards than nurses is not just a matter of doctors' good integral luck: although it may be true sometimes of some doctors that the rewards they reap are the result of good integral luck, this is not what generally accounts for those rewards being quite substantial. Therefore, there are no reasons to revise our judgement that doctors deserve their high rewards, as there would be if integral luck were at work.

This suggestion, however, overlooks the role of circumstantial luck, which affects what rewards individuals reap in two ways. First, it affects the market rewards nurses and doctors reap, respectively, in that those rewards are a function of factors that are beyond individuals' control, and which

---

[36] This is what Miller seems to suggest. The objection from integral luck would, if we accept this reply, be an objection against the third claim of the contribution argument rather than the second: it would undermine the claim that the free market rewards in accordance with the demands of desert as contribution, rather than the claim that a distribution of rewards justified by the contribution principle is just. So, even then, it would be a problem for the contribution argument.

individuals cannot be held responsible for, such as the actual supply and demand of nurses and doctors. And second, it affects, in various ways, *any one individual's* chance of becoming a nurse or a doctor, since an individual's occupational choice is seriously constrained by factors such as her natural talents and various forms of brute external luck. Someone who may have wanted to become a doctor may be unable to do so because of external luck, or because she is untalented, or both. And, even if her performance as a nurse may have less market value, her receiving less rewards than someone more talented and luckier who has become a doctor is not justified by desert, since she did not have a fair opportunity to become more deserving. If desert is to justify a distribution of benefits and burdens across individuals, it must be desert acquired against a background in which circumstantial luck is minimised.

This suggestion has been criticised by Miller. He acknowledges that, to the extent that luck is under human control, we have reason to reduce its scope, but then shirks the implications of this suggestion by stating that '[d]esert is strengthened when opportunities to become deserving themselves depend on the initiative and choice of individuals, *and are not artificially distributed by some other human agency*'.[37] We have reason to contest this claim: if individuals do not have a fair opportunity to be deserving, we cannot rest assured that inequalities that arise between them really reflect unequal deserts, rather than unfair advantage of some over others.

So long as a distribution of differential market earnings is one that reflects people's differential deserts, where those differential deserts are acquired against a background of circumstantial luck, the contribution argument fails as an argument for the justice of the market. The contribution argument rests on an interpretation of desert which makes true the claim that market earnings reflect people's deserts at the expense of the justice-informing nature of desert. Desert as a defensible principle of distributive justice is a notion of active desert that respects the fair opportunity requirement, and should thus have application over a distribution of differential benefits and burdens across individuals. A principle of desert of that sort would require the elimination of precisely the sort of circumstantial luck which instead determines differentials in market earnings, and which

---

[37] Miller, *Principles*, p. 145. As should be apparent by now, I do not agree with the contention that circumstantial luck *reduces desert*. Rather, I would make the following claim. To the extent that circumstantial luck is in the background, then the distribution of rewards matching people's deserts is unjust. Or, as I have sometimes put this point, to the extent that we adopt a notion of desert which allows the impact of circumstantial luck to determine people's differential deserts, that notion is not a notion of desert that can justify a distribution of burdens and benefits.

the contribution argument tries to establish, unsuccessfully, is reconcilable with desert. The resulting argument is not one which shows that a market distribution of burdens and benefits is just.

4. SUMMARY

Before turning, in the next chapters, to examine the entitlement-based justification of the free market, let me briefly summarise the main conclusions of my analysis so far. In this and the previous chapter I have analysed two main arguments that try to justify market distributions of incomes by appeal to desert, and have argued that neither of them is successful. My main focus, in analysing these justifications, has been on their contention that the principle of desert each favours is a defensible principle of justice. That contention, as I have shown, can be analysed as two other separate ones. First, desert as compensation and desert as contribution are *eligible principles of desert*, that is, they meet the three eligibility constraints I identified in chapter 1, so that they could lend themselves, in principle, to informing what justice requires. Second, a distribution of rewards that satisfies the principles of compensation and contribution, respectively, is just. This second point could be put in a different way, namely, that compensation and contribution, respectively, in order to be defensible or attractive principles of justice, must satisfy the fair opportunity and the comparative justice constraints. A principle of desert that meets these constraints is not liable to some potentially fatal objections that have been advanced against the possibility of adopting desert, and can justify inequalities as just.

As far as the interpretations of desert adopted by the compensatory and the contribution arguments are concerned, I have argued that desert as compensation is not eligible as a candidate principle of desert, since it is not an independent and distinctive notion of desert. Compensatory desert claims are claims that express an independently formulated demand of justice, where what justice requires is determined independently of compensatory desert. As far as desert as reward for productive contribution is concerned, I have suggested that some of the arguments that are offered in its favour support only the general claim to the effect that people should be rewarded for the performance of productive or socially useful activities, rather than the specific claim to the effect that people should be rewarded in accordance with the value of their productive contribution. We have less reason than is often thought to believe that the contribution principle is really an independent and distinctive principle of desert, since its claims seem the expression of demands of commutative justice, or, in other cases, of a principle of non-discrimination.

Further, I have argued that both the compensatory desert and the contribution argument are unsuccessful to the extent that the distributions of rewards they recommend fall foul of the fair opportunity requirement that is associated with a defensible principle of desert, as well as of the comparative justice requirement. Even if the notion of compensatory desert were a defensible notion of desert, a market distribution of those rewards would not be just, because individuals' differential deserts are not deserts that those individuals had a fair opportunity to acquire. Similarly, even if the market rewarded individuals proportionally with the value of their productive contribution, a distribution of differential deserts is one that is underpinned by circumstantial luck, the elimination of which would be required for that distribution to be a just one.

I started my discussion of desert in chapter 1 by pointing to how the notion of desert is used in a variety of different contexts, with different meanings and connotations. I suggested that we should not dismiss some uses of desert as non-genuine or sham, but that, in order to consider which notion of desert is defensible as a principle of justice that can justify market outcomes, we should proceed carefully in delimiting and examining the notion of desert that can serve as a principle of distributive justice, and that can be defended in light of some objections that have been moved against the possibility of adopting desert. There are, of course, some senses of 'desert' on which it is true that the free market gives individuals what they deserve. But many appeals to this principle are indefensible. They wrongly proceed as if all interpretations of desert were equally eligible as principles of justice, while in fact many of them are parasitic on some independent conception of justice, or are institutional, so that they cannot inform what justice requires. Other interpretations of desert, while eligible, in principle, to inform what justice requires, are indefensible, suggesting as they do that justice does not require that people be given a fair opportunity to deserve, and that people should be treated as equals relative to their deserts. It is up to defenders of the free market to show, not only that there is *some* usage of desert such that the market may be said to satisfy it, but that this usage is one that meets certain plausible constraints. Neither the compensatory desert argument nor the contribution arguments succeed in showing this.

CHAPTER 4

Liberty and entitlements in the libertarian justification of the free market

I. FROM DESERT TO ENTITLEMENT AS GROUNDS FOR JUSTIFYING FREE MARKET OUTCOMES

The defence of the market, says Jan Narveson, is the first, if not the only, thing on the libertarian agenda. However, he goes on to add, to defend some market activity is trivial: libertarians aim at justifying no less than a full market society.[1] This ambitious libertarian project, to which I now turn, may seem to be more likely to succeed in providing a justification of free market outcomes than the desert-based arguments I have examined so far. By resting their case for the justice of free markets on the appeal to a substantive principle of justice, desert-based arguments must show that a distribution of rewards matches a pattern or distribution of deserts. This, as I have shown, raises serious problems where the distribution of rewards is one generated by the free market, since a market-generated distribution of rewards is deeply and pervasively influenced by the effects of luck, so that it is unlikely to match a distribution of differential deserts. I have also shown that attempts at overcoming this problem and trying to render desert compatible with luck stretch the notion of desert in an indefensible way.

None of these difficulties seem to beset libertarian arguments for the free market. These are entitlement-based, that is, they set out to justify the free market by appealing to antecedently established entitlements of individuals, the market being the process whereby these rights are exchanged without being infringed. In this view, the market is seen as 'part and parcel' of

---

[1] J. Narveson, *The Libertarian Idea* (Philadelphia: Temple University Press, 1988) and 'The Justice of the Market: Comments on Gray and Radin', in J. W. Chapman and J. R. Pennock (eds.), *Markets and Justice. Nomos* XXXI (New York University Press, 1989), pp. 250–76. Recall that by 'market' is meant nothing other than the subset of activities in which rights to do various things with various objects are traded, and a free market is one in which agents have full private property rights. A full market society is one where everything is owned by individuals (whether as individuals or as members of voluntary associations).

the exercise of pre-given rights.[2] By holding that justice consists simply in the requirement to respect those rights, the libertarian argument forgoes appeal to any substantive principle and relies instead on a pure procedural theory of distributive justice.[3] The distinctive characteristic of a pure procedural theory of justice is that there is no independent criterion for determining what a just division or distribution is, that is, no criterion defined separately from, and prior to, the procedure which is then to be followed. There is only 'a correct or fair procedure such that the outcome is likewise correct or fair, *whatever it is, provided that the procedure has been properly followed*'.[4] A distribution is just, for the libertarian, when it has been brought about as a result of everyone's rights being respected. There is no pattern which the distribution of rewards has to match, and no independent principle by which to judge the justice of that distribution. For this reason, the libertarian argument for the market appears to be appealingly clear-cut and robust: a strictly non-consequentialist justification such as the libertarian one has the advantage of being independent of empirical regularities. Market transactions themselves may be good or bad, but they are always legitimate independently of such considerations insofar as they are sanctioned by antecedently given rights.[5]

Whilst differing from desert-based arguments in relying on a procedural, rather than a substantive, conception of justice, entitlement-based defences of the market share with desert-based ones two important and related features, which I have mentioned before. First, both rest on *historical* conceptions of justice, so that it matters, for the justice of a given distribution, how that distribution came about. Secondly, both adopt non-comparative principles of distributive justice, claiming that justice consists in giving separate individuals their due. As a result, both claim to give pride of place to personal responsibility, since both conceive of justice as requiring respect of individuals by giving them their due, where what their due is depends on what they have done. It remains to be seen, then, whether entitlements and the related notions of freedom and choice that libertarians appeal to can indeed give adequate expression to a commitment to treating individuals as responsible agents, which libertarians as much as desert theorists claim to embrace, and whether they can provide the grounds for justifying the free market.

[2] See A. Sen, 'The Moral Standing of the Market', in E. F. Paul, F. D. Miller and J. Paul (eds.), *Ethics and Economics* (Oxford: Blackwell, 1985), pp. 1–19; Alan Gibbard, 'What's Morally Special About Free Exchange?', in Paul *et al.* (eds.), *Ethics and Economics*, pp. 20–8.
[3] For a definition of pure, perfect and imperfect procedural theories of justice, see J. Rawls, *A Theory of Justice* (Oxford University Press, 1972), pp. 85–6.
[4] *Ibid.*, p. 86, emphasis mine.   [5] Sen, 'Moral Standing of the Market'.

In what follows I subject to scrutiny the libertarian apologetics of the free market largely through an examination of Robert Nozick's defence of the market in *Anarchy, State, and Utopia*.[6] Nozick's version of libertarianism clearly does not exhaust the libertarian stance, neither in its right version nor, obviously, in its very close rival – left-libertarianism – which, in recent years, has flourished in various forms, attracting very sophisticated supporters.[7] Some of what I say in what follows will consider, and have a bearing upon, arguments for the free market other than Nozick's that appeal to self-ownership, liberty and voluntariness. My main aim is to show how the libertarian defence of the unbridled market, insofar as it appeals to notions of voluntariness and freedom, fails.[8]

Before undertaking that critique I must begin by providing a characterisation of the libertarian defence of the market that I will subject to examination. Such a defence is, as I have mentioned, entitlement-based, and the entitlement theories of justice defended by libertarians typically treat at length questions regarding original rights and principles of just acquisition, and view the issue of the conditions under which the transfer of original rights should occur as a derivative one. The present chapter aims to offer an outline of the libertarian defence of the free market in which freedom and voluntariness play a significant role, thereby focusing on the conditions under which justice is supposedly preserved in transfer. After reconstructing Nozick's defence of the free market society in section 2, I turn, in section 3, to consider how the right-libertarianism defended by Nozick differs from, and is challenged by, left-libertarianism's alternative account of original rights and just acquisition. This is done with a view both to locating Nozick's arguments and to cast light on the nature and relevance of the ones I develop. Whilst some of what I say in what follows could well be endorsed by left-libertarians, the latter, too, so I suggest, have paid insufficient attention to the question of justice in transfer. I then conclude the chapter, in section 4, by making a case for why libertarians – both right and left – should give more attention to justice in transfer, and suggest that the attempt to circumvent the appeal to voluntariness as an independent justificatory principle for the free market renders libertarianism unappealing and ultimately incoherent.

---

[6] R. Nozick, *Anarchy, State, and Utopia* (Oxford: Blackwell, 1974); henceforth cited as *ASU*.
[7] Three book-length defences of different versions of left-libertarianism are H. Steiner, *An Essay on Rights* (Oxford: Blackwell, 1994); P. Van Parijs, *Real Freedom for All. What (If Anything) Can Justify Capitalism?* (Oxford: Clarendon Press, 1995); and M. Otsuka, *Libertarianism Without Inequality* (Oxford University Press, 2003). In what follows, by 'libertarianism' *simpliciter* I refer to right-libertarianism.
[8] Throughout I use 'freedom' and 'liberty' interchangeably.

The present chapter, then, sets the stage for the following two chapters, which criticise the libertarian argument as I characterise it here. That argument is one which freedom and voluntariness have pride of place: libertarians claim to be defenders of a free society and allege that a free society is a free market society. This is because, so the argument runs, in a free market society all (or nearly all) interferences with individuals are going to be voluntarily consented to, so there is going to be no limitation of individuals' freedom.[9] Underpinning this contention is a voluntariness requirement, namely, the claim that voluntariness is a necessary and sufficient condition for the legitimacy of nearly all obligations and interference with individuals.

2. THE LIBERTARIAN DEFENCE OF THE FREE MARKET: MORAL FOUNDATIONS AND STRUCTURE

There is no chapter or section in the entire *Anarchy, State, and Utopia* dedicated to a discussion of 'the market'. Nozick's primary aim in his book is to show that the minimal state is justified, and no other state with more powers than that is. He proceeds in two stages, first tracing the steps whereby a minimal state-like institution would arise from a situation of anarchy *via* a competition among several private associations for protection, and then moving on to considering and rejecting the possibility that that association should have any powers beyond those acquired in this process, by responding to John Rawls' theory of justice. In both steps, the yardstick for the legitimacy of institutions and their formation are what Nozick calls moral constraints, that is, inviolable and pre-given individual rights. These also underlie Nozick's defence of the free market, which is, however, derivative and indirect and an implication of Nozick's theory of justice, 'the entitlement theory'.[10] The latter is grounded in an intuitively appealing idea, namely, the conviction that it is never possible to justify non-consented-to interpersonal sacrifices of individuals. By making this conviction the driving idea in the elaboration of a theory of justice, Nozick sets himself against not only the utilitarian tradition, but also, or so he thinks, against the Rawlsian Difference Principle. Nozick turns against Rawls the same accusation the latter had directed against utilitarianism: for although Rawls attempts to build his theory on Kantian bases, his Difference Principle, Nozick claims, ends up sacrificing the most advantaged members of society in order to

---

[9] In what follows I talk about 'consent' and 'choice' interchangeably.   [10] *ASU*, pp. 150–3.

compensate for the least advantaged ones. Just like utilitarians, Rawls himself, so Nozick claims, fails to take seriously the separateness of persons.[11]

Nozick's entitlement theory, like other libertarian theories, is characterised by the following four main features, which Peter Vallentyne has identified.[12] First, it is individualist, insofar as it takes individual agents, and not communities or states or societies, to be the object of fundamental moral concern. Libertarianism purports to assign 'ultimate and irreducible moral importance to each person's life'.[13] Second, libertarianism, including Nozick's, is rights-based, in that it takes the concern for individuals it enjoins to be adequately expressed by assigning inviolable rights to persons, in contrast to goal-based moralities.[14] Nozick argues that the concern for the separateness of persons his libertarianism expresses supports ascribing inviolable entitlements to individuals. These entitlements are incorporated in the theory of justice in the form of moral side constraints, which, in Eric Mack's words, are 'rights-correlative obligations', that is, they are constraints placed upon the actions to be performed, as opposed to being rights that are incorporated into a moral goal.[15] A theory that postulates rights in the latter way results in what Nozick calls a 'utilitarianism of rights', because, although it aims at minimising the violation of rights, it would nonetheless allow for the infringement of rights if this were to serve to lessen their overall violation in society.[16] Third, libertarianism is property-rights-based, holding that the relevant rights, including the right to liberty, are property rights.[17] Further, it recognises that those rights include original rights and created derivative rights, and, as a result, the libertarian theory of justice

---

[11] *Ibid.*, chapter 3; Rawls, *Theory of Justice*, sections 5, 6 and 30.

[12] See P. Vallentyne, 'Left-Libertarian Theories of Justice' (unpublished manuscript, 1999). There is a published French version of this manuscript. See P. Vallentyne, 'Le Libertarisme de gauche et la justice', *Revue Economique* 50 (1999), pp. 859–78.

[13] E. Mack, 'Moral Individualism and Libertarian Theory', in T. R. Machan and D. B. Rasmussen (eds.), *Liberty for the 21st Century. Contemporary Libertarian Thought* (Maryland: Rowman & Littlefield, 1995), pp. 41–58. See also T. R. Machan, *Individuals and their Rights* (La Salle, Ill.: Open Court, 1989).

[14] See Mack, 'Moral Individualism' and 'Self-Ownership and the Right to Property', *The Monist* 73 (1990), pp. 519–43. Here Mack insists that 'within any large-scale pluralist society, the special sharing of goals that exists among particular individuals and groups will not even begin to provide for goal-based rules or prescriptions having general interpersonal force across that society' (p. 521). Mack's belief in the agent-relativity of value underpins his commitment to rights-based individualism.

[15] E. Mack, 'How to Derive Libertarian Rights', in J. Paul (ed.), *Reading Nozick* (Oxford: Blackwell, 1982), pp. 286–302. Note that moral side constraints need not be rights-based, like the ones Nozick endorses: there can be duties without correlative waivable rights.

[16] *ASU*, pp. 28–30. An instance of the 'utilitarianism of rights' would be Ronald Dworkin's theory; see R. Dworkin, *Taking Rights Seriously* (London: Duckworth, 1977).

[17] See, for instance, Narveson, *Libertarian Idea*, p. 66, and 'Contracting for Liberty', in Machan and Rasmussen (eds.), *Liberty for the 21st Century*; J. Hospers, 'What Libertarianism Is', in Machan and Rasmussen (eds.), *Liberty for the 21st Century*; Steiner, *Essay on Rights*, at pp. 39, 52 and 91.

is historical, viewing the justice of holdings to depend on how those hold-ings were acquired and transferred.[18] Finally, libertarianism endorses full self-ownership: the most fundamental entitlement is that to one's natural assets and talents. Libertarians inherit the concept of self-ownership from John Locke, who, in Nozick's words, viewed a person as having 'a right to decide what would become of himself and what he would do, and as hav-ing a right to reap the benefits of what he did'.[19] According to Nozick, the natural right of self-ownership has its moral foundation in the separateness of persons.[20]

Since the contention that the right of self-ownership is a natural right with which all individuals are endowed is the distinctive characteristic of the libertarian position, both right and left, and a crucial element in the libertarian justification of the market, it is worth clarifying what exactly this right is and what motivates its adoption.

As G. A. Cohen has pointed out, the concept of self-ownership is a reflexive one, denoting a person's moral relation to herself.[21] That relation is fleshed out as one of ownership, congruently with libertarianism's con-tention, which I have just mentioned, that all rights are property rights. Libertarianism claims to enjoin respect for individuals as beings with 'a spe-cial moral jurisdiction over [themselves]',[22] and, since to own something is to have the right to do with it as one pleases, respect for individuals' moral jurisdiction over themselves takes the form of a recognition of them as self-owners. As one libertarian puts it: 'At a fundamental moral level autonomous agents are (initially, at least) self-owning in the sense of hav-ing moral authority to decide how to live their lives (within the constraints of the rights of others).'[23] The concept of self-ownership has been criticised for being indeterminate. Following Cohen, I assume that this indetermi-nacy may be overcome, and indeed, as we have just seen, libertarianism is characterised by the endorsement of a *full* and *universal* self-ownership.[24]

---

[18] See H. Steiner, 'Liberty and Equality', *Political Studies* 29 (1981), pp. 555–69.

[19] *ASU*, p. 171. See John Locke, *Two Treatises of Government*, edited by Peter Laslett (Cambridge University Press, 1988), pp. 287–8.

[20] *ASU*, p. 33; R. Nozick, 'On the Randian Argument', in Paul (ed.), *Reading Nozick*, pp. 206–31.

[21] As argued by G. A. Cohen, *Self-Ownership, Freedom, and Equality* (Cambridge University Press, 1995), chapter 9.

[22] Mack, 'Self-Ownership and the Right to Property', p. 522.

[23] P. Vallentyne, 'Self-Ownership and Equality: Brute Luck, Gifts, Universal Dominance, and Leximin', *Ethics* 107 (1997), pp. 321–43, at p. 321.

[24] For the claim that self-ownership is indeterminate, see R. J. Arneson, 'Lockean Self-Ownership: Towards a Demolition', *Political Studies* 39 (1991), pp. 36–54; A. Ryan, 'Self-Ownership, Autonomy, and Property Rights', *Social Philosophy and Policy* 11 (1994), pp. 241–58. Cohen replies in *Self-Ownership*, pp. 213–17.

That is, *all* individuals have *full* private property rights over themselves. According to Cohen, the thesis of self-ownership then holds that[25]

> Each person is the morally rightful owner of himself. He possesses over himself, as a matter of moral right, all those rights that a slaveholder has over a complete chattel slave as a matter of legal right, and he is entitled, morally speaking, to dispose over himself in the way such a slaveholder is entitled, legally speaking, to dispose over his slave.[26]

Full self-ownership, then, includes both rights of control over, and use of, one's mental and physical powers, and the right to what one can reap by applying those powers, both on one's own and through unregulated exchanges with others. Nozick and other libertarians think that only by positing individuals' rights of self-ownership as side constraints, rather than the minimisation of their violation as a goal, is the Kantian principle that persons are ends and not means really satisfied and personal autonomy respected. The idea is thus respected that persons 'may not be sacrificed or used for the achieving of other ends without their consent. Individuals are inviolable.'[27]

If we grant individuals full self-ownership, what follows from it?

As I have shown, self-ownership rights protect an area in which a person may not be *forced* to do anything, although they do allow interference aimed at securing other people's self-ownership rights. This means that non-consented-to obligations, with the exception of those non-consented-to obligations that are the correlative of others' rights, are seen as illegitimate, insofar as they are taken to amount to acquiring partial property rights in someone. At the same time, the principle of self-ownership implies a principle of self-responsibility, whereby each individual is alone responsible for himself, duties on others being of a merely negative sort.[28] The thesis of self-ownership, in other words, states that although all are required not

---

[25] The distinction between the concept and the thesis of self-ownership has been made by Cohen, *Self-Ownership*, p. 290.

[26] *Ibid.*, p. 68.

[27] *ASU*, p. 31. This respect for individuals is grounded in the recognition that they possess certain distinctly human characteristics which are valuable and which require protection. These characteristics, according to Nozick, include rationality, free will and moral agency, as well as the capacity to guide their life in accordance with some overall conception they themselves formulate. These features – and the conviction of their worth – provide the foundations to moral side constraints and to the entitlements which these protect. *Ibid.*, pp. 48–50.

[28] J. Child, 'Can Libertarianism Sustain a Fraud Standard?', *Ethics* 104 (1994), pp. 722–38, see pp. 728–9 in particular. For the appeal to self-responsibility, see also T. Machan, 'The Virtue of Freedom in Capitalism', *Journal of Applied Philosophy* 3 (1986), pp. 49–58. I return to the relation between self-ownership, freedom and responsibility in section 4 below, and explore it in greater depth in chapter 6 below.

to harm others, no one is required to assist anyone else.[29] As Cohen has remarked, '[t]he polemically crucial right of self-ownership is the right not to be (forced to) supply product or service to anyone'.[30]

Cohen and some libertarians, including Nozick, also hold that self-ownership, protecting as it does one's right not to be forced to assist others, is inconsistent with redistributive income taxation as such, which is other-assisting: 'I do not (fully) own myself if I am required to give others (part of) what I earn by applying my powers.'[31] As I will show below, this latter claim has been challenged by left-libertarians, who insist that redistributive taxation on income *is* compatible with respect of full self-ownership. But according to right-libertarians such as Nozick, the endorsement of full self-ownership is inconsistent with a tax on earned market income as such, which requires that, whenever an individual uses his powers for his benefit, he should also use them for someone else's benefit to a certain degree. Libertarianism's endorsement of full self-ownership has then been argued to be inextricably linked with a defence of the market: 'market competition', says Cohen, 'is the social soul of self-ownership'.[32]

Nozick believes that, besides being endowed with rights of self-ownership, individuals have potentially very extensive full private property rights in external resources, which they come to acquire either by appropriating previously unowned resources (congruently with a fairly generous principle of justice in acquisition, which requires only that the appropriator compensates others up to the point where they are no worse off than they would have been had the resource not been appropriated), or as a result of others' transfers of justly held resources (in line with a principle of justice in transfer that proscribes force and fraud).[33] With these resources, too, individuals may do as they please, since their having *full* private property rights in them simply means that these resources are theirs to do with as they

---

[29] As Richard Arneson puts it, 'Self-ownership is the moral principle that one ought to be left free to do whatever one chooses so long as non-consenting other persons are not thereby harmed, in specified ways.' Arneson, 'Lockean Self-Ownership', p. 36; see also J. Waldron, *The Right to Private Property* (Oxford University Press, 1988), p. 388. On some of the issues surrounding this articulation of the principle of self-ownership, see Cohen, *Self-Ownership*, pp. 226–8. I look at Nozick's harm criterion in chapter 5 below.

[30] Cohen, *Self-Ownership*, p. 215. See also R. Arneson, 'Property Rights in Persons', *Social Philosophy and Policy* 9 (1992), pp. 201–30. Arneson refers to the obligations proscribed by self-ownership as 'pure obligations to aid others', which, he claims, give the beneficiaries limited property rights in the body of the person whose presumed obligation the law enforces.

[31] Cohen, *Self-Ownership*, p. 216.   [32] *Ibid.*, p. 227.

[33] See *ASU*, pp. 150–3 for a statement of the principles of justice in acquisition, transfer and rectification that make up the entitlement theory. See also *ASU*, pp. 174–82 on justice in acquisition. For a critical discussion of Nozick's theory of justice in acquisition, see Cohen, *Self-Ownership*, chapter 3. I illustrate this point further in the next section.

like; as a result, *any* taxation other than the taxation necessary to protect and enforce everyone's private property rights in themselves and in their resources is rights-violating and equivalent to theft.

Respect of individuals' full self-ownership rights and of their private property rights in external resources, in accordance with the principles of justice in acquisition and of justice in transfer specified by the entitlement theory, is all that justice requires. So long as the conditions for just acquisition and transfer are met, justice is preserved. Whatever distribution results from the recursive application of these principles is a just one. As Nozick remarks, 'the total result is the product of many individual decisions which the different individuals involved are entitled to make';[34] furthermore, 'a distribution is just if everyone is entitled to the holdings they possess under the distribution'.[35] Both these points convey the idea, albeit from two different angles,[36] that there is for Nozick no subject of justice other than individual acts, and that a society realises an overall just distribution simply insofar as its members are all individually entitled to their holdings, over time and across society at any particular time. There is no social justice as distinct from individual justice, and no subject other than individual acts to which judgements of justice apply, but only a sum of individual transactions, the overall result of which is declared to be just by virtue of these transactions having occurred in conformity with just procedures.

Furthermore, Nozick believes that respecting liberty requires no more than respecting people's private property rights (in themselves and over justly acquired and transferred holdings) and therefore justice. Because liberty is identified with self-ownership, justice is regarded as being exhausted by the claims of liberty. If laid out in the form of premises and conclusion, the argument would be as follows:

(1)   Individuals have rights of self-ownership and to their natural assets, and hence, to whatever they produce through these;

(2)   Liberty is curtailed if and to the extent that individuals' rights are violated;

(3)   Justice requires respect for rights and hence, respect for liberty;

therefore,

(4)   As long as there is liberty, there is justice.

---

[34] *ASU*, p. 150.   [35] *Ibid.*, p. 151.

[36] By this I mean that while the first point captures the 'historical' aspect of the recursive application of the principles of justice, that is, the justice-preserving character of transactions *over time*, the second point refers to the justice-sufficing character of individual entitlements *at any given time*.

With these points in mind, we are in a position to see clearly how a justification of the unbridled market follows from Nozick's endorsement of the view that individuals have full private property rights in themselves and in external resources. The free market, being nothing but the exercise of full private property rights, realises liberty and justice alike. The free market respects, indeed is *required by*, justice, since justice demands that individuals be left free to exercise rights over their justly held resources, which is what individuals do on the free market. Being the sphere of voluntariness, the free market hosts only mutually advantageous, or productive, exchange, and hence exchange that is demanded by, and respects, individuals' inviolable rights.[37] Voluntary exchange, together with gift, is the only legitimate, and justice-preserving, allocative mechanism, and both are allowed by the principle of justice in transfer, which proscribes force and fraud.

3. LIBERTARIANISM, SELF-OWNERSHIP AND WORLD-OWNERSHIP

The libertarian defence of the market, as I have just mentioned, rests on the endorsement of full self-ownership rights, a defence of unlimited private ownership of external resources, or world ownership (in accordance with the demands of the principle of justice in acquisition), and the contention that all that justice requires is respect of private property rights (in accordance with the principle of justice in transfer, which requires that transfers be voluntary, that is, free of force and fraud). A critique of the libertarian defence of the unbridled market can then proceed at different levels, which it is helpful to distinguish here so as to clarify how my own treatment of the libertarian argument differs from others that have been offered.

One line of critique focuses on the foundational moral principles adopted by libertarians and casts doubt on the attractiveness of the principle of self-ownership. Some commentators, for example, have argued that the notion of self-ownership is inconsistent, or that it is not a plausible interpretation of the Kantian principle that individuals should not be treated as means only, or of autonomy.[38] Insofar as libertarianism's appeal partly derives from its contention that a commitment to self-ownership, the Kantian principle and

---

[37] On free market transactions as mutually advantageous transactions and productive exchange, see *ASU*, pp. 84–7; Mack, 'Moral Individualism'; Narveson, 'Contracting for Liberty'; and R. E. Lane, 'Market Choice and Human Choice', in Chapman and Pennock (eds.), *Markets and Justice*, pp. 226–49.

[38] See Arneson, 'Lockean Self-Ownership'; Ryan, 'Self-Ownership, Autonomy, and Property Rights'; Cohen, *Self-Ownership*, chapter 9.

the value of autonomy are inextricably linked, that appeal is accordingly diminished. Another line of critique consists in challenging the principle of justice in acquisition defended by Nozick, and the related argument for unlimited world ownership, or in arguing that Nozick assumes exactly the full private property rights in external resources that he needs to justify.[39] Yet another involves targeting the principle of justice in transfer by casting doubt on the contention that voluntariness preserves justice.[40]

My own critique of the libertarian defence of the free market grants the libertarian all the contentions that these alternative critiques aim to challenge. I assume the plausibility of full self-ownership, the justifiability of world ownership and the coherence of the claim that the voluntariness of transactions is both a necessary and a sufficient condition for their justice. But, I argue, these assumptions do not sustain the unbridled market in the way libertarians claim they do. In order to press this critique I will need to bring out more fully the way in which freedom and voluntariness are used by libertarians to justify the free market. But before doing that in the next section, it is worth pausing briefly here to consider the second of the three main lines of critique of the libertarian defence I have just identified, which attacks the argument from self-ownership to unlimited world-ownership, or unlimited full private property rights in external resources. This critique, which partly revolves around a critical examination of what is a defensible principle of justice in acquisition, has recently attracted considerable attention. It lies at the heart of left-libertarian theories, and an examination of it, besides shedding light on some of the key notions and claims that are deployed by libertarians, will help to both locate Nozick's arguments within the spectrum of libertarian theories and to clarify what implications my own critique will have for libertarian arguments other than Nozick's.

Left-libertarians, like right-libertarians, endorse the view of justice as property-rights-based, and the contention that individuals have full self-ownership rights. They contest, however, the supposed irreconcilability of self-ownership with any redistributive measures, which Nozick and other right-libertarians defend. As an introduction to an illustration of the left-libertarian position, notice that even if individuals are assigned self-ownership rights, further argument is needed to justify private property

---

[39] O. O'Neill, 'Nozick's Entitlements', in Paul (ed.), *Reading Nozick*, pp. 305–22; C. C. Ryan, 'Yours, Mine and Ours: Property Rights and Individual Liberty', in Paul (ed.), *Reading Nozick*, pp. 323–44.

[40] See Cohen, *Self-Ownership*, chapter 2, where Cohen denies that just steps (i.e. from which force and fraud are absent) and market transactions are justice-preserving. Cohen refers to freedom, rather than voluntariness, as justice-preserving, something I wish to avoid given that I distinguish between freedom and voluntariness. See chapter 6 below for a discussion of that distinction and for an examination of Cohen's view.

rights in external resources. Different libertarian theories proceed differently here. On the one hand there are those theories that try to justify entitlements to extra-personal resources by accounting for those entitlements on the basis of the exercise of the right of self-ownership or some aspect of self-ownership.[41] On the other hand there are accounts that justify entitlements to extra-personal resources by appealing to some other natural right individuals are assigned alongside the right of self-ownership, such as a right to the practice of private property or a right to an equal share of natural resources, which right may or may not share its moral foundations with the right of self-ownership.[42]

Whichever of these two approaches is adopted, the question of whether self-ownership, or another natural right which may or may not share its moral foundations with self-ownership, justify *full* private property rights in extra-personal resources is an open one.[43] And, so left-libertarians argue, full self-ownership is reconcilable with less than full private property rights in external resources, and, consequently, with redistributive measures entailed by encumbered world-ownership.

The most general formulation of the claim that underpins the left-libertarian strategy is then that full self-ownership is compatible with any arrangement in terms of ownership over external resources, though, as we will see, some arrangements make that self-ownership nugatory or worthless.[44] Nothing at all follows, as far as ownership of extra-personal

---

[41] Nozick's theory is an example, as well as other Lockean arguments and those that appeal to world-ownership as an extension of the right to one's body or the right to liberty. See J. Christman, 'Can Ownership be Justified by Natural Rights?', *Philosophy and Public Affairs* 15 (1986), pp. 156–77, for an illustration and critique of some of these arguments.

[42] Examples are the theories of Mack and Steiner. See Mack, 'Self-Ownership and the Right of Property', and Steiner, *An Essay on Rights*. Steiner grounds both the right of self-ownership and the right to an equal share of natural resources in the principle of equal liberty.

[43] For a negative answer to this question, see Christman, 'Can Ownership be Justified?'; and A. Gibbard, 'Natural Property Rights', *Nous* 10 (1976), pp. 77–86. Christman also provides an argument to the effect that we have reason to endorse less than full self-ownership. In particular, he argues that a concern with promoting individual autonomy and liberty warrants granting rights of use and of control over one's mind and body, but not the right to reap untaxed income from these. See J. Christman, *The Myth of Property: Toward an Egalitarian Theory of Ownership* (Oxford University Press, 1994). David Gauthier may be viewed as putting forward a more moderate version of this claim, in that he questions not the inclusion of income rights *tout court* as constitutive of self-ownership, but only of the right to factor rent. That right, he argues, is not part of a right to one's basic endowments. See D. Gauthier, *Morals by Agreement* (Oxford University Press, 1986), pp. 346–8. Since these arguments question full self-ownership, which I am granting to libertarians, I leave them aside here.

[44] Throughout, self-ownership is assumed to include ownership of one's entire body. Notice that self-owning individuals are assumed to be world-interactive. Interestingly, Mack acknowledges the importance for self-ownership of the fact that agents' talents are fundamentally 'world-interactive', and argues that for this reason an anti-disablement proviso is needed. A version of this proviso,

resources is concerned, from self-ownership alone: the fact that individuals are self-owners does not justify their acquiring private property rights in worldly resources.[45] Whether private property rights in external resources are justified, and to what extent inequality is generated, depend on the regime of external resources and on the rules for just acquisition.

Hence Cohen has argued that self-ownership is compatible with an egalitarian regime of natural resources where the latter are jointly owned, and where self-ownership is prevented from generating inequality. This, however, is achieved, according to Cohen, at the cost of self-ownership being rendered nugatory, since in this world no one would be able to do anything without the consent of others.[46] The argument is nonetheless crucial, in that it shows that full self-ownership is compatible with an egalitarian distribution of worldly resources. Further, as Cohen points out, the nugatory self-ownership of individuals under a regime of joint ownership of external resource is equivalent to the nugatory self-ownership of propertyless proletarians under capitalism, so the right-libertarian cannot object to the proposed reconciliation of self-ownership and joint-ownership of external resources on the grounds that self-ownership is, under that regime, merely formal.[47]

Self-ownership may also be reconciled with other egalitarian regimes of external resources, under which a robust self-ownership is preserved. This argument starts, as right-libertarian theories do, with common-use-based conceptions of natural resources, and permits unilateral appropriation, that is, appropriation without the consent of others. Whilst the principles of justice in acquisition defended by right-libertarians allow for large inequalities in world-ownership to arise,[48] alternative principles of justice in acquisition informed by egalitarian concerns, which left-libertarians endorse, curtail those inequalities to various degrees. The two prominent alternatives to the right-libertarian view, which I would like to mention only briefly here,

---

which he calls the self-ownership proviso, is, he believes, part of the theory of self-ownership, not of the theory of acquisition. See Mack, 'Self-Ownership Proviso'.

[45] Vallentyne, 'Left-Libertarian Theories of Justice'.   [46] Cohen, *Self-Ownership*, chapter 4.

[47] *Ibid.*, especially pp. 99–102.

[48] Nozick's interpretation of the Lockean proviso on appropriation requires only that compensation be paid to those that are worse off than they would have been had no appropriation occurred. Other right-libertarians stipulate even weaker conditions for appropriation. See, for instance, I. Kirzner, 'Entrepreneurship, Entitlement, and Economic Justice', in Paul (ed.), *Reading Nozick*, pp. 383–411, and 'The Nature of Profits: Some Economic Insights and their Ethical Implications', in R. Cowan and M. J. Rizzo (eds.), *Profits and Morality* (University of Chicago Press, 1995), pp. 22–47. Jan Narveson, too, holds that a resource being put to socially productive use is a sufficient ground for legitimate appropriation. See J. Narveson, 'Egalitarianism: Partial, Counterproductive, and Baseless', in A. Mason (ed.), *Ideals of Equality* (Oxford: Blackwell, 1998), pp. 79–94.

are the Georgist libertarian and the full benefit taxation conceptions. On the Georgist conception, defended by Hillel Steiner, individuals, besides having rights of full self-ownership, also have rights to an equal share of natural resources. In a fully appropriated world, according to Steiner, 'each person's original right to an equal portion of initially unowned things amounts to a right to an equal share of their total *value*'.[49] Steiner's left-libertarianism, then, posits a requirement on legitimate appropriation that provides a justification for exacting payments which contribute to a global fund, which redistributes wealth so as to satisfy every individual's right to an equal share of the value of natural resources.[50]

Although Steiner's theory does accommodate some egalitarian concerns, it only equalises external resources at the 'starting gate' of individuals' lives. It does not fully equalise personal resources, but only that part of individuals' differential talents and capacities that are due to a differential distribution of germ-line genetic information, which he considers as an appropriated natural resource.[51] However, as I said earlier, since it is possible to concede that individuals have full self-ownership rights without this entailing that they have full private property rights in external resources, a reconciliation of full self-ownership and more demanding egalitarian commitments than Steiner's may be achieved.

The second main variant of left-libertarianism I would like to mention sets out to show precisely this. On this view, equalisation of people's differential personal resources is operated not by encroaching on the unencumbered use of those resources but *via* a differential compensatory distribution of external resources.[52] In this spirit, Michael Otsuka has offered a very convincing argument for the reconciliation of a robust self-ownership with

---

[49] Steiner, *Essay on Rights*, p. 236. Steiner draws on Henry George's theory of ownership. See H. George, *Progress and Poverty*, edited by A. W. Madsen, Centenary Edition (London: Hogarth Press, 1979).

[50] That fund, according to Steiner, would be further swollen by two other just taxes, namely, would-be bequests, the taxation of which is justified on the grounds that dead persons do not have rights, and a payment on germ-line genetic information, which is argued to be a natural resource which parents appropriate, so that their ownership of their children, like their ownership of external resources, is an encumbered title. See Steiner, *Essay on Rights*, pp. 249–61, and p. 274. See also H. Steiner, 'Three Just Taxes', in P. Van Parijs (ed.), *Arguing for Basic Income* (London and New York: Verso, 1992), pp. 81–92. Note that the tax on genetic information Steiner justifies is different from 'talent pooling', and does not contravene full self-ownership.

[51] Steiner's account therefore differs from those accounts, like John Rawls', which treat advantages due to superior (or inferior) natural endowments and those due to propitious (or disadvantaging) social factors on a par. The distinction between these two is emphasised by Steiner in his 'Choice and Circumstance', in A. Mason (ed.), *Ideals of Equality* (Oxford: Blackwell, 1998). Unlike Steiner's theory, which prescribes an equal distribution of the global fund, Philippe Van Parijs' version of the Georgist conception prescribes that the global fund provide for compensation for unchosen disadvantage before the remainder is equally divided. See Van Parijs, *Real Freedom for All*.

[52] Vallentyne favours this approach. See Vallentyne, 'Left-Libertarian Theories of Justice'.

strong egalitarian concerns, which are incorporated in the theory of just acquisition through the elaboration of an egalitarian proviso.[53]

The conclusions defended by left-libertarians are compatible with the conclusions of my arguments. What I argue in what follows is that an unbridled market, one in which agents have unlimited full private property rights and where no redistributive taxation takes place, is not the realm of freedom and voluntariness right-libertarians claim it is. Right-libertarians' concerns with ensuring that justice is preserved through voluntary exchange, then, justifies ensuring that the conditions for voluntary choices are protected. And left-libertarians' main conclusions, as I have just suggested, are that some redistributive measures that are demanded by equality are compatible with full self-ownership, unlike what right-libertarians suggest. This means that under a left-libertarian regime, individuals will less likely find themselves in the limited choice circumstances in which their choices would be forced ones. Left-libertarians may then accept the conclusions I defend, and underline that they escape the objections to which right-libertarians are susceptible.

In what follows I will neither be directly concerned with the left-libertarian project, nor will I appeal to considerations of equality as relevant for justice in acquisition. My project is substantially different from that of left-libertarians. Whilst they endorse full self-ownership but contest unlimited full private property rights in external resources and start with egalitarian commitments, I assume *both* full self-ownership and unlimited world-ownership, and do not appeal to considerations of equality. My main concern in what follows consists in assessing the entitlement-based defence of the free market by means of right-libertarianism's own standards, namely, its avowed commitment to liberty and free choice.

Despite these differences between the left-libertarian project and mine, however, I will, at times, refer to what left-libertarians say about that part of their views which is relevantly similar to right-libertarians. And some of what I say will have some bearing for left-libertarians, as well as for right-libertarians, for the following reasons. Left-libertarians' main disagreement with right-libertarians concerns what original rights, if any, beyond those of self-ownership individuals have and/or what the defensible theory of justice in acquisition is. As far as the principle of justice in transfer is concerned, however, left-libertarians have so far had little to say that is different from right-libertarians: they, too, endorse the view that justice in transfer requires that transactions be voluntary, but have dedicated little

---

[53] See Otsuka, *Libertarianism Without Inequality*, chapter 1.

attention to precisely what this voluntariness requirement amounts to. As a result, left-libertarians, as much as right-libertarians (and, I shall claim later, critics of libertarianism), have neglected to flesh out the implications of some key libertarian commitments.

4. FREEDOM AND VOLUNTARINESS IN THE LIBERTARIAN JUSTIFICATION

Libertarians define libertarianism as 'the moral and political outlook holding that individual liberty is the only proper concern of coercive institutions',[54] and claim that the society which they defend, the free market society, respects freedom and realises justice: 'a politically just community is one in which the lives and creative energies of free men and women are for no one other than themselves and those whom they choose'.[55] In their eulogy of the free society, or, what is said to be the same thing, of the free market, libertarians appeal to a host of related notions, the most recurrent of which are freedom, individual rights, voluntariness, autonomy and responsibility.[56] With some exceptions, the exact meaning of, and relationship between, these notions are left largely unexplored. I would now like to bring out fully the role of voluntariness in the libertarian defence of the free market, and to illustrate how a concern with voluntariness is supposedly related to a respect for liberty and a concern with property rights. This prepares the ground for the critique of the libertarian defence of the free market that will be developed in the next two chapters, where that defence is seen as claiming that the free market society is a society in which there are no limitations of individuals' freedom, because all (supposed) interferences with individuals are going to be voluntarily consented-to interferences.[57]

Consider, first of all, the crucial role of the notion of voluntariness in the libertarian argument. In outlining the main features of Nozick's entitlement theory in section two above, the notions of voluntariness and voluntary exchange have appeared to be important ones. Nozick's thoroughgoing concern in his book is best described as a desire to establish that individuals cannot be claimed to incur any obligations towards their fellow human beings to which they have not consented and which they have

---

[54] Narveson, *Libertarian Idea*, p. xi.

[55] T. R. Machan and D. B. Rasmussen, 'Introduction', in Machan and Rasmussen (eds.), *Liberty for the 21st Century*, p. xi.

[56] 'The market is not a separate institution in the free society. It simply *is* the free society.' Cf. Narveson, 'Justice of the Market', p. 266.

[57] Interferences that are the enforcement of natural rights-correlative obligations are exempted from having to be consented to.

not voluntarily undertaken. We have seen how this contention rests on the belief, which Nozick unquestioningly assumes as a moral basis for his theory and which constitutes the well-known opening sentence of his book, that 'individuals have rights, and there are things no person or group may do to them (without violating their rights)'.[58] Interference with conduct protected by these rights is only legitimate when the individuals themselves choose to allow that interference. Hence, respect for individuals is in this view tightly linked to a minimal imposition of non-voluntary obligations and the protection of negative individual liberty. Further, Nozick thinks that individual liberty thus understood exhausts the requirement of justice. This means that all a theory of justice in transfer needs to comprise are principles that embody strict requirements of voluntariness for the transfer of goods and services.

Given this outlook, the free market, together with the practices of gift-making and charity, appear as the forms of exchange most consonant with respect for the values of liberty and the principles of justice, since voluntariness is so central to their functioning that non-voluntary transfers are ruled out by definition. As Thomas Scanlon points out, the notion of free exchange that is inherently associated with the market leads Nozick to see the latter as the fundamental form of social co-operation, in that it is one in which individuals enter freely and in which they themselves establish the terms of their co-operation through bargaining.[59]

The close connection between liberty, voluntariness and justice is also emphasised by other libertarians, including left-libertarians. Steiner, for example, and although he devotes less attention than Nozick to the issue of voluntary exchange, endorses the libertarian commitment to eliminating or reducing non-voluntary obligations: libertarians, he says, are committed to a negative conception of liberty, and 'it is the essence of such a commitment that most, if not all, of the restrictions to which an individual is subject should be restrictions which he has contractually incurred'.[60] Admittedly, Steiner is now sceptical about both what exactly a 'commitment to liberty' *per se* means and about the possibility of *quantifying* obligations (which would be necessary in order to minimise uncontracted enforceable obligations).[61] Despite this, however, he is still committed to the distinctly

[58] *ASU*, p. ix.

[59] T. M. Scanlon, 'Liberty, Contract, and Contribution', in G. Dworkin, G. Bermant and P. G. Brown (eds.), *Markets and Morals* (New York: Halsted Press, 1977), pp. 43–67.

[60] Steiner, 'Liberty and Equality', p. 555.

[61] Private correspondence. Steiner now claims only that libertarians are committed to a right to equal freedom and thus to the uncontracted obligations which that right entails.

libertarian view that being subject to uncontracted enforceable obligations limits an individual's freedom. In a similar spirit, the right-libertarian John Hospers remarks that 'the right to liberty is the right to live one's life in accordance with one's voluntary choices, as long as one does not, in so doing, violate the equal rights of others'.[62]

Although, as I will argue later in this book, freedom and voluntariness are in *some* relation, I believe that the distinction between these two notions, as well as their relation, warrants more attention than libertarians have given it. I conceive of the distinction between freedom and voluntariness as one between freedom as 'being free to do something', on the one hand, and freedom as 'doing something freely, or voluntarily', on the other.[63] By making that distinction, and by analysing closely the relation between freedom and voluntariness and related notions such as coercion and responsibility, much insight is gained about the cogency, or lack thereof, of the libertarian defence of the free market.

One very preliminary observation in this respect, which can serve by way of introduction, is as follows. Libertarians claim to accord pride of place to freedom in their political philosophy. In fact, Cohen has argued, self-ownership rather than freedom as such is what lies at the basis of the libertarian edifice.[64] The libertarian rejoins by insisting that self-ownership *is* a doctrine of liberty.[65] In its most plausible form, this rejoinder takes the form of an argument to the effect that rights, including self-ownership rights, prescribe distributions of pure negative freedom.[66]

But notice now that pure negative freedom is limited by *all* enforceable obligations, whether or not these obligations have been voluntarily consented to, and libertarians insist that what they are concerned with are uncontracted enforceable obligations. This does not mean, of course, that if the concern is with uncontracted enforceable obligations, then pure negative freedom is irrelevant. But it clearly does mean that what ultimately exercises the libertarian is not the limitation of pure negative freedom *per se*, which every enforceable obligation involves, but only that subset of freedom-limiting interference that is licensed by self-ownership and legitimate private property rights themselves, which one has not consented to and which, therefore, so the libertarian claims, is illegitimate. And there are two possible reasons, which libertarians conflate but which are best

---

[62] Hospers, 'Contracting for Liberty'.   [63] Chapter 6 elaborates and defends this distinction.

[64] Cohen, *Self-Ownership*, p. 67.

[65] J. Narveson, 'Libertarianism vs. Marxism: Reflections on G. A. Cohen's *Self-Ownership, Freedom and Equality*', *Journal of Ethics* 2 (1998), pp. 1–16, see especially pp. 7–9.

[66] Steiner, *Essay on Rights*, p. 58.

kept separate, why the criterion for what counts as legitimate freedom-limiting interference should be the voluntariness requirement.[67] The first is a concern with autonomy and sovereignty over self, which supports the conviction that individuals must choose voluntarily what happens to them; the second is a concern with individuals' fundamental rights as rights of *property*, in themselves and in extra-personal resources, which rights are seen as freely transferable and as waivable. It is because they are concerned with respecting individuals' autonomy and/or ownership rights that libertarians see voluntariness as a necessary and sufficient requirement for all interferences (with the exception of those interferences that are the enforcement of natural rights-correlative obligations), and, so I will argue in chapter 6, (pure negative) freedom, or freedom 'as such', is important to the extent that it is necessary for voluntariness.

Libertarians, as I have mentioned when illustrating Nozick's view earlier in this chapter, hold that self-ownership is an interpretation of autonomy, and claim that ascribing self-ownership rights to people is both necessary and sufficient for respecting their autonomy. But if, as seems to be the case, the contention that self-ownership is an interpretation of autonomy is flawed, and insofar as, therefore, libertarianism's commitment to the voluntariness requirement is grounded in the endorsement of self-ownership rather than of autonomy, there is then a sense in which it is indeed true that self-ownership rather than freedom as such is what lies at the basis of the libertarian edifice. For it is the endorsement of self-ownership, and not the commitment to freedom as such, that underpins the libertarian concern with proscribing uncontracted enforceable obligations, and it is the latter concern which, in turn, justifies a preoccupation with securing for people some negative freedom.

In what follows I assume that self-ownership is at the basis of the libertarian edifice, and argue that even if we assume the plausibility of the principle of self-ownership and the coherence of the claim that the voluntariness of transactions is both a necessary and a sufficient condition for their justice, these assumptions do not support the unbridled market in the way libertarians claim they do. I argue that the claim that the free market

---

[67] See Cohen, *Self-Ownership*, chapter 10, where Cohen separates the notion of being an autonomous being, of not being a slave, and of being an end and not a means, from the concept of self-ownership. A similar argument is offered by Andrew Levine, 'Capitalist Persons', *Social Philosophy and Policy* 6 (1988), pp. 39–59. Levine identifies two ideal types of persons – the Lockean and the Kantian – and argues that the intuitions conveyed by the idea of self-ownership constitutive of the Lockean person can be better supported by the alternative conceptions embodied in the Kantian idea of the person. See also J. H. Reiman, 'The Fallacy of Libertarian Capitalism', *Ethics* 92 (1981), pp. 85–95, where Reiman argues that there is a tension between libertarianism and the Kantian principle.

society is a society in which freedom and voluntariness are respected rests on a flawed account of voluntary choice and of its relationship to freedom. When these notions and their relationship are properly understood, we are led to a re-evaluation of the status of the free market as the realm of voluntary exchange and away from the libertarian fixation with the absence of coercion, which supposedly characterises the free market. Furthermore, I suggest that an account of voluntary choice which can play some role in settling questions of responsibility is different from the one defended by libertarians.

To this critique of the libertarian defence of the free market, it may be thought, libertarians may reply by forgoing any appeal to notions of autonomy, freedom and voluntariness. They could insist that even if the free market is not the realm of freedom it seems at first, it is nonetheless legitimate by virtue of the principle of self-ownership enjoining the free exchange of private property rights. Libertarians could then ignore arguments that show that liberty and autonomy are not realised in the unbridled market, and suggest that their only concern is with the exchange of legitimate rights *per se*. An argument of this sort would have to rely on a clear-cut separation between the principles of self-ownership, autonomy and liberty. Such a separation may well be plausible, in that self-ownership seems meaningful independently of notions of both liberty and autonomy.[68] Further, libertarians could abandon the appeal to voluntariness altogether. They could state that transactions are justice-preserving only insofar as they are rights-respecting, whether or not they happen to be voluntary.[69]

I do not think that being forced into this move would be welcomed by most libertarians. Most of them, as I have shown, do appeal to both autonomy and voluntariness as central notions in the defence of the free market. Nozick, for instance, clearly and repeatedly relates side constraints, separateness of persons, self-ownership, the principle of consent and the Kantian principle that individuals are ends and not only means.[70] If nothing else,

---

[68] Think of the following example. Two individuals, A and B, inhabit distant planets, on one of which, inhabited by A, natural resources are much richer. A is able to cultivate the fertile land and thus live a plentiful life. Suppose further that resources could be moved from one planet to the other. Were someone to put forward the suggestion that A should transfer some goods he has produced to B, who has been less lucky and inhabits a sterile planet, the question would arise: 'What does A have to do with it?' Objecting to the transfer in this way makes reference to self-ownership, not to liberty or autonomy. I leave aside the issue of whether self-ownership is a plausible interpretation of the principle of autonomy, and go on to assume that what motivates the libertarians' concern with voluntariness is an endorsement of self-ownership. If our concern is with personal autonomy, then I believe that we have reason to reconsider too exclusive an emphasis on voluntariness.

[69] This suggestion was made to me by Alan Wertheimer and Andrew Williams.

[70] See *ASU*, chapter 3.

giving up the appeal to notions of autonomy, freedom and voluntariness would certainly deprive libertarianism of much of its appeal. In fact, however, I do not think that this move is open to libertarians, for the following three reasons.

First, libertarians want to disallow fraud and, certainly, coercion, but not all fraud and coercion constitute infringement of (libertarian) rights.[71] If the reasons for disallowing fraud and coercion nonetheless are, as I believe they should be, grounded in a concern with ensuring that people make voluntary choices, then voluntariness reappears in the libertarian argument. The libertarian would have to provide principled grounds for disallowing coercion and fraud while permitting other types of non-voluntary transactions as justice-preserving, where those grounds are not that the only justice-disrupting transactions are rights-infringing ones.

Second, even if libertarians did renounce a proscription of fraud and non-rights-infringing coercion in their principle of justice in transfer, notions of voluntariness and force are still preserved in their account. After all, the appeal to choice is integral to the thesis of self-ownership and the libertarian emphasis on property rights alike. At the basis of the assignment of self-ownership rights to individuals, as shown earlier, is the conviction that individuals should not be used by others in certain ways, that they should have a moral space in which to exercise their powers and make decisions without interference from others. What the principle of self-ownership purports to capture, it should be recalled, is the importance of ensuring that individuals not be *forced* to supply service to others. A commitment to ensuring that individuals make voluntary, not forced, choices, therefore, is what underlies the very ascription of self-ownership rights to persons.[72]

---

[71] On the problems libertarianism encounters in trying to proscribe fraud, see Child, 'Can Libertarianism Sustain a Fraud Standard?'

[72] This very concern with ensuring that self-owning individuals be well placed to make voluntary choices is what is invoked when it is claimed that self-ownership should be 'robust' rather than 'nugatory', which I mentioned when discussing left-libertarianism. The point I am pressing here could then be rephrased as follows: the importance of ensuring that people make voluntary choices lies at the basis of libertarians' commitment to endowing individuals with robust, as opposed to nugatory, self-ownership. Rephrasing the point this way should not lead us to overlook that what moves libertarians is a concern with the importance of protecting people's capacity to make voluntary choices by endowing them with certain property rights, rather than a concern with property rights as such, regardless of how possession and exercise of these rights affects the voluntariness of choice. I therefore take issue with Otsuka's suggestion that Nozick's argument against redistributive taxation 'is not essentially a complaint that such taxation is on a par with forced labour but rather the complaint that such taxation violates one's rights of ownership *simpliciter*'. See Otsuka, *Libertarianism Without Inequality*, p. 17. That contrast, I am suggesting, is misleading, for rights of ownership are supposed to protect an area in which people are not forced. I return to Nozick's complaint against taxation and forced labour in chapter 5 below.

This commitment results in the conviction that individuals should be free from interference that they have not voluntarily allowed, and free to do anything they choose with themselves so long as they do not infringe other people's rights. But the conviction that individuals should not be used by others in certain ways, and should not be forced to supply services to others, which is what motivates vesting individuals with self-ownership rights in the first place, also justifies a concern with the conditions under which the transfer of rights occur.

Hence, even if we agreed with Steiner that historical entitlement principles of transfer and rectification are 'simply implications of the conceptual fact that rights vest their owners with powers of waiver and redress',[73] the very same reasons that justify assigning certain rights to individuals are also reasons for examining carefully what a principle of transfer should stipulate and what it should prescribe, and proscribe, for the motivation behind the allocation of those rights to be respected. If a commitment to respecting full self-ownership justifies holding that voluntariness in transfer is all that is required to preserve justice, we must ask under what conditions transfers respect voluntariness.

Thirdly and finally, libertarianism lays claim to being a political philosophy with a commitment to personal responsibility, and that commitment is tightly linked with the role libertarians claim to assign to freedom and voluntariness. As Steiner emphasises, there is a close link between personal responsibility and historical entitlement theories, and that link lies in the 'pivotal role' which is accorded by both to persons' actions. The principle of justice in transfer (and the principle of rectification) distributes personal responsibility to agents. In order for them to do this, actions have to be of a certain sort, and therefore, the antecedent conditions of acting must be arranged in a certain way. Steiner believes that the required arrangement consists in ensuring that agents are equally free, thus implying that liberty is necessary for responsibility.[74] The concern with responsibility also underpins the special attention libertarianism dedicates to tort law.[75] An account of justice in transfer that made no appeal to freedom and to the

---

[73] Steiner, *Essay on Rights*, p. 226.

[74] *Ibid.*, p. 226. Steiner also implies that freedom is sufficient for responsibility. I discuss these issues in chapter 6 below. On the claim that libertarianism is committed to making room for responsibility, see also Machan, 'Virtue of Freedom in Capitalism'.

[75] See Steiner, 'Choice and Circumstance'; S. P. Perry, 'Libertarianism, Entitlement, and Responsibility', *Philosophy and Public Affairs* 26 (1997), pp. 351–95; R. A. Epstein, 'Luck', *Social Philosophy and Policy* 6 (1988), pp. 17–38; L. Katz, 'Responsibility and Consent: The Libertarian's Problem with Freedom of Contract', *Social Philosophy and Policy* 16 (1999), pp. 94–117.

voluntariness in the transfer of rights would not preserve that link with responsibility.

In its standard formulation, libertarianism does lay much emphasis on freedom and voluntariness in providing the moral foundations for original rights and in defending the society in which those rights are allegedly respected. Libertarians claim that a free market society is a society in which all or nearly all interferences with people are going to be voluntarily consented to, so there is going to be no or nearly no limitation of people's freedom. They also claim that a free market society, being one in which individuals are subject to a minimal imposition of uncontracted enforceable obligations, is one which respects their rights, so that a free market society is also a just society. As has appeared, these claims crucially rest on the contention that individuals have certain rights, and that, in virtue of individuals having those rights, voluntariness is both a necessary and a sufficient obligation for the legitimacy of almost all interference with individuals. It is this voluntariness requirement that the market is said to satisfy.

CHAPTER 5

The moralised defence of the free market: a critique

I. THE LIBERTARIAN THESIS

In the previous chapter I characterised the libertarian defence of the free market as one in which freedom and voluntariness have pride of place. I now turn to an examination of that defence. My aim in this chapter is to show how the libertarian contention that a free market society is one where liberty and justice are realised because all (supposed) limitations of freedom derive from specific voluntary undertakings, is vitiated by indefensible definitions of freedom, harm and voluntariness. More precisely, I here do three main things: first, I argue that the libertarian justification of the unbridled market is underpinned by a rights-definition of voluntariness, alongside the more familiar rights-definition of freedom; second, I examine the notion of rights-defined voluntariness, and argue that it should be rejected; and finally, I show how two of Nozick's central contentions in the defence of the unbridled market – namely, that taxation is on a par with forced labour, and that workers are not forced to sell their labour – rest on the rights-definition of voluntariness and that their force is therefore undermined.[1]

In undertaking this critical examination of the libertarian argument for the free market it is helpful to start by identifying the main steps in which it unfolds, and briefly discussing how two challenges that may be raised against that argument are avoided by libertarians by using moralised definitions of harm and freedom. Recall first of all that Nozick's criticism of patterned principles of justice is that these violate individuals' entitlements by giving some people claims over other people's activities 'independently

---

[1] Throughout, I will use interchangeably the terms 'morally defined', 'rights-defined' and 'moralised' voluntariness, and similarly with freedom. With respect to both freedom and voluntariness, I hold that there is a problem in defining them through *rights*. With respect to freedom only, I also assume, for current purposes, that a non-moralised definition, as well as a non-rights-based one, is preferable to a moralised one. This, as I said earlier, is because libertarians claim to appeal to non-moralised negative freedom, and I am proceeding on this, and other, shared premises.

of whether the other persons *enter into particular relationships* that give rise to these claims, and independently of whether they *voluntarily* take these claims upon themselves, in charity or in exchange for something'.[2] Others' claims on us, according to Nozick, are only justified when they are claims we have given rise to by voluntarily consenting to them, with the exception, as I have previously mentioned, of claims to having one's (libertarian) rights respected, which ground legitimate unchosen enforceable obligations.[3] Voluntary choice is a demand of self-ownership, and non-contractual enforceable obligations are a curtailment of self-ownership and a threat to autonomy.[4]

This voluntariness requirement is alleged to be satisfied only by the free market, the realm of contractual exchange *par excellence*. The free market society, Nozick believes, is one where liberty and justice are realised because all (supposed) limitations on freedom derive from specific voluntary undertakings, a claim I will refer to, from now on, as 'the libertarian thesis'. The argument for the thesis, in a nutshell, is as follows.

(1)   All obligations and interferences with individuals must be voluntarily consented to by the affected parties, with the exception of those obligations that are correlative to other individuals' rights and those interferences that are justified for the enforcement of those rights (the voluntariness requirement);[5]

(2)   The free market satisfies the voluntariness requirement;

(3)   A society in which the voluntariness requirement is satisfied is one where no freedom is curtailed;

---

[2] R. Nozick, *Anarchy, State, and Utopia* (Oxford: Blackwell, 1974), p. 18, emphasis mine. Henceforth cited as *ASU*.

[3] Throughout, by 'obligation' I will refer to 'enforceable obligation'. Note that the fact that the obligations in question are *enforceable* is what grounds the requirement that they be consented to, or chosen, for them to be legitimate (with the stated exception). Having enforceable obligations makes one liable to legitimate interference, that is, at least that interference which is required to enforce the obligation, and consent is therefore needed for the interference which those obligations allow to be justified. Because I only talk about enforceable obligations, and because of the latter's connection to interference, in what follows I talk about enforceable obligations and legitimate interference interchangeably. It is of course possible for libertarians to hold that individuals have unchosen non-enforceable obligations. That is not a contention I examine in what follows, since I am concerned with the claims libertarianism makes as a *political* morality; that is, as a political philosophy that is concerned with ascertaining what is the scope of obligations that may be legitimately enforced by a political authority.

[4] As I suggested in chapter 4 above, self-ownership and autonomy are, in my view, distinct, and an endorsement of either could ground a concern with uncontracted enforceable obligations. In this chapter I assume that the endorsement of full self-ownership is at the basis of the libertarian argument, and do not focus on the problems that may arise for the libertarian defence of the free market if libertarians' concern with voluntariness were motivated by a commitment to autonomy as distinct from self-ownership.

[5] Throughout, by 'rights' I refer to the negative rights libertarians endorse.

therefore,

(4)   A free market society is a society in which no freedom is curtailed.[6]

In this chapter I argue that, even if we endorse (1), (4) does not follow, because both (2) and (3) are liable to objections. I also suggest that we can see Nozick's attempt to defend his argument against those objections as what motivates his use of moralised definitions of harm, freedom and voluntariness, and that that attempt is ultimately unsuccessful.

Let me start with the following important challenges to the libertarian thesis, which target the claim that the free market satisfies the voluntariness requirement (claim 2) and the claim that a society in which the voluntariness requirement is satisfied is one in which no one's freedom is curtailed (claim 3). In a free market society, not all relevant interferences are voluntarily consented to, since non-consenting individuals are variously affected by others' voluntarily entered into transactions. Moreover, some of the ways in which they are affected are freedom-curtailing, so that it is not true that a free market society is one in which no one's freedom is curtailed. Consider, in particular, the following two main ways in which some non-consenting individuals have their freedom curtailed or are otherwise affected in a rights-respecting free market society.

First, the institutions of promising and of private property, which support the free market envisaged by Nozick, affect individuals beyond those directly involved.[7] The obligation the promise creates in the promisor may come into conflict with other claims which weigh on the promisor, so that the promise, besides creating the new rights in the promisee, also results in the conflicting claims being set aside. Nozick himself provides an example of this type of case, in which person P, towards whom I have an obligation, has the power to release me from that obligation unless he has promised Q that he will not.[8] In this case, P's promising to Q considerably alters my situation, by depriving P of the power of releasing me from my obligation. In these cases, as Thomas Scanlon remarks, it seems that 'if [conflicting

---

[6] Of course, Robert Nozick also claims that freedom exhausts justice, and that a free society is therefore a just society. I do not here take issue with that claim. For a critique of it, see G. A. Cohen, *Self-Ownership, Freedom, and Equality* (Cambridge University Press, 1995), chapters 1 and 2.

[7] With both promising and private property, there are two general issues concerning the role which consent has in those institutions being created in the first place. The first regards the non-contractual moral grounding of those institutions; the second the non-consented-to duty of non-interference which is correlative to rights of private property and rights created by free exchange. I do not deal with these issues here, for I am concerned not with the justification of those institutions but rather with ascertaining the degree to which, when those institutions *are* in place, some individuals' situations are altered in ways that extend beyond their being under an uncontracted rights-correlative duty.

[8] *ASU*, pp. 91–2.

obligations] can be set aside at all by voluntary agreement, [they] cannot be amended merely by consent of the promisor and promisee. At the very least more general consent would be required'.[9] Similar arguments may be adduced concerning the effects on third parties of the acquisition and transfer of private property rights.[10] Consider, for instance, the case of Cary, who benefits from Audrey's permission to walk across Audrey's privately owned field. On Audrey's sale of her land to Burt, Cary loses such a right, as Burt forbids him to walk over his property. Cary's freedom is thereby limited without him having consented to this. This casts doubt on both (2) and (3) above.

A second way in which third parties are affected by transactions they have not consented to is through externalities and spill-overs of other people's voluntary exchanges. An externality is defined as an 'unintended and not fully voluntary effect of some agent's action on others'.[11] Externalities may be caused by an individual or a group; they may be positive or negative depending on whether the effects are beneficial or harmful, respectively; and they are distinguished into pecuniary and non-pecuniary ones, the former being those whose consequences are mediated *via* markets, the latter those whose consequences are created outside them, although they, too, may result from market activities. For example, the threat to employment that results from the introduction of a new technology, which makes some of the workforce redundant, is a negative pecuniary externality; the pollution that the new technology causes is a negative non-pecuniary externality. Pecuniary externalities, admittedly, where the individuals who suffer from them are all market actors who are affected by others' entering into competition with them, are claimed to be justified by the fact that market actors have *chosen*, by entering the market, to undergo certain risks.[12] Cases where individuals are affected by pecuniary externalities are thereby represented as instances in which the affected parties have, in a sense, consented to the imposition of the burden or the interference at issue.[13]

---

[9] T. M. Scanlon, 'Liberty, Contract, and Contribution', in G. Dworkin, G. Bermant and P. G. Brown (eds.), *Markets and Morals* (New York: Halsted Press, 1977), pp. 43–67, at p. 48.

[10] See Scanlon, 'Liberty'; A. Gibbard, 'Natural Property Rights', *Nous* 10 (1976), pp. 77–86.

[11] D. M. Hausman, 'When Jack and Jill Make a Deal', *Social Philosophy and Policy* 9 (1992), pp. 95–113, at p. 97. A similar definition is offered by Charles Fried, according to whom externalities are 'unintended impositions incidental to the pursuit of some other end'. See C. Fried, 'Difficulties in the Economic Analysis of Rights', in Dworkin *et al.* (eds.), *Markets and Morals*, p. 192.

[12] As Hayek puts it, 'once we have agreed to play the game and profited from its results it is a moral obligation on us to abide by the results, even if they turn against us'. F. A. Hayek, 'The Principles of a Liberal Social Order', *Politico* 31 (1966), pp. 601–17, at p. 611. As the next chapter will show, this claim is, in fact, hardly plausible.

[13] This sort of case is treated in section 3 below, which deals with limited choice.

Non-pecuniary externalities, by contrast, are clearly instances of affecting non-consenting others. A widely discussed example of one such externality is pollution. The decision of a landowner to build a factory on his privately owned estate is legitimate, for the landowner, it is assumed, acts within his rights, but it may, as a side-effect, pollute the surrounding environment and affect others in harmful ways. Another sort of non-pecuniary externality is that created by the marketisation of certain goods and services. Individuals are affected by others' decisions to make something available on the market; if a certain item is up for sale, this may result in changes in people's perception of the item in question, and, sometimes, of people themselves and of their relations to other people.[14] According to Nozick, so long as an individual voluntarily chooses to sell his blood or his organs, this transaction is legitimate and should be allowed. But making such goods available on the market may be objectionable on the grounds that this results in a degradation of personhood, or because of a concern with altruism and the value of solidarity. Even if these externalities are not freedom-curtailing, their occurrence challenges (2) above, which states that the free market satisfies the voluntariness requirement. It is not true, that is, that all interferences to which people are subject in a free market society have been voluntarily chosen or consented to by them.

2. RIGHTS-DEFINED HARM AND RIGHTS-DEFINED FREEDOM

The contentions that the free market satisfies the voluntariness requirement, and that in a free market society no one's freedom is curtailed, then, can both be challenged. Yet, in spite of the presence of non-consented-to interferences in a free market society, Nozick contends that the latter is one where all (supposed) limitations of freedom derive from specific voluntary undertakings. This is because, first, he delimits the range of interferences that would have to be voluntarily consented to through the use of a rights-based harm criterion; and second, by using a rights-definition of freedom, Nozick claims that non-consented-to interferences that are exempt from the voluntariness requirement are not freedom-curtailing. His argument would now run as follows.

(1a)   Only potentially right-infringing interferences with individuals is harmful (on the rights-based harm criterion) and freedom-curtailing (on the

[14] E. Anderson, *Value in Ethics and Economics* (Harvard University Press, 1993), M. J. Radin, *Contested Commodities* (Harvard University Press, 1996).

rights-based definition of freedom),[15] and must therefore be voluntarily consented to by the affected parties (the qualified voluntariness requirement);[16]

(2)   The free market satisfies the (qualified) voluntariness requirement;

(3)   A society in which the (qualified) voluntariness requirement is satisfied is one where no freedom is curtailed;

therefore,

(4)   A free market society is a society in which no freedom is curtailed.

Let us consider again the various ways in which, as I observed earlier, non-consenting individuals are affected by others' voluntarily consented-to exchanges. I said earlier that the presence of non-consented-to interference challenged the claim that the free market satisfies the voluntariness requirement. But once the voluntariness requirement is qualified, so as to only posit consent as a necessary condition for the legitimacy of a narrower range of interference with individuals, namely, rights-infringing interference, then the contention that the (qualified) voluntariness requirement is satisfied holds. Hence, while acknowledging that individuals affect others on a great number of occasions, Nozick suggests that any non-rights-violating form of affecting others is legitimate and does not require the consent of those affected. When discussing equality of opportunity, for instance, Nozick distinguishes between the case in which someone with better opportunities blocks or impedes someone with worse opportunities from becoming better off, and the case where someone worsens another's situation by stealing from him.[17]

---

[15] The rights-definition of freedom entails that consented-to interference is not viewed as freedom-curtailing interference: if only rights-infringing interference curtails freedom, then consented-to interference, being non-rights-infringing interference (consent opens borders), is not freedom-curtailing interference. Hence, because of his moralised definition of freedom, Nozick overlooks *both* the fact that some non-consented-to interference is freedom curtailing, *and* the fact that consented-to interference, too, limits freedom, where freedom is pure negative freedom. As I have already mentioned in chapter 4, other libertarians, too, claim, in my view mistakenly, that consented-to interference is not freedom curtailing. One need not endorse a moralised definition of freedom to hold that position, though endorsing the moralised definition entails it.

[16] It is no longer necessary, here, unlike with the original voluntariness requirement, to exempt from the demands of the voluntariness requirement those obligations that are the correlative of others' rights. This is because, if only potentially *rights-infringing* interferences need consenting to, those obligations are automatically exempt: any interference that is the correlative of others' libertarian rights is *not* rights-infringing, since individuals do not have rights to breach others' libertarian rights. If they breach those rights, they forfeit theirs, and interference is justified.

[17] *ASU*, p. 237. Compare this with the statement that 'to be at *social* liberty, liberty in relation to one's fellows, is for them to refrain from impeding one's effort'. Cf. J. Narveson, 'Contracting for Liberty', in T. R. Machan and D. B. Rasmussen (eds.), *Liberty for the 21st Century. Contemporary Libertarian Thought* (Maryland: Rowman & Littlefield, 1995), pp. 19–39, at p. 26.

Externalities, then, would only be deemed problematic where someone's rights are violated as a result, thus being viewed as harmful.[18] A non-harmful and hence legitimate externality, on this account, would occur in the case in which, for example, as a result of others' legitimate actions, a person is left unemployed. However much some individuals' transactions may affect others, then, so long as those others are not harmed (that is, their rights are not infringed), there is no injustice (since only rights infringement raises problems of justice) and no justification for restricting those transactions or only allowing them conditionally upon the affected parties' consent.

Nozick's use of a rights-based criterion of harm is liable to a number of objections. First, a rights-definition of harm does not seem to do justice to the ordinary sense in which we use this notion and to its significance. It is counter-intuitive to insist that being left unemployed is not harmful while having one of many pencils one owns stolen is, even if we grant that rights are violated in the second but not in the first case. As Daniel Hausman has remarked, cases of negative pecuniary externalities that legitimately arise through the exchange of private property rights and which have profound deleterious effects on people's lives surely do raise concerns of justice.[19] So, and even if we grant libertarians their view of rights, we have reason to contest their contention that only cases where rights are violated should count as relevant for justice: there are evidently cases in which individuals are harmed, although their (libertarian) rights have not been violated, and which do seem to raise questions of justice.

The second difficulty with the rights-based harm criterion is one of consistency. Whilst Nozick explicitly states that he intends 'harm' to refer to rights-violating interference only, and that individuals should be left free to act as they wish so long as they do not harm others, he nonetheless allows some instances of seemingly non-rights-violating affecting of others as justifiably prevented.[20] This emerges in the discussion of the fear which the knowledge that violation of rights goes unpunished creates in people.[21] In this context, Nozick suggests that what calls for intervention is not only the realised fear of those who have undergone, say, physical injury, but also the fear of potential victims. And here he contemplates not only the fear resulting from the prospect of having one's rights violated, but also the emotional distress associated with being humiliated, shamed, disgraced,

---

[18] Nozick's discussion of pollution is limited to those cases where rights have indeed been infringed. See *ASU*, pp. 79–81.

[19] Hausman, 'When Jack and Jill Made a Deal', p. 104.   [20] See *ASU*, chapter 5, note 12, at p. 341.

[21] *ASU*, pp. 65–71. Fear-inducing activity is an instance of 'affecting others'.

embarrassed and so on.[22] If these considerations are given any weight at any stage, it is difficult to see how Nozick can then overlook them in other cases of non-rights-violating interference.

The rights-based harm criterion, then, seems both implausible as a criterion of what counts as unjust interference and inconsistent with Nozick's own goal of characterising as harmful certain non-rights-infringing forms of affecting others. These reservations would remain even if Nozick accepted that rights infringement alone, rather than harmfulness, is what he should appeal to for determining whether or not other-affecting actions should be voluntarily consented to by the affected parties.[23] For even if Nozick subscribed to a qualified voluntariness requirement that makes no mention of harm at all, and stated simply that only potentially right-infringing interferences with individuals must be voluntarily consented to by the affected parties, we may complain that at least some non-rights-violating but harmful conduct surely gives rise to concerns of justice and point to the fact that Nozick himself wants to allow for this.

But let us leave this problem aside now, and assume that Nozick could coherently justify exempting some cases of non-consented-to interference from having to satisfy the voluntariness requirement by appeal to something like his harm criterion. Even then, it would still be true that that interference could be freedom-curtailing interference. The negative freedom of the would-be walker is limited by the landowner's property rights (in that the landowner prevents the would-be walker from walking on his private property), even if that curtailment of freedom were legitimately exempted from having to be consented to (on the rights-based harm criterion).

Now, it is because he uses a rights-definition of freedom that Nozick claims that when the only non-consented-to interferences are interferences that are sanctioned by the modified voluntariness requirement, then no one's freedom is curtailed. On Nozick's rights-definition of freedom, not just any interference with an agent limits her freedom. Rather, an individual's freedom is curtailed only insofar as he is prevented from doing what he has a right to do. Thus, punishing a thief by either exacting compensation or through imprisonment does not in this view amount to limiting his freedom. Similarly, the passer-by's freedom is not being limited by forbidding him to walk over a landowner's property, while the landowner's freedom would indeed be curtailed if an inheritance tax were introduced. He has a right to his property, while the passer-by does not have a right to walk across someone else's property. By inscribing the notion of freedom in a

---

[22] *ASU*, p. 70.   [23] I thank Peter Vallentyne for bringing this point to my attention.

theory of rights, Nozick can discriminate between freedom-curtailing and non-freedom-curtailing interference, and justify the latter without being committed to the view that at least some individuals' freedom is curtailed in a libertarian society.

It is worth noting that Nozick is not alone in offering a moralised definition of freedom. Alan Wertheimer, for instance, expounds a similar view in his avowedly moralised 'two-pronged theory of coercion'.[24] Other libertarians, too, wrongly infer, from their contention that rights protect freedom, that freedom is to be defined through rights, so that the only freedom-curtailing interference is rights-infringing interference.[25] Another moralised definition of freedom is defended by David Miller, who claims that an individual is made unfree only by those obstacles for which some other person or persons can be held *morally* responsible.[26] Miller thus builds moral considerations – in his case, attributions of moral responsibility – into judgements of freedom and unfreedom. However, he suggests that his view avoids the problems incurred by Nozick's moralised definition, on the grounds that his view does, while Nozick's does not, make a distinction between unfreedom and *justified* unfreedom.[27] This is because, while the attribution of moral responsibility to the constraining agent identifies a case in which the constrained party is made unfree, Miller suggests that to say that someone is morally responsible for something does not mean that he is blameable for it, but only that he is liable to blame if he does not provide a justification for his conduct. But while it is true that Miller's view allows us to talk about justified freedom-curtailing interference where

[24] Commenting on Nozick's view, Wertheimer notes that, although it may be wrong, 'it is neither arbitrary nor bizarre. In effect, his view captures the theory of coercion that characterises virtually the entire corpus of American law'. See A. Wertheimer, *Coercion* (Princeton University Press, 1987), p. 201. A moralised account of freedom is also upheld by R. E. Lane, 'Market Choice and Human Choice', in J. W. Chapman and J. R. Pennock (eds.), *Markets and Justice* (New York University Press, 1989), pp. 226–49.

[25] See J. Hospers, 'What Libertarianism Is', in Machan and Rasmussen (eds.), *Liberty for the 21st Century*, pp. 5–17. In a similar vein, Murray Rothbard suggests: 'Freedom is a condition in which a person's ownership rights in his own body and his legitimate material property are not invaded, are not aggressed against.' See M. Rothbard, *For a New Liberty* (New York: Macmillan, 1973), p. 43.

[26] D. Miller, 'Constraints on Freedom', *Ethics* 94 (1983), pp. 66–86.

[27] That distinction is also retained on the moralised definition of freedom defended by Eric Mack, according to whom 'individual I's liberty consists in the absence of those interferences that violate his rights *or would violate his rights had those rights not been waived or forfeited by I*.' See E. Mack, 'Moral Individualism and Libertarian Theory', in Machan and Rasmussen (eds.), *Liberty for the 21st Century*, pp. 41–58, in note 1 at p. 57, emphasis mine. Mack can thus suggest that a justly incarcerated individual's freedom is curtailed. For the distinction between the moral responsibility view of freedom and the moralised definition of freedom detected in Nozick, see K. Kristjánsson, *Social Freedom: The Responsibility View* (Cambridge University Press, 1996), pp. 19–20; I. Carter, *A Measure of Freedom* (Oxford University Press, 1999), p. 236.

Nozick's would not, Miller's definition of freedom, too, excludes a range of interference from qualifying as freedom-curtailing in the first place. For instance, on the assumption that he is not morally responsible for his action, a shopkeeper who raises his price as a result of a wholesale price rise of some commodity does not infringe the freedom of his customers because he has acted 'within his rights'.[28]

Nozick's use of a moralised definition of freedom has been subjected to sustained criticism, and I will rehearse the difficulties it incurs only summarily here.[29] One criticism is a charge of circularity: Nozick intends to show that considerations of freedom support arguments for private property rights, but that argument cannot be based on neutrally defined liberty, for on neutrally defined liberty, some people's freedom is curtailed by others' legitimate exercise of their property rights. By adopting, instead, a rights-definition of freedom, Nozick already assumes in the very definition of freedom what his argument is supposed to show, namely, that a concern with protecting people's freedom requires that their private property rights be respected. These difficulties are often illustrated by focusing on the Wilt Chamberlain argument, where Nozick aims to establish that liberty upsets patterns. Nozick invites us to imagine that we start with whatever patterned or end-state distribution we favour, whether in accordance with desert or needs, or an equal one, and then supposes that people freely choose to pay Wilt Chamberlain to watch him play basketball. The resulting inequality is the result of people's exercise of their liberty; the latter is what would have to be sacrificed to restore the patterned distribution (so as to ensure that everyone has what they deserve, what they need, or an equal share).[30] But what definition of liberty is Nozick appealing to here? If the liberty at issue is rights-defined freedom, then the Wilt Chamberlain argument presupposes exactly the rights it is supposed to justify. For if individuals have encumbered, rather than full, ownership rights over the resources they command, they may well not be permitted to transfer those resources at will in the first place. If, instead, the Wilt Chamberlain example relies on a neutral

---

[28] Miller, 'Constraints on Freedom', p. 79.

[29] See G. A. Cohen, 'Capitalism, Freedom, and the Proletariat', in D. Miller (ed.), *Liberty* (Oxford University Press, 1991), pp. 163–82, at pp. 170–2; Cohen, *Self-Ownership*, pp. 60–5; W. Kymlicka, *Contemporary Political Philosophy* (Oxford: Clarendon Press, 1990), chapter 4; T. M. Scanlon, 'Nozick on Rights, Liberty, and Property', in J. Paul (ed.), *Reading Nozick* (Oxford: Blackwell, 1982), pp. 107–29; J. Child, 'Can Libertarianism Sustain a Fraud Standard?', *Ethics* 104 (1994), pp. 722–38; C. C. Ryan, 'Yours, Mine, and Ours: Property Rights and Individual Liberty', in Paul (ed.), *Reading Nozick*, pp. 323–43. For a criticism of Cohen's view, see J. Gray, 'Marxian Freedom, Individual Liberty, and the End of Alienation', *Social Philosophy and Policy* 3 (1986), pp. 161–78, to which Cohen replies in *Self-Ownership*, chapter 2, section 3.

[30] *ASU*, pp. 160–4.

definition of freedom, this is inconsistent with Nozick's use of a rights-definition of freedom. Moreover, the Wilt Chamberlain argument would fail, as the pattern-disrupting distribution would not necessarily ensue.

Aside from problems of inconsistency and circularity which Nozick's argument incurs by using a moralised definition of freedom, the latter is objectionable on the grounds that it does not allow us to distinguish between justified and unjustified freedom-curtailing interference, and thus obscures the fact that a libertarian society is not a society in which no freedom is curtailed.

Nozick's statement that in a free market society there are no limitations of freedom because all interferences and obligations (except those that are the correlative of individuals' rights) are voluntarily consented to, then, faces the objections that in a free market society there is much non-consented-to interference, and that some of this is freedom-curtailing interference. Nozick's – and other libertarians' – way of circumventing that objection rests on restricting the scope of the voluntariness requirement to rights-infringing or border-crossing interference only, and on a flawed moralised definition of freedom.

3. MARKET CHOICE AND RIGHTS-DEFINED VOLUNTARINESS

We have seen that, in a free market society, much freedom is curtailed, and this is true even if the modified voluntariness requirement were satisfied, that is, even if all obligations and interferences that would be border-crossing (or rights-violating or harmful) in the absence of consent were actually consented to. I now turn to explore an objection to the claim that the free market satisfies even the modified voluntariness requirement. Even where the range of interference that should be voluntarily consented to is limited to potentially boundary-crossing interference only, in fact, much voluntariness is vitiated in a free market society. This is because, where everything is owned by individuals or by private associations of individuals, there are many situations of limited choice, in which the nature of the options that are available to many individuals is such as to vitiate the voluntariness of their choices. An action or a choice is non-voluntary, or forced, I suggest, if and only if it is done because there is no acceptable alternative to it, where the standard of acceptability is an objective one. In particular, let us assume here that an option that involves sacrificing some basic need is *not* an acceptable one. So, for example, someone who accepts a hazardous job to avoid remaining unemployed in a context in which there is no unemployment safety net can hardly be said to be making a voluntary choice.[31]

Whilst such cases of limited choice well illustrate the issue by pointing to situations where the choice is made under pressure of dire circumstances, it may be suggested that there is a sense in which market transactions *as such* are instances of limited choice. Individuals cannot be said to choose market transactions, insofar as they do not (standardly) have an acceptable alternative option but to take part in those transactions. The decision to participate in market transactions, then, hardly counts as a voluntary choice, given that there is no possibility of opting out of the market game, as there is to opt out of playing the Lottery. As G. A. Cohen suggests, 'entering the market lottery is always a (possibly dispreferred) way of doing something else' – earning one's living, obtaining a place to live, getting the means for realising one's plans.[32] Moreover, and crucially, there is no safe option to stay out of the market in the same way as there is a safe option to abstain from playing the Lottery.

If these objections against the alleged voluntariness of market choice are justified, the consequences for Nozick's defence of the free market are serious indeed. If individuals cannot be said to voluntarily choose to engage in market transactions, then the harmful or deleterious consequences that accompany these transactions remain unjustified and cannot be considered as merely the unpleasant side effect of just – just because voluntary, that is – transactions. Negative pecuniary externalities, which I mentioned in the previous section, can no longer be constructed as the result of risks one chooses to take voluntarily when deciding to participate in the market. Someone's decision to take on both the benefits and the risks associated with the workings of the free market would only count as voluntary insofar as the person in question had some acceptable alternative, which most people, in a free market society, do not have.

Whilst this kind of objection to Nozick's view may have plausibility, in what follows I do not pursue this point further, and I do not suggest that all market transactions are forced insofar as participating in the market is not a voluntary choice. I do not want to make such a sweeping claim for two reasons. First, as will appear, I do not maintain that, *whenever* an individual has no acceptable alternative, then he is forced to choose as he does. It is possible for someone to have no acceptable alternative to what he does, but nonetheless to do what he does voluntarily. So, while the fact that someone

---

[31] I discuss this notion of voluntariness in greater depth in the next chapter.
[32] Cohen, *Self-Ownership*, p. 49.

is forced entails that he has no acceptable alternative, the converse does not hold: the fact that someone has no acceptable alternative does not entail that he is forced.[33] And second, this claim is just too sweeping. It is true that the great majority of individuals do not choose to participate in the market, but I do not think that that is what we should concentrate on. What we are concerned with, in my view, is the problem presented by *some* transactions that occur in a free market society, such as the case of a worker choosing a hazardous job, which constitute limited choice situations in a way in which other market transactions do not.

Nozick's response to the limited choice problem is to dismiss any such considerations. He states:

Whether a person's actions are voluntary depends on what it is that limits its alternatives . . . Other people's actions place limits on one's available opportunities. Whether this makes one's resulting action non-voluntary depends upon whether these others had the right to act as they did.[34]

According to Nozick, then, the fact that one chooses among very unattractive or unacceptable options is not sufficient to render choices non-voluntary. Rather, choices are non-voluntary only if they are made among alternatives that resulted from others not acting within their rights.[35]

The rights-definition of voluntariness used by Nozick is different from the rights-definition of freedom examined in the previous section. Whilst the rights-definition of freedom gives a restricted meaning to what counts as a limitation of freedom, the rights-definition of voluntariness provides a restricted account of what counts as non-voluntary choice.[36] The former shows that interferences with the actions of individuals who do not have the right to perform those actions are not infringements of their liberty. It covers those cases where *no* consent has been given to interference, and contends that, unlike cases where this would count as a limitation of freedom and hence be illegitimate, there are instances of non-consented-to interferences that are not freedom-curtailing, and, therefore, are legitimate. The

---

[33] I return to this point in chapter 6, sections 1 and 4.   [34] *ASU*, p. 262.

[35] On this analysis, as I. A. Macdonald remarks, 'we can ask questions about the voluntariness of choices only within a theory of rights'. I. A. Macdonald, 'Rights, Rights of Enforcement, and Nozick's Critique of the "Principle of Fairness"', *South African Journal of Philosophy* 3 (1984), pp. 47–53.

[36] Throughout, I use the attribute 'non-voluntary', which I prefer over 'involuntary'. This is because, I think, 'involuntary' is more readily associated with 'non-volitional'. This is an association which I would like to avoid, as the cases of vitiated voluntariness which I consider do not involve choices which are 'unwilled' in the sense in which reflexes, for example, are. By 'non-voluntary' choice I mean a choice that is volitional but not voluntary, where the conditions for voluntariness are over and above those for volition. See below chapter 6, section 4 for an elaboration of this point.

rights-definition of voluntariness, by contrast, deals with cases where consent *has* indeed been given, but where the agent seems to face a restricted choice. It denies that such restricted choice undermines the voluntariness of the action and asserts that as long as the choice was restricted as a result of others' acting within their rights, it is to be considered as voluntary.

Despite being different, and despite playing two different roles in Nozick's defence of the market, the rights-definition of freedom and the rights-definition of voluntariness have failed to be distinguished, either by Nozick himself or by his critics.[37] The two definitions, of course, are related: both freedom and voluntariness are defined by Nozick by reference to rights and indeed, so I argue in what follows, Nozick can be seen to derive his rights-definition of voluntariness from his rights-definition of freedom. He believes that freedom, rights-defined, will guarantee voluntariness, rights-defined, so there is going to be no case where freedom is intact but where voluntariness is not. However, as I will show, insofar as it derives a statement about voluntariness from moralised freedom, the rights-definition of voluntariness rests on a mistake. This is because morally defined freedom does not guarantee voluntariness. Furthermore, and independently from considerations about the coherence of the notion of rights-defined voluntariness, the latter is problematic insofar as it introduces an element of circularity in Nozick's 'voluntarism yardstick of justice in transfer',[38] which holds that, so long as transfers of justly acquired rights are voluntary, the resulting distribution of rights is also just.

Voluntariness and freedom of the constrained agent

Let us first of all recall what the two definitions state:

(1)   An individual is rendered unfree (his freedom is curtailed) when prevented from doing x only if he has a right to do x (rights-definition of freedom);

(2)   An individual acts non-voluntarily only if the choice that is available to him is the result of the actions of others that have acted outside their rights (rights-definition of voluntariness).

---

[37] Hence Cohen, when arguing that Nozick adopts the rights-definition of freedom, quotes as evidence the passage from Nozick (*ASU*, p. 262), where the latter offers a rights-definition of voluntariness. Steiner makes a similar mistake. See H. Steiner, *An Essay on Rights* (Oxford: Blackwell, 1994), p. 12.

[38] This term for the contention that voluntariness preserves justice is Israel Kirzner's. See I. M. Kirzner, 'Entrepreneurship, Entitlement, and Economic Justice', in Paul (ed.), *Reading Nozick*, pp. 383–411.

These two definitions address two related questions: 'Are individuals made unfree just by *any* interference or constraints?', and 'Are individuals' actions made non-voluntary just by *any* restraint on their choice conditions?' To these questions, they both provide a negative answer. The rights-definition of freedom states that one is only made unfree by interference or constraints that violate one's rights. The rights-definition of voluntariness states that one's choices are non-voluntary only if they are restrained by things others do that they do not have a right to do.[39]

Notice that while both the rights-definition of freedom and the rights-definition of voluntariness, obviously, are grounded in rights, the sets of rights by *direct* reference to which they are articulated, and the *type* of rights invoked, are not the same. In the case of the rights-definition of freedom, the reference is to the *claim* rights of the agent himself, and only derivatively and indirectly to the *liberty* rights of others. Someone has a claim right to do *x* if and only if she has a right to be free from interference with doing *x*; someone has a liberty right to do *x* (is at liberty to do *x*) if and only if she is under no enforceable obligation not to do *x*.[40] So, for example, if Audrey has no claim right to do *x*, she is not made unfree when she is obstructed by Burt in her performance of *x*. Audrey is only rendered unfree by Burt's interference when she does have a claim right to do *x*, and Burt,

---

[39] Note that the rights-definition of voluntariness tells us only when an agent's action is *not* rendered non-voluntary, but does not tell us when an agent's action *is* voluntary, that is, it does not offer us sufficient conditions to regard an action as voluntary. Nozick may presumably allow, for instance, for the fact that ignorance undermines voluntariness. Nozick, in fact, swings between two views of the status of rights-defined voluntariness. At some points, he seems to ascribe to the crude view according to which non-rights violation is a sufficient as well as a necessary condition of voluntariness: as long as others have acted within their rights, an action is declared as voluntary. (This is implied, for instance, by Nozick's statement that if facts of nature limit our alternatives, we *act voluntarily*. Cf. *ASU*, p. 262.) At other times, Nozick seems to subscribe to the more plausible view that non-rights violation is only a necessary but not a sufficient condition for voluntariness. Whilst both views are present in Nozick's arguments, this does not affect my critique of rights-defined voluntariness, insofar as this is aimed at Nozick's treatment of how *constrained choice situations* affect voluntariness. Both the crude and the more plausible interpretations, in fact, imply that the contention I set out to criticise is present, namely, that non-rights-violating choice restriction does not undermine voluntariness.

[40] Note that I am here defining a 'liberty right' as 'being free of an *enforceable* obligation or duty not to do what one is at liberty to do'. This is compatible with one's having a *moral* but unenforceable obligation not to do what one is at liberty (in the present sense) to do. Since, as I said earlier, I am here concerned only with libertarianism's claims about enforceable obligations, I use the narrower sense of 'liberty rights'. So, an employer acts within his liberty rights (as I understand them here), according to Nozick, when he makes an abysmal job offer to someone who is desperately seeking a job, that is, he does not breach others' claim rights; but this is compatible with contending that he has an unenforceable moral obligation to make a more generous job offer, and is liable to blame if he does not. The *locus classicus* of the distinction between claim rights and liberties is W. N. Hohfeld's *Fundamental Legal Conceptions as Applied in Judicial Reasoning* (Westport, Conn.: Greenwood Press, 1978, first published by Yale University Press in 1919).

consequently, has no liberty right to obstruct Audrey (that is, he has an obligation *not to* obstruct Audrey).[41]

With the rights-definition of voluntariness, by contrast, the rights by direct reference to which the voluntariness of an action is defined are not the claim rights of the agent himself, but rather the liberty rights of those who restrict the ranges of options facing the agent. If they have acted within their liberty rights, this *also* means that they have not infringed the agent's claim rights by acting as they have done. That is, they have acted in ways which they had no enforceable obligation *not* to act in, and have therefore not infringed any of the agent's claim rights.

These observations about the different sets of rights which are primary in the definitions of freedom and voluntariness, besides clarifying the definitions themselves, also shed light on the way the two notions, though different, are related. In particular, I would like to claim that the rights-definition of voluntariness presupposes the rights-definition of freedom, and that Nozick defines voluntariness through rights *because* he assumes that freedom guarantees voluntariness.[42]

Consider the following example. Suppose that W is a worker who chooses to sell her labour to employer E. The choice facing W is either to work for E at a very low wage, or to be unemployed and eventually starve. We want to establish whether W's choice to work for E can be deemed voluntary. Consider, then, the standard case, as Nozick conceives it, in which E, by offering the low wage to W, acts within his rights. E, because he acts within his rights, does not violate W's rights. On the rights-definition of freedom, this means that E does not render W unfree. Hence, Nozick concludes, W's choice to work for Burt is voluntary. For the sake of clarity, let us sketch the main steps of this reasoning.

(1)   If E acts within his rights, he does not infringe W's rights;

(2)   If W's rights are not infringed by E's actions, then E's affecting of W does not render W unfree (on the rights-definition of freedom);

(3)   If W is not rendered unfree, then W acts voluntarily;

---

[41] Note that this is compatible with the fact that Audrey may lack the right to do x *because* Burt has an exclusive right over who should do *x*. The explanation of why Audrey does not have the claim right may itself make reference to others', including Burt's, claim rights. But we need not know *why* Audrey has or lacks the claim right in question to know whether Audrey is rendered unfree when interfered with.

[42] From now on, and having made this distinction, I will talk about 'rights' *simpliciter*, except where it is necessary to draw attention to the fact that the rights in questions are claim rights and liberty rights, respectively.

therefore,

(4) W does not act non-voluntarily if E, by limiting W's choice, has acted within his rights.

However, (3) is false. The fact that W is not unfree on a rights-definition of freedom does not settle the question of the voluntariness of W's actions. This is because morally defined freedom does not guarantee voluntariness (nor does unfreedom, where unfreedom is morally defined, necessarily undermine voluntariness). To see this, consider the case in which justly imprisoned prisoner P, not having any right to leave prison, is therefore, on the rights-definition of freedom, not made unfree to leave his cell by guardian G. This does not mean, however, that P's remaining in prison and deciding not to escape, *because* of G's preventing him from leaving, is a voluntary choice. Or imagine the case in which P has decided to escape from prison and is then recaptured. This is not an infringement of P's (moralised) freedom, although P's voluntary decision has been undermined, that is, P's remaining in prison is a not a voluntary choice.

Conversely, P may have gained the right to leave prison, and hence be rendered unfree if guardian G prevents him from leaving, and yet his staying in prison, it seems, may be voluntary. Perhaps P has grown attached to his prison mates and routine, and genuinely prefers that over the loneliness of his home. He willingly stays in prison although he has the right to leave and although G, by preventing P from leaving, makes P unfree. These examples show that the fact that an agent's rights have not been violated by someone else's limiting his options does not settle the question of the voluntariness of the choice. Therefore, (3) is unjustified.

The attempt to infer judgements about voluntariness from considerations of moralised freedom, resulting in a moralised definition of voluntariness, is also found in Wertheimer's account, which I mentioned earlier. According to Wertheimer, 'one acts voluntarily when responding to morally permissible threats'.[43] This follows from the fact that, on his moralised theory of coercion, morally permissible threats can be recast as offers, and offers, Wertheimer holds, do not restrict freedom. Hence, if someone is made a morally permissible threat, his freedom is not restricted. And if someone's freedom is not restricted, he acts voluntarily. Wertheimer too, then, elaborates a rights-definition of voluntariness, and he does so for reasons very similar to those I am attributing to Nozick: starting with a moralised definition of freedom, and with the view that freedom guarantees voluntariness,

---

[43] Wertheimer, *Coercion*, p. 250.

he concludes that 'B acts voluntarily when B succumbs to a proposal that A has a right to make, even if it is one which B finds unattractive and would prefer not to receive'.[44] But in this case as much as with Nozick's, and despite Wertheimer's attempt to articulate a connection between moralised coercion and voluntariness, the fact that someone is not made unfree on a moralised definition does not tell us anything about voluntariness.[45]

I would like to suggest that the reason why voluntariness is not necessarily related to freedom morally defined is explained by the fact that the notion of freedom as 'being free to do something', of which I take the rights-definition of freedom to be a version, is in a complex relation to voluntariness, and by the fact that freedom does not guarantee voluntariness.[46] As I will show in the next chapter, where I develop this point further, judgements about freedom and judgements of voluntariness can sometimes pull in different directions.

Voluntariness and freedom of the constraining agent

We can make sense of the rights-definition of voluntariness, then, as something Nozick may endorse because of his endorsement of the rights-definition of freedom. One may try to extract claims about voluntariness from claims of (moralised) freedom. But in so doing, one simply tells us nothing relevant about voluntariness. We may know that the choice facing an agent is restricted as a result of others having acted within their rights, and without, therefore, the agent's rights having been violated. But this does not entitle us to say anything as to whether the agent has acted free*ly* or voluntarily. (As I have suggested, something else is needed in order to assess whether voluntariness is vitiated in limited choice situations: we need to know whether the agent's choices in these situations were made because no other acceptable alternative was available.)

What might lead us to take the answer to the question of whether a person's options are limited as a result of others' acting within their rights to

---

[44] *Ibid.*, p. 301.

[45] Wertheimer tries to articulate a connection between coercion and voluntariness through an analysis of voluntariness which makes reference to hierarchical preferences, such that voluntary action is viewed as action in accordance with one's moral principles. On this view, it is crucial that, when responding to a morally permissible threat, the coerced agent is '*himself* morally committed to the principles which grant A the right to make the proposal'. Wertheimer, *Coercion*, p. 301. I do not believe that Wertheimer's attempt at explaining the connection between coercion and voluntariness is successful, but I cannot defend this claim here. For a brief treatment of the relationship between voluntariness and hierarchical preferences, however, see below chapter 6, section 2.

[46] This point is developed below in chapter 6, section 1.

settle the question of whether that person acts voluntarily? One reason why Nozick may be tempted into the rights-definition of voluntariness is that he is concerned about the freedom of those who restrict people's choices. He may worry that, if we deem that the voluntariness of someone's choice can be undermined as a result of someone else acting within his rights, then this may justify interfering with the latter person, and *this* interference would count as freedom-curtailing on Nozick's own rights-based definition of freedom.

By way of illustration, consider again the case of worker W and employer E. By saying that E acts within his rights when he offers W a poorly paid hazardous job, we are suggesting that he has no enforceable obligation to abstain from offering W the deal he offers him. If E has no enforceable obligation to abstain from making W the dire offer, E is also likely to have a right to be free from *some forms* of interference aimed at preventing him from making this offer (although, of course, someone may affect the likelihood of his offer being successful by making another, better offer).[47] If W's choice were deemed non-voluntary, and since voluntariness is a necessary condition for justifiable interference with anyone, then, by Nozick's own lights, we should prevent E from making the offer he makes to W (for example, by requiring that he offer at least minimum wage rates to W), and we would thereby be restricting E's freedom. To avoid this conclusion, Nozick suggests that, when E acts within his rights, W's choice is voluntary. But, of course, wanting to avoid the conclusion that E's freedom should be curtailed is not a good reason to define voluntariness through rights.

Nozick, in my view, would have better admitted that W's choice may sometimes be rendered non-voluntary, on a non-rights-defined notion of voluntariness, by E's action, and yet insist that W's acting non-voluntarily does not qualify as a limitation of W's freedom, morally defined, as no rights of W's have been violated. This might have more plausibility than his arguing that, because W's rights have not been violated, then W, not having been made unfree, acts voluntarily. After all, arguing what I suggest

---

[47] Although liberties do not *entail* claim rights, they are often protected by various obligations placed on others, or by what H. L. A. Hart has referred to as a 'protective perimeter' of obligations. H. L. A. Hart, *Essays on Bentham: Studies in Jurisprudence and Political Theory* (Oxford: Clarendon Press, 1982), pp. 171–3. These include at least those obligations entailed by the claim rights held by the person who has the liberty right. For example, E's liberty right to offer a low wage to W is protected by others' obligation not to violate his various claim rights not to be killed or to have his property stolen from him. This means that others cannot interfere with E's making of his offer to W by killing him, maiming him, or violating his property rights in any way, though they may interfere with E's (successful) making of the offer by outbidding him.

would simply amount to allowing the rights-definition of freedom to do all the required ideological work. The rights-definition of freedom as Nozick articulates it states that not all non-consented-to interference counts as a limitation of freedom. Now, it would also state that not all vitiated voluntariness is a case of reduced freedom. Obviously, such an argument would still be riddled with all the problems which the rights-definition of freedom incurs.[48] Possibly, Nozick eschews this conclusion because he wants to retain some room for voluntariness. But the rights-definition of voluntariness is one step too many even if we accept the rights-definition of freedom. Not only is it not convincing for common sense: Nozick's own rights-definition of freedom provides no support for it.

One final comment on the problems incurred by the rights-definition of voluntariness is in order. The use of the rights-definition of voluntariness is also problematic for Nozick's account in another way, independently from the issue of the plausibility of the notion. If considerations of rights are introduced for defining something as voluntary, then the voluntarism yardstick of justice is undermined. This is because, if we adopt the rights-definition of voluntariness, then, in order to know whether an action is voluntary, we need to know whether the options facing an individual were brought about by other individuals acting in accordance with their rights. Hence, considerations of justice, that is, of whether rights are respected, come in before we define something as voluntary, and are indeed needed in order to establish whether something is voluntary. However, once we have relied on considerations of individuals' rights in order to declare an action as voluntary, it is pointless to then refer to voluntariness in order to establish that the transaction, being voluntary, is just.

Hence, if voluntariness is rights-defined, it ceases to do any substantive work in establishing whether a transaction is just. What we are really focusing on is whether individuals act within their rights: if they do, then resulting actions are going to be declared as voluntary. But to then insist that, because they are voluntary, they preserve justice, adds nothing that is not already contained in the definition of voluntariness itself. The voluntarism

---

[48] Yet another possibility for Nozick would be to admit that W's action may be non-voluntary (on a non-rights-based definition of voluntariness), *and* that this may limit W's freedom (on a non-rights-based definition of freedom), but to insist nonetheless that imposing restrictions on E to avoid this would require violating his rights, and is therefore unjustified. Here, again, Nozick would base his case on a commitment to the protection of rights, rather than on any appeal to voluntariness or freedom. For reasons I outlined in the previous chapter, I think this move would not be welcomed by libertarians, as it renders libertarianism considerably less attractive and undercuts the very rationale at the basis of assigning individuals the fundamental libertarian rights.

yardstick of justice, then, would already assume what it is supposed to test, namely, claims of individuals' rights and of justice.

4. TAXATION AND FORCED LABOUR

So far I have argued that Nozick employs a flawed rights-definition of voluntariness, alongside the more familiar rights-definition of freedom. I now bring these points to bear on the analysis of two of Nozick's most forceful arguments in favour of the free market, namely, his claim that workers are not forced to sell their labour, and his contention that taxation is on a par with forced labour. I show that both these arguments make use of the rights-definition of voluntariness, and argue that they are therefore ultimately unsuccessful.

Choosing to marry and choosing whom to marry

There is an argument Nozick offers when making his case for the rights-definition of voluntariness that would seem to readily command agreement. By drawing an analogy between a worker's choice to work and an individual's choice of which person to marry, Nozick's intention is to show that we would endorse judgements based on the rights-definition of voluntariness for the marriage case and then to convince us that the worker's choice is similar in the relevant respects.[49] We should thus endorse Nozick's contention that the worker acts voluntarily.

I shall argue that the analogy is misguided, and that, once this is exposed, the force of Nozick's example is eroded. In particular, I argue, first, that there are two different sets of choices involved here, one concerning the choice of the moves within the game, and the other concerning the choice of participating in the game. Second, once we have distinguished between these two sets of choices, Nozick's application of the rights-definition of voluntariness to each one of the two cases can be better assessed. I suggest that in both cases, if individuals face a limited choice, and even if that situation of limited choice has been brought about by others acting within their rights, we should deny that a voluntary choice has, in fact, been made.

Nozick starts with twenty-six women and twenty-six men each wanting to be married, each group ranked from A to Z for the women and A_1 to Z_1 for men, where the ranking criterion is their desirability as marriage partners. A voluntarily marries A_1; B would like to marry A_1 but by their

49 *ASU*, p. 263.

choice, A and A_1 have removed this option from B, who will then voluntarily marry B_1. This goes on until Z and Z_1 only are left.

Each prefers any one of the twenty-five other partners who by their choices have removed themselves from consideration by Z and Z_1. Z and Z_1 voluntarily choose to marry each other. The fact that their only other alternative is (in their view) much worse, and the fact that others chose to exercise their rights in certain ways, thereby shaping the external environment of options in which Z and Z_1 choose, does not mean that they did not marry voluntarily.[50]

Nozick then quickly extends the same observations to the case of market exchanges between workers and owners of capital. But this is most puzzling.

My first claim is that in the marriage case, Nozick misrepresents the doubts we face when asking about the voluntariness of Z's and Z_1's actions. The doubt is not whether they *married* voluntarily. Rather, the doubt is whether they married *that particular partner* voluntarily, that is, whether they voluntarily chose to marry the particular partner that they married. That Z and Z_1 marry voluntarily, we know from the beginning: Nozick starts off with the specification that there are fifty-two people 'each wanting to be married'. The voluntariness of this choice is not undermined, because Z and Z_1 want to marry, and the option of not marrying, for all we know, is open to them.

The question as to whether Z and Z_1 marry voluntarily would arise in a different situation. This is the case in which the twenty-six men and twenty-six women at issue were induced into marriage in the first place, by, say, having strong social ostracism attached to being unmarried.[51] They could then each be left the choice as to which of the twenty-six members of the other sex to marry. Indeed, there may be an unlimited number of highly desirable partners, not limited by others' choices. Nonetheless, the question would arise as to whether they have married voluntarily.

In both these instances, the choice facing the prospective bride or bridegroom is voluntary, under the rights-definition of voluntariness. That is, in both cases those who have restricted the alternatives have acted within their rights: in the first case, each individual had decided whom to choose as partner; in the second case, a number of individuals working together under a certain system of social rules attach negative pay-offs to the choice of remaining unmarried. These pay-offs, however, do not, we can suppose, amount to an infringement of rights in Nozick's sense.

---

[50] *Ibid.*

[51] We can, for the sake of simplicity, imagine a situation in which the social ostracism attached to being unmarried is such as to result in a dire material situation for the ostracised one, leading to isolation from the labour market and, eventually, starvation.

There is, however, a considerable difference between the two marriage cases. This results from the fact that in each case a different set of choices is at issue. In the first marriage case, the choice of opting out of the game is available and the choice of choosing which move to make within the game, also in principle available, turns out to be constrained by other players' legitimate moves. In the second marriage case, by contrast, the first choice is not available. The choice of moves within the game is in principle available, whether or not it is then constrained by others' moves, as in the first case. And market exchanges between the worker and the owner of capital approximate to the second, rather than the first, of the two cases.

Hence, the analogy that Nozick offers between the marriage example and the worker's selling his labour to the owner of capital is misguided. In Nozick's marriage case, the choice that is restricted by other individuals' action is that of which partner to marry, against a background in which the choice to marry or not to marry is available. The worker faces a diametrically opposed situation: he may on many occasions choose which entrepreneur to sell his labour to, but within a framework of constraint. His 'wish' to sell his labour power is a preference resembling that of the future bridegroom who has not chosen to marry, but who is given a choice as to whom to marry. The limited choice he faces is not limited because he only has one entrepreneur who wants to employ him, against a background in which he can choose to abstain from selling his labour; it is limited because he can only sell his labour or starve.

Since, as we can now see, the two examples are relevantly disanalogous, Nozick cannot point to the conclusions reached in the marriage example and enjoin us to reach similar conclusions in the case of the worker deciding whether to sell his labour. In Nozick's marriage example, the fifty-two individuals involved all have an acceptable alternative to marrying any particular person; *ex hypothesi*, they have the option of remaining unmarried. In the light of this, the fact that Z and Z_I are, for each other, the least preferred partners, is irrelevant for ascertaining the voluntariness of Z's and Z_I's choice. Each could have chosen to remain unmarried, since remaining unmarried is, we assume, an acceptable option; their choice of marrying each other is, therefore, a voluntary one.[52]

[52] In a previous treatment of Nozick's rights definition of voluntariness and his marriage example, I suggested that Z and Z_I do not choose voluntarily to marry one another, because they are each other's least preferred partner. (S. Olsaretti, 'Freedom, Force and Choice: Against the Rights-Based Definition of Voluntariness', *Journal of Political Philosophy* 6 (1998), pp. 53–78.) This was because, in my treatment of the example, I followed Nozick's contention that a choice made among options which one does not like very much is non-voluntary. In fact, I do not endorse that contention, and

Consider, by contrast, the second marriage scenario I constructed a few moments ago, in which the option of remaining unmarried is an unacceptable one. In that scenario, Z's and Z_1's situation looks different, and we may well say, now, that they do not choose to marry each other voluntarily, if each marries the other only because the alternative – that of remaining unmarried – is unacceptable. In this case, the fact that others have acted within their rights in limiting Z's and Z_1's options of which partner to marry is irrelevant: what makes the choice a forced one is the fact that here, unlike in the first scenario, Z and Z_1 have no acceptable alternative to marrying each other. (Whether the absence of choice of partners is or is not an injustice is an entirely different matter, and indeed one that may make reference to whether others had the right to act as they did.[53] But such considerations do not tell us anything about whether Z and Z_1 may choose to remain single rather than marrying.)

The second version of the marriage example is what most limited choice market transactions look like. Individuals have no acceptable alternative to participating, but may voluntarily exercise their choice of whom to marry and whom to sell their labour power to, respectively. Does the worker voluntarily sell his labour power, then? Nozick, as could be expected, employs his rights-definition of voluntariness to answer this question:

'Z is faced with working or starving; the choices and actions of all other persons do not add up to providing Z with some other option. (He may have various options about what job to take.) Does Z choose to work voluntarily? . . . Z does choose voluntarily if the other individuals A through Y each acted voluntarily and within their rights.'[54]

Nozick's reply is riddled with the problems that the rights-definition of voluntariness incurs. Summarily, these are, first, that by making voluntariness a function of rights, Nozick introduces considerations of justice at too

accordingly, I now hold that, in the example as Nozick presents it, Z and Z_I do choose to marry each other voluntarily. This is because Z and Z_I, we are assuming, have the (acceptable) alternative of not marrying, and, presumably, the option of marrying each other is also acceptable (although less desirable than the option of marrying other people). Their choice, then, *is* voluntary. A choice is non-voluntary, I have suggested, if and only if it is made because there is no acceptable alternative to it. Note, however, that even if we accepted Nozick's definition of voluntariness, it would still be the case that the marriage example is relevantly different from the worker's example, since the former example *assumes* that the (acceptable) alternative to marrying one's least favoured partner is available (one could remain unmarried), whereas, in the latter, it is precisely lack of an acceptable alternative to selling one's labour that makes the worker's choice of whether or not to sell his labour a forced one.

[53] Notice that if Nozick *assumes* that the voluntariness of the choice of partners depends on whether others have the right to act as they do, then he may not ask whether it is an injustice, as this would make reference to those rights that Nozick has already built into his definition of voluntariness.

[54] *ASU*, p. 263.

early a stage in the argument, so as to make the voluntarism yardstick of justice in transfer circular and the notion of voluntariness redundant from a justificatory point of view. And second, the fact that others have acted within their rights does not support the conclusion that Z acts voluntarily. At most, as I have shown, it shows that Z is not rendered unfree on a rights-definition of freedom, but this does not justify deeming his action as voluntary. What we want to know about Z is not whether he is free to sell his labour power; we want to know whether he decides to sell it *freely* or voluntarily.

In the passage quoted above, the concern that underlies Nozick's adoption of the rights-definition of voluntariness is most evident. This is that *others have acted voluntarily*, and that therefore, disrupting their voluntary transactions would constitute an infringement of *their* freedom. But as I have said, this cannot justify the conclusion that Z the worker must have acted voluntarily.

Is taxation on a par with forced labour?

The use of a rights-definition of voluntariness is crucial in a second of Nozick's main claims, namely, his contention that taxation is on a par with forced labour. Non-consented-to taxation is a special case of interference, one which Nozick thinks amounts to a serious limitation of freedom and infringement of rights. This is because redistributive taxation contravenes rights of self-ownership by making some people aid others. Taxation also involves a special case of limited options, one which, Nozick maintains, renders the choice among them non-voluntary. It is particularly the latter aspect of the issue that I am concerned with here.

Nozick's well-known contention is as follows: 'Taxation of earnings from labor is on par with forced labor . . . taking the earnings of *n* hours of labour is like taking *n* hours from the person; it is like forcing the person to work *n* hours for another person'.[55] Notice that two different claims may be made about why taxation is illegitimate interference:

(1)   Taxation is non-consented-to interference. I pay taxes under threat of punishment in the form of fines or imprisonment for fiscal evasion. But, *ex hypothesi*, I have not consented to this obligation. My rights are therefore infringed and my freedom limited.

This, however, does not quite amount to saying that taxation is on a par with forced labour. (1) states that taxation is a sort of interference with people's lives that, being non-consented-to, limits their (rights-based) freedom. But

---

[55] *Ibid.*, p. 169.

Nozick also wants to say that people are made to work n extra hours, that is, they face no choice but to work n extra hours. He thus also needs to claim the following:

(2)   Taxation forces people to work extra hours for someone else's purpose. Admittedly, it may be said, people do have an alternative to paying taxes. They can avoid taxation altogether by working only so as to earn just enough for satisfying their basic needs.[56] This, however, is not an acceptable choice. It cannot be said that I choose to pay taxes because I choose to work more than just enough for earning mere subsistence (and not pay any taxes). The nature of this alleged choice is such that I cannot be said to voluntarily choose being taxed since I prefer being taxed over mere subsistence.

Note that (1) is a statement about interference with rights-based freedom; (2), however, is a claim about limited choice. Whilst (1) states that non-consented-to interference is freedom-curtailing, because rights-infringing, (2) states that what looks like the choice of being taxed cannot be considered as such.

We can endorse both claims as they stand. On a neutral definition of freedom, interference with someone constitutes a limitation of their liberty. We can also, on a non-rights-definition of voluntariness, endorse the claim that availability of the option of mere subsistence does not render the choice to work more hours and be taxed a voluntary one. Mere subsistence is a meagre option, and choosing it over taxed well-being does not seem a reasonable choice. This is why we agree that the person does not freely decide to work more and thereby earn enough to satisfy his preferences.

However convincing, this is not the sort of argument to which Nozick himself subscribes. He considers the view that underlies the suggestion that one cannot be said to choose to be taxed by choosing to earn more than a minimum for subsistence. This is the view according to which 'people are forced to do something *whenever* the alternatives they face are considerably worse'.[57] But Nozick dismisses it as incorrect. This is unsurprising, because, if he endorsed this view, he would also have to acknowledge that other instances of limited choice vitiate the voluntariness of decision. But Nozick would consider other cases of a structurally identical choice situation as perfectly legitimate.

Consider the case of an eccentric landowner, who agrees with a share-cropper that, if the latter only harvests just enough for subsistence, he will

---

[56] Notice that taxation normally begins *before* subsistence has been earned; Nozick himself, however, concentrates on the hypothesis of a tax on everything above the amount necessary for basic needs.

[57] *ASU*, p. 169. I take issue with this way of conceiving the issue of limited choice below in chapter 6, section 4.

not have to give any share of the crop to the landowner. If the sharecropper decides to harvest beyond that level, however, he will have to hand over a 50 per cent share of his crop to the landowner. In this case, just as with the taxation case, the farmer will, if he wants to earn more than just enough for basic subsistence, need to work twice as long; he will be forced to work *n* hours for another's purpose. But Nozick would deny that in this case the farmer has been *forced*: what makes the case of taxation a case of forced labour is neither the fact that it is non-consented-to, nor the fact that the alternative is considerably worse and no choice can be said to have been made. Rather,

> The fact that others intentionally intervene, in violation of a side constraint against aggression, to threaten force to limit the alternatives, in this case to paying taxes or (presumably the worse alternative) bare subsistence, makes the taxation system one of forced labor and distinguishes it from other cases of limited choices which are not forcings.[58]

Nozick's contention that taxation is forced labour, then, rests on the rights-definition of voluntariness.[59] It is not the nature of the choice itself, but rather the fact that those who limit the choice do not act within their rights, that makes it a case of forcing. On this account of why taxation is on a par with forced labour, Nozick's conviction that voluntariness is guaranteed by freedom, so that an infringement of (moralised) freedom results in the judgement that the voluntariness of the choice has been undermined, appears very clearly. The limited choice faced by the tax-payer vitiates voluntariness because taxation is a mechanism that curtails people's freedom.

Nozick's rights-based version of the contention that taxation is forced labour is riddled with the flaws that the rights-definition of voluntariness incurs. Why should the fact that others have acted outside their rights make the choice less voluntary than if others had limited the choice in a similar way, but by acting within their rights? Admittedly, Nozick thinks that others, on a rights-definition of freedom, make the taxed person unfree, because they do not have the right to 'fine' him. But as I have suggested,

---

[58] *ASU*, p. 169.

[59] It might be said that there is a relevant difference between the sharecropper and the tax-payer, since there are many landlords but only one tax collector. As a result, the sharecropper has the possibility of making various voluntary choices (concerning which landlord to work for), which the tax-payer lacks. Whilst this may be true, this difference does not justify treating the sharecropper's choice of whether or not to accept the work conditions offered by landowners as voluntary, and the tax-payer's choice of whether or not z to pay tax as non-voluntary, as I argued by reference to the marriage example.

the fact that someone is made unfree on a rights-definition of freedom has no bearing on the voluntariness of choice. Nozick's reasons for suggesting that the limited choice involved in taxation does not count as voluntary, resting on his rights-definition of voluntariness, are unpersuasive. He wants to assert that not every sort of non-consented-to interference and not every sort of under-rewarded labour is forced labour. His line of argument to make just this claim, however, is implausible. The claim that taxation is like forced labour, if it can be accepted, can be accepted as an instance of the claim of the choice-restricting nature of mechanisms that interfere with people's lives and that limit their choices between unreasonable alternatives. There is nothing special about taxation that uniquely makes *it* forced labour: rights-defined voluntariness cannot provide that special grounding.

We must conclude, then, that the libertarian claim that a free market society is one in which no freedom is curtailed and in which justice is realised because all (supposed) limitations of freedom derive from specific voluntary undertakings is multiply problematic. In particular, I have shown that, first, the scope of voluntariness is more restricted than may appear at first, in that the class of interference that must satisfy the voluntariness requirement is limited to interference that would infringe libertarian rights; other non-consented-to interference is not deemed as freedom-curtailing on the rights-definition of freedom. Second, the contention in question is only true on a flawed rights-definition of voluntariness, distinct from that of freedom, which sanctions as legitimate choices the voluntariness of which is, in fact, vitiated. And finally, the libertarian contention rests on an incorrect account of the relationship between freedom and voluntariness. It overlooks the fact that that freedom is curtailed by interference whether or not that interference is consented-to interference, and that rights-defined freedom does not guarantee voluntariness. The relation between freedom and voluntariness is a point that warrants further investigation, and to which I turn in the next chapter.

CHAPTER 6

The free market, force and choice: beyond libertarians and their critics

I. FREEDOM AND VOLUNTARINESS: A DISTINCTION

In the last chapter I argued that Nozick's defence of the free market rests on the use of implausible rights-based definitions of freedom and of voluntariness. In this chapter I develop further my critique of the libertarian argument by showing that, quite aside from the problems surrounding its defining of freedom and voluntariness through rights, that defence reflects an unsatisfactory understanding of the central notions it utilises, namely, those of voluntary choice, freedom and coercion. In particular, libertarians have, first, tended to resolve questions of voluntariness by appeal to questions of freedom, thereby ignoring that these two notions are distinct, and that freedom does not suffice for voluntariness. Second, they have singled out coercion as the only illegitimate form of interference, and have failed to appreciate that part of what makes coercion troubling is also found in other types of forcings.

Once these mistakes are revealed, the case for the free market is considerably weakened. Libertarians hold that freedom is sufficient for voluntariness – so that giving people options is enough to ensure that they choose voluntarily – and that the free market, hosting only mutually advantageous exchanges, rather than coercive transactions, is the realm of freedom. But these contentions cannot be defended. A satisfactory account of voluntary choice, I argue, reflects the fact that freedom does not suffice for voluntariness, and that there are non-voluntary choices other than coerced ones that warrant our concern. Insofar as libertarians take the voluntariness of choice to be a necessary condition for the legitimacy of interference with individuals, so that only voluntary choices are justice-preserving and responsibility-grounding, they then have reason to support not the free market, in which the voluntariness of many choices is vitiated, but rather those circumstances in which every one is provided with a range of acceptable options and is thereby enabled to make voluntary choices.

I proceed as follows. In the remainder of this section I argue that we should draw a distinction between freedom and voluntariness, and in the next, that this distinction helps us to understand the notion of coercion and its relevance. I then turn, in the third section, to show that critics of libertarianism, as much as libertarians themselves, have not taken note of the distinct role played by voluntary choice, and of the extent to which coercion is only one among other relevant types of forcings. Finally, in section 4 I tease out the implications of the account of voluntary choice I think is defensible and which underlies my critique of libertarianism, so as to defend it against some possible objections libertarians may raise, and in favour of reverting to their narrower focus on coercion and on the claim that freedom suffices for voluntariness.

Let me start first of all, then, by noting the distinction between freedom and voluntariness. In the previous chapter I have shown that morally defined freedom cannot guarantee voluntariness. I now want to put forward a broader claim to the effect that the reason why morally defined freedom cannot guarantee voluntariness is because freedom understood as 'being free to do something', of which the moralised definition is a version, does not guarantee voluntariness. The mistake at the basis of the moralised definition of voluntariness is twofold: voluntariness is defined through rights; *and* questions of voluntariness are conflated with questions of freedom. The first mistake is a consequence of the second: insofar as one holds that freedom guarantees voluntariness,[1] and that rights define the domain of each person's freedom, then the rights-definition of voluntariness follows naturally. I would now like to focus on the second mistake, namely, the conflation between freedom and voluntariness.

That a satisfactory account of choice needs to make a sharp distinction between freedom and voluntariness is shown by the following two examples, which depict situations where judgements of freedom and voluntariness pull in different directions.

> *The Desert City.* Daisy is the inhabitant of a city, located in the middle of a desert, which she is free to leave. However Daisy, who would wish to leave, knows with absolute certainty that if she leaves the city, she will not be able to survive the hardship of the desert and she will die. Her choice to remain in the city is not a voluntary one.

> *The Wired City.* Wendy is the inhabitant of a city fenced with electrifying wire, which she is unfree to leave. However, her city has all that anyone could ever ask for, and Wendy, who is perfectly happy with her life there, has no wish of leaving it. She voluntarily remains in her city.

[1] By this, of course, I have in mind the conviction that, if an agent has the relevant freedom(s), *and she acts*, then she has acted voluntarily or freely.

In the first example, freedom does not suffice for voluntariness; in the second, unfreedom (that is, lack of the freedom to not perform the action one does perform) does not undermine voluntariness.

A satisfactory account of voluntary choice, I suggest, has to steer away from two opposed but similarly misguided tendencies. The first is to conflate questions of voluntariness with questions of freedom, to suppose that, *given* that the agent whose voluntary choice is under discussion is free to act as he does, and does what he does, it follows that he acts voluntarily. The second mistake that is sometimes made consists in (rightly) separating questions of freedom and questions of voluntariness, and in then (wrongly) suggesting that there are no structural features of an individual's 'choice conditions' which are of moral interest.[2] I suggest, by contrast, that considerations about the choice conditions an individual faces are germane to the voluntariness of her choice, and, for that reason, do have moral significance. An account of voluntariness that can deal with cases of limited choice needs to specify precisely under what conditions an individual's choice counts as voluntary: given that the individual has made a choice or given his consent, there is a genuine issue as to whether the conditions under which this choice was carried out vitiate its voluntariness.

When, then, is a choice voluntary? As I anticipated in the last chapter, I suggest that a choice is voluntary if and only if it is not made *because* there is no acceptable alternative to it. Conversely, a claim that a person was forced to do x (she did x non-voluntarily) means that she did x because she had no acceptable alternative to it.[3] Claims of force, in my view, are claims of vitiated voluntariness, not of curtailed freedom. Notice that when we refer to someone acting voluntarily (or freely), we refer both to voluntary *choice* and to voluntary *doings*. Both the case in which an individual voluntarily chooses the option he chooses among a pool of them, and the case in

---

[2] See, for example, A. Wertheimer, *Coercion* (Princeton University Press, 1987), p. 201.
[3] My definitions could be restated as follows. A person is forced to do x if and only if (i) there is no acceptable alternative to doing x; *and* (ii) the fact that there is no acceptable alternative to doing x motivates that person. A person chooses to do x voluntarily if and only if (i) there is an acceptable alternative to doing x, and she knows this when she does x; *or* (ii) x is an option which she finds very attractive or choiceworthy, and which she is motivated to choose by the fact that she finds it very attractive or choiceworthy. Note that if a person chooses a course of action out of mixed motives when faced with one or more unacceptable options, then, in order to ascertain whether she has chosen voluntarily, we would ask whether she would have made that choice even if she had had an acceptable alternative. So, for example, suppose that Burt faces the choice of whether to become a teacher on the one hand and suffer hardship on the other, and chooses the former both because he likes the prospect of being a teacher and because the alternative is unacceptable. Is Burt's choice forced? The answer is affirmative only if, had Burt an acceptable alternative to becoming a teacher, he would choose that over becoming a teacher.

which, although no choice among several options is involved, an individual nonetheless does the thing he does voluntarily, are cases in which the individual acts voluntarily, that is, he does not act as he does because no acceptable alternative is available. As I suggested before, the standard of acceptability by which options are assessed is an objective one that views basic needs satisfactions as central, so that choices made so as to avoid having one's basic needs go unmet are non-voluntary ones.[4]

This definition of voluntariness needs further specification, and I will develop it somewhat more fully at the end of this chapter. For the moment, however, this definition will do. What I want to emphasise here is the distinction between claims of freedom, which are claims about the options an individual faces, and claims of voluntariness, which are claims about how the nature of those options affect an individual's will. In other words, freedom is about the options we face, whereas voluntariness is about the choices we make.[5] Judgements of freedom identify the circumstances in which an individual is situated; judgements of voluntariness and of force, by contrast, are primarily claims about why an agent acts as she does.

Freedom and voluntariness, then, are distinct. Freedom does not guarantee voluntariness; and unfreedom does not undermine it. *Some* freedom, however, is necessary for *some* voluntariness. In order for P to do *x* voluntarily, it must be the case that P is free to do *x*. This, it must be noted, is not a claim about the relationship between freedom and voluntariness, but about freedom and action. For P to do *x* at all, whether voluntarily or non-voluntarily, it must be the case that P is free to do *x*. Once we recognise this, we are able to make sense of G. A. Cohen's claim that when someone is forced to do something, she is free to do it.[6] The truth of that claim hinges, quite simply, on this: if someone is forced to do something, then she does that thing. And if she does that thing, she was free to do that thing. We cannot do what we are not free to do. Insofar as voluntariness is a quality of our *actions*, and insofar as, in order to act, we must be free to act, then the freedom to do *x* is required for someone to do *x* voluntarily. But, as I suggested above, it is not always necessary that someone be free to do anything else, including not-*x*, in order to choose to do *x* voluntarily.

---

[4] When talking about actions, choices or consent, I use 'non-voluntary' and 'forced' interchangeably.

[5] The term 'choice' is ambiguously used to refer both to an option and to the choosing of an option. In order to avoid this ambiguity, throughout I use 'choice' to refer to 'the choosing of an option'.

[6] G. A. Cohen, "Are Disadvantaged Workers who take Hazardous Jobs Forced to take Hazardous Jobs?", in *History, Labour and Freedom* (Oxford: Clarendon Press, 1988), pp. 239–54; G. A. Cohen, 'Capitalism, Freedom, and the Proletariat', in D. Miller (ed.), *Liberty* (Oxford University Press, 1991), pp. 163–82. Section 3 below analyses this claim in more detail.

Hence my emphasis on the fact that *some* freedom is necessary for some voluntariness.

Further, it is the case that even this limited freedom is not always necessary for voluntariness. Since voluntariness can be a quality of our choices as well as our actions, and since choices do not necessarily result in action, it is possible for someone to *choose to do* something voluntarily, even if she does not, after all, do that thing, and she is not free to do it. Hence my emphasis on the fact that some freedom is necessary for *some* voluntariness. Since in what follows I am going to be concerned with the voluntariness of actions that people in fact do perform, the freedom to perform those actions is a necessary condition for those actions to have been carried out voluntarily.

But the distinction between freedom and voluntariness remains crucial. First, 'being free to do *x*' is a necessary condition for 'doing *x* voluntarily, or freely' only because 'being free to do *x*' is a necessary condition for 'doing *x*' at all. The required freedom is not required for voluntariness as such, but for action generally. Second, no other freedom than the freedom to do *x* is necessary.[7] And finally and most interestingly, even if the freedom to do *x* is a necessary condition for someone to do *x* voluntarily, it is not a sufficient one. Freedom does not guarantee voluntariness.

2. COERCION AND VOLUNTARY CHOICE

The distinction between freedom and voluntariness, so I believe, helps us to better understand the concept of coercion, by which I refer to the deliberate interference of one person with another, typically through the use of threat of force.[8] Coercion, as I have mentioned, is often taken by libertarians to be the paradigmatic form of illegitimate, justice-disrupting interference. As one libertarian states, 'the essential ingredient in all this [in the libertarian idea] is freedom from coercion by others. This is one's basic and inalienable right'.[9] Libertarians also claim that coercion involves

---

[7] This, of course, will depend on the individual's preferences. See section 4 below.

[8] 'Coercion' is sometimes used more loosely, so as to refer to the deliberate interference of one person with another, without necessarily involving the use of threat. Even when they use the notion of coercion so defined, libertarians subscribe to the view that choices made in response to offers and choices made in limited choice circumstances not deliberately created by other agents do not count as coercive. These two claims are the ones I focus on in what follows, when contesting libertarians' emphasis on coercion as the only type of forcing. The fact that I take 'coercion' to refer to interference that typically involves the use of threat, therefore, does not matter for my argument below.

[9] J. Hospers, 'What Libertarianism Is', in T. R. Machan and D. B. Rasmussen (eds.), *Liberty for the 21st Century. Contemporary Libertarian Thought* (Maryland: Rowman & Littlefield, 1995), pp. 5–17, at p. 8.

a loss of negative freedom, and imply that, in the absence of coercion, all transactions are voluntary. They then conclude that, since the free market hosts only mutually advantageous and therefore non-coercive transactions, it is a realm in which freedom and voluntariness alike are respected.[10]

However, just how coercion affects freedom, voluntariness or both are questions that merit more careful examination than libertarians have given them. To see this, consider the following example. Burt's coercive threat to Audrey to do y if Audrey does x leads Audrey to abstain from doing x, since she wants to avoid y. However, unbeknown to Audrey, Burt is bluffing and would be unable to carry through his threat. In this case, Audrey has been coerced not to do x, although it is also true that she was not rendered unfree by Burt.[11] Unlike freedom, voluntariness is always undermined by coercion, *independently* of whether the agent who is coerced not to do x has been rendered unfree to do anything. In the example above, Audrey has acted non-voluntarily. Does it mean, then, that coercion is characterised by undermined voluntariness rather than unfreedom? Does a commitment to protecting people against coercion therefore require something altogether different from giving them freedom? And if coercion does undermine voluntariness and the latter is what makes coercion illegitimate, should we not also ask whether it is sufficient, to ensure that people make voluntary choices, that they not be coerced?

In what follows I claim that, standardly, where threats are not bluffings, coercion does involve a loss of freedom. Nonetheless, I suggest that when we talk about an individual being coerced, we are primarily making claims of vitiated voluntariness, so that coercion is really a type of forcing. This has the following implications for the libertarian defence of the free market: since coercion is primarily a type of forcing, and since the concern behind condemning coercion lies (at least in part) in the fact that the coerced agent has not chosen voluntarily, then that concern also seems to justify taking seriously cases of vitiated voluntariness where coercion is not present. Libertarians overlook this important fact and wrongly conclude, from the fact that coercion is not present on the free market, that all free market transactions are voluntary and justice-preserving. In fact, libertarians' own anti-coercion stance justifies a concern with reducing the

[10] John Hospers, for example, holds that the right to liberty is 'the right to live one's life in accordance with one's voluntary choices', and thinks that this will be guaranteed when there is no coercion; see Hospers, 'What Libertarianism Is', p. 8. In a similar vein, the classical liberal Milton Friedman says that the free market achieves co-operation without coercion and through voluntary interaction. M. Friedman, *Capitalism and Freedom* (University of Chicago Press, 1962, 1982), pp. 12–14.

[11] The example draws on Robert Nozick's. See R. Nozick, 'Coercion', in P. Laslett and W. Runciman (eds.), *Philosophy, Politics, and Society*, 4th series (Oxford: Blackwell, 1967), pp. 101–35.

forced transactions individuals enter in a free market society as much as it minimises the coercive interference by the more-than-minimal state.

Consider, first of all, in what sense a coercive situation is, standardly, one in which freedom is curtailed, even where freedom is negative freedom.[12] When Audrey is threatened, and the threat is not a bluffing, she loses the freedom to carry out a complex action, namely, the freedom not to comply with the threat *and* not be penalised. The complex freedom of keeping her money and walking away unharmed is removed from her.[13] That coercion involves the loss of some freedom, then, seems undeniable. This suggestion has been contested by Hillel Steiner. According to Steiner, it is not the threat, but its execution, that removes the mentioned complex freedom.[14] But this does not square with a negative definition of when someone is unfree to do an action, which Steiner himself defends and which, we are assuming, most libertarians endorse. A person is describable as unfree to do an action, Steiner claims, if and only if his doing an action is rendered impossible by the action of another person. And, he goes on to add, an action is rendered impossible by another action 'if the latter either (i) does occur, or (ii) would occur if the former were attempted, and the latter's occurrence implies the impossibility of the former's occurrence'.[15]

On this account of when a person is unfree to do an action, Audrey is unfree to do the complex action of keeping her money and walking away unharmed if this action is rendered impossible by Burt's action. And Audrey's complex action is indeed rendered impossible by Burt if (i) Burt executes the threat; (ii) Burt would execute the threat if Audrey attempted to carry through her complex action. Now, since (ii) obtains in our situation, in which Audrey is threatened by Burt *and* Burt would, *ex hypothesi* – remember that in this case Burt is *not* bluffing[16] – execute his threat if Audrey failed to comply with it, it is true that she loses the freedom to do the relevant complex action.[17] She is less free than she was before the threat. Coercive interference, that is, the issuing of threats, reduces freedom in this

---

[12] As I have said before, I make this assumption so as to proceed within a shared framework, and libertarians often claim that they favour a negative conception of freedom.

[13] See J. P. Day, 'Threats, Offers, Law, Opinion and Liberty', *American Philosophical Quarterly* 14 (1977), pp. 257–72, to which Hillel Steiner replies with the contention I criticise shortly.

[14] H. Steiner, *An Essay on Rights* (Oxford: Blackwell, 1994), p. 29.   [15] *Ibid.*, p. 8.

[16] And, of course, other things being equal. I assume throughout that other factors that may come in the way of Burt's removing Audrey's complex freedom (such as Burt dying before he can execute the threat) are not at issue.

[17] Strictly speaking, it is true that the execution of the threat is what makes Audrey's action impossible. But it remains true that, when Burt decides to threaten Audrey (and Burt is not bluffing), Audrey is unfree to do the relevant complex action.

sense: it changes the options an individual faces by removing the freedom to perform some complex action.[18]

So, I suggest, a coercive situation is one in which the threatened individual does lose some freedom, namely, the complex freedom not to comply with the threat and to remain unharmed. But notice now that this sense in which coercive interference reduces freedom is the sense in which, as a result of that interference, individuals are placed in limited choice situations, in which the eligibility of the options that are available to them motivates them to comply, if the threat is coercive. Whilst, in these limited choice situations, individuals are free to do what they are coerced into doing, as well as free to do what they are threatened they should not do, they are forced to act in a particular way.

In this sense, claims of coercion are primarily claims of vitiated voluntariness. Consider, once again, the example of Audrey, who is threatened by Burt with being killed if she fails to hand over her money to him. Audrey is no longer free not to hand over her money and to leave unharmed, but she is still free both to hand over her money and not to hand it over. Since being killed is not an acceptable option, she complies. She chooses to hand over his money because the alternative is not acceptable: she is coerced into handing over her money. Neither of the two above-mentioned freedoms is lost when Audrey is threatened, as shown by the fact that it would be possible for her to choose either one. But of the freedoms she still has, one is unacceptable, and Audrey does not voluntarily, or freely, choose to hand over her money. Coercion, then, is a type of forcing, namely, one that involves the use of threats. Whilst coercion always involves the use of threats, not all threats are coercive, because not all threats constitute forcings. Not all threats, in other words, are effective, that is, they may not succeed in motivating the victim as they are meant to. It follows that while coercion necessarily undermines voluntariness, not all threats do.[19]

---

[18] There is, I believe, one further reason to resist Steiner's suggestion that the execution of threats, rather than the issuing of them, is what removes Audrey's complex freedom, and that is as follows: Steiner's thesis that the execution of threats is freedom-removing results in the counterintuitive suggestion that a person is only rendered unfree by threats when she has not been coerced. This is because the execution of the threat (and hence, on Steiner's view, the removal of Audrey's freedom to do the complex action) would only be carried out if Audrey had failed to comply with the threat, that is, the threat had failed to be coercive, and Audrey would not have been *coerced* by Burt, though she would, now, be rendered unfree by Burt to carry out the complex action. For another account of why threats reduce freedom, also developed in reply to Steiner, see I. Carter, *A Measure of Freedom* (Oxford University Press, 1999), pp. 224–32.

[19] It might be suggested that threats can be coercive even when they fail to motivate the victim, in that they may nonetheless influence her. I would want to say that these threats do constrain and burden a person's choices, so as to make these choices less free than they would be in the absence of these constraints. I thank Peter Vallentyne for bringing this point to my attention.

The fact that coercion is primarily a type of forcing is, in my view, compatible with our tendency to say that coercion makes individuals less free than they otherwise would be, insofar as in so doing we appeal to the idea that, when we are coerced, our *freedom of choice* is curtailed. This is a different way of saying that, when we are coerced, we are forced to choose what we choose. Freedom of choice is a quality of our choices, and it is nothing other than the notion of voluntariness I have been referring to. To say of a choice that it was a free choice is to suggest that the individual in question chose what he chose freely or voluntarily. In the sense of freedom of choice as a quality of our choices, Audrey's choice of handing over the money is not going to be a free one, insofar as she was coerced into giving her money. We would say that she did not make a free choice, and thereby reassert that coercion is a type of forcing.[20]

The fact that coercion is one type of forcing, however, should not make us overlook the fact that it is only one type of forcing, which is what libertarians seem to do when they single out coercive exchanges as justice-disrupting exchanges, while deeming forced exchanges that do not involve coercion to be justice-preserving. Voluntariness is undermined by things other than coercion. In support of this claim, let me now consider some possible reasons for deeming coercion to be relevantly different from other types of forcings. Libertarians could adduce these as reasons for the emphasis they have placed on coercion, as distinct from other types of forcings, but, as I argue, their case would be a weak one. There are two main respects in which, libertarians could argue, coercion is a special type of forcing.

First, coercion, where the latter refers to force that involves threats, is always characterised by the fact that there is *someone doing the coercing*. This is not necessarily the case with all force, which, as I said, is a matter of constrained choices. So, for instance, I may be forced to accept an offer but (i) the offer does not force me; (ii) the person who makes the offer is not forcing me to accept it. Hence, the spectrum of cases of force is wider than the subset of coercion. With coercion, there is always someone who is intentionally altering my options (through the use of threats) so as to get me to do something I do not want to do. This, one may argue, makes

---

[20] 'Freedom of choice' may also be taken to refer to freedom as 'being free to do something', so as to identify the conjunction of two freedoms of that type. Since 'freedom of choice' is regularly used both to refer to a conjunction of freedoms and to refer to the quality of our choices, I am not suggesting that one usage should be preferred over the other as the correct one. All I am emphasising here is that, in the sense of freedom of choice as a quality of the choices we make, coercion may be said to make us less free, in that, when we are forced to choose something because we are threatened with an unacceptable alternative, our choice is not a free one.

coercion especially bad, since it involves the subordination of one's will to that of another person.[21]

This feature of coercion, however, does not justify treating it as the only kind of justice-disrupting interference with a person. We may grant that the subordination of one's will to that of another person, which coercion always involves, makes the latter bad, but it is not true that *only* coercion involves such subordination. Some cases of forced acceptance of offers, too, are cases in which one's purposes and will are subordinated to those of another person. Insofar as the nature of the offer someone makes to someone in limited choice circumstances is informed by awareness that the recipient of the offer cannot but accept it, the recipient's will is indeed subordinated to the offer-maker's. Furthermore, even in those cases of forcings where no one is intentionally forcing anyone, or directly or deliberately benefiting from the forced person's being in the position in which she is forced to make the choices she makes, this should not make it any less true that, in a relevant sense, the agent in question is forced to act as she does. Insofar as the voluntariness of choice is a necessary condition for justifiable interference with individuals – and this is what libertarians suggest is the case – cases of forced offers are as problematic as cases of coercion. We may overlook this point and proceed, in these matters, with a bias in favour of linking questions of force with questions of deliberate interference, because this is how we proceed in defining freedom. We expect that with cases of acting voluntarily, too, we should look for the deliberate imposition of constraints by human agents in order to identify instances of failures to act voluntarily. Hence the bias towards the idea that coercion is the only type of forcing.

The second line of argument for treating only coercion as voluntariness-undermining is as follows. It might be said that coercion is distinctive in that, insofar as it involves the use of threats, it is characterised by the fact that non-compliance with threats standardly leaves one worse off than one was or would have been in the pre-proposal (pre-threat) situation. Threats are fundamentally different from offers, the acceptance of which makes agents better off than they would have been in the absence of the offer. This difference between threats and offers accounts, one might say, for the fact that coercion and forcings in response to offers differ insofar as agents *standardly* regret receiving threats, but they do not *standardly* regret

---

[21] For an account of this aspect of coercion, see, for example, F. A. Hayek, *The Constitution of Liberty* (London: Routledge & Kegan Paul, 1960). Here Hayek states: 'Coercion is evil precisely because it . . . eliminates an individual as a thinking and valuing person and makes him a bare tool in the achievement of the ends of another' (p. 21).

receiving offers. Indeed, the presumed regret accompanying the receipt of threats, and not, in the standard case, the receipt of offers, is often pointed to when characterising coercion. It is further suggested that this feature is what supports the claim that, when coerced, an individual does not act voluntarily, whereas, at least in the standard case, an individual who responds to an offer does act voluntarily insofar as he does not regret receiving it.[22]

Whilst I agree that a feeling of regret may *in most cases* distinguish the receipt of threats from the receipt of offers, I do not think that this supports singling out coercion as the only type of justice-disrupting force, for the following three reasons. First, insofar as we are concerned with whether someone chooses voluntarily, and with how an agent's deliberations are affected, the fact that an agent regrets receiving a threat but not receiving an offer is irrelevant. Even though Audrey may not regret receiving an offer, she may nonetheless regret having to act in the constrained conditions in which she finds herself. In other words, Audrey may regret *having to accept* the offer just as much as she would regret having to comply with a threat. And that seems to be more relevant, in characterising the voluntariness of the individual's choice, than the presumed regret accompanying the *receipt* of offers and threats. At best, if we are concerned with regret in this context, we are concerned with *regretting the reasons for one's action*, and that may be present with all types of forcings, in response to offers as much as in response to threats.

The second reason why appealing to the regret that supposedly accompanies the receipt of threats but not offers does not justify libertarians' exclusive focus on coercion is as follows. Regretting the reasons for one's actions is relevant not for the voluntariness of choice but for autonomy, where the latter is defined as a second-order capacity to act in accordance with one's first-order preferences. Being in a limited-choice situation, and hence, having to act on first-order preferences that one may regret acting upon, may be disruptive of a person's autonomy. But whether one does or does not regret acting upon certain reasons does not determine whether that action is voluntary. For example, I may be forced to give up smoking because of a prohibitive tax on tobacco, but nonetheless not regret that, insofar as I have a second-order preference to give up smoking. My choice to give up smoking, we may say, was forced, but that may nonetheless not

---

[22] See, for example, G. Dworkin, 'Acting Freely', *Noûs* 4 (1970), pp. 367–83. Gerald Dworkin talks of 'acting freely' in a different sense from the one I have been referring to. He claims: 'A does X freely if A does X for reasons which he doesn't mind acting from' (p. 381). Cohen also adopts this view in 'Are Disadvantaged Workers?', p. 243. See the next section below for a discussion of Cohen's view.

prove a reason for regret, and, as a result, my ability to act autonomously may not be threatened. Where regret is indeed present, and where one regrets the reasons for one's own actions, what is at stake is the autonomy of an individual, not the voluntariness of her choices.[23]

This last remark points to a third reason why the appeal to regret does not successfully justify viewing the acceptance of threats but not of offers as cases of force: it is not always true that we regret receiving threats but not offers. I may well regret receiving offers and not regret receiving threats, depending on how the receipt of either affects my other plans and desires. I may regret receiving an offer that I decide, on reflection, not to accept, but in the light of which my current situation no longer looks as desirable as it did before the offer was made to me. And I may not regret receiving a threat that allows me to act in a way which I endorse, but which others would deem unacceptable.[24] The proposed basis for distinguishing threats from offers, then, does not have general applicability.

Neither the fact that, when individuals are coerced, they are coerced by *someone*, nor the fact that compliance with threats typically makes individuals worse off than they were in the pre-threat situation, justify singling out coercion as the only type of justice-disrupting interference with persons. Insofar as we are concerned with the voluntariness of people's choices, there are no grounds for treating coercion as if it were the only type of forcing.

3. FREEDOM, COERCION AND VOLUNTARINESS IN TWO CRITIQUES OF LIBERTARIANISM

So far I have claimed that a satisfactory account of voluntariness must reflect the fact that claims of voluntariness and of force on the one hand, and claims of freedom and unfreedom on the other, are distinct. But, as I have said, this distinction has been overlooked by critics of libertarianism as much as by libertarians themselves. Critics of Nozick's moralised definition of freedom have failed to identify the moralised definition of

---

[23] Some of the ambiguity in this area may be the result of the fact that the notion of 'acting voluntarily' or 'acting freely' are applied to refer to both first- and second-order preferences, or preferences about preferences.

[24] I am grateful to Raymond Geuss for bringing this point to my attention. Note that the cases at issue are not cases where the threat fails to be coercive, in the sense that it is not what motivates me: rather, the threat is coercive, in the sense that, in its absence, I would have acted differently, but it is still true that I welcome the threat.

voluntariness, and, in fact, have referred to the passage in which Nozick appeals most clearly to rights-defined voluntariness as an illustration of his use of rights-defined freedom.[25] This is because, like Nozick, they have failed to distinguish between freedom and voluntariness. Further, they have contributed to clouding the distinction between freedom and voluntariness by presenting their discussion of Nozick's account as one of 'the moralised theory of coercion'.[26] Since coercion is thought to undermine both freedom and voluntariness, the issue of the conditions for voluntary choice has been presented as being primarily an issue about coercion, thus resulting in – or at least reinforcing – the contention that coercion exhausts non-voluntariness. The debate is further muddled due to the ambiguous use of the idea of 'being forced', which is sometimes equated with that of 'being coerced', sometimes broadly opposed to the idea of 'being free' and yet at other times opposed to the idea of 'acting voluntarily'. In this section I would like to bring what I have said about freedom, voluntariness and coercion to bear on the assessment of some existing critiques of libertarianism.

Consider, first, G. A. Cohen's discussion of libertarianism. It is indicative of the confusion between freedom and voluntariness that Cohen, who has been a main critic of the libertarian use of the moralised definition of freedom, has failed to notice the extent to which his critique of Nozick, and his own thesis about freedom, actually rests on notions of voluntariness rather than freedom.[27] This is very apparent in one of Cohen's central claims, namely, his interpretation of what 'being forced' means, and in his claim, which I have already mentioned, that when one is forced to do something, one is free to do that thing. According to Cohen, someone is forced to do something if she has no reasonable or acceptable alternative to doing something, which is compatible with saying that she is free to do that thing. As Cohen points out, the dispute between the Left and Right

---

[25] Hence, as I said earlier, when arguing that Nozick adopts the rights-definition of freedom in the previous chapter, Cohen quotes as evidence the passage from Nozick (*Anarchy, State, and Utopia* (Oxford: Blackwell, 1974), p. 262) where the latter offers a rights-definition of voluntariness. Steiner makes the same mistake. See Steiner, *Essay on Rights*, p. 12. Notice that, in an earlier piece, Steiner does object to Nozick's moralised definition of voluntariness (Cf. H. Steiner, 'Capitalism, Justice and Equal Starts', *Social Philosophy and Policy* 5 (1987), pp. 49–71, at p. 55, note 8), but there he does not address the question of the relationship between freedom and voluntariness. Although I have not defended here the adoption of a negative conception of freedom, I believe that one reason for adopting such a conception lies in the fact that, by so doing, we can draw a clear distinction between freedom and voluntariness and thereby achieve greater clarity about many otherwise ambiguous claims about freedom.

[26] See Wertheimer, *Coercion*; D. Zimmerman, 'Coercive Wage Offers', *Philosophy and Public Affairs* 10 (1981), pp. 121–45.

[27] In what follows I focus on Cohen's remarks in 'Are Disadvantaged Workers?'.

about whether workers are forced to take hazardous jobs is the result of a failure to see that *both* Left and Right are right, insofar as workers are free, as well as forced, to take hazardous jobs.[28]

I too would endorse that claim. Unlike Cohen, however, I believe that its truth is nothing but an illustration of the distinction between being free to do something and doing something voluntarily. Workers are free to take hazardous jobs – they are not prevented from taking those jobs – and yet, because, *ex hypothesi*, they take them *because* they have no acceptable alternative, they are also forced to take them, that is, their choice to take those jobs is not a voluntary one. Cohen identifies an important point, but the way he makes sense of it is misguided.[29] He implies that 'being forced to do something' makes one unfree on the first sense of freedom, rather than it being an explanatory claim, one about the vitiated voluntariness of people's choices.

The claim that workers are both free and forced to sell their labour may well show, as Cohen says, that both the Left and the Right are right, insofar as each can uphold the claim that is dear to them. But the reason why they can each uphold their favoured claim lies in nothing other than the distinction between freedom and voluntariness, so the fact that workers are free to sell their labour does not imply that, when they sell their labour, they sell it voluntarily. When the Right and the Left each insist on claiming that establishing that workers are free to sell their labour could either support or refute the claim that workers are forced to sell their labour, they are both mistaken, insofar as they both imply that judgements of freedom suffice to settle judgements about voluntariness and force.[30]

---

[28] Some contributions in labour history commit a mistake along these lines, by focusing on labour as 'free' as opposed to 'coerced'. Further, since what they actually focus on are issues of *legal* freedoms, they overlook how labour that is free in this sense may nonetheless be forced labour. And, by opposing free labour with coerced labour, they also suggest that coercion is the only form of unfreedom and the only type of forcing. See: R. J. Steinfeld and S. L. Engerman, 'Labor – Free or Coerced? A Historical Reassessment of Differences and Similarities', in T. Brass and M. van der Linden (eds.), *Free and Unfree Labour. The Debate Continues* (Bern: Peter Lang, 1997), pp. 11–42; R. J. Steinfeld, *The Invention of Free Labor* (Chapel Hill: University of North Carolina Press, 1991).

[29] Cohen himself does draw a distinction between 'being free to do something' and 'doing something freely', but this is a different distinction from the one I have referred to. Cohen has in mind the distinction drawn by Dworkin which I mentioned earlier. By 'acting freely', Dworkin, and Cohen, refer to acting on desires with which the agent identifies. See Cohen, 'Are Disadvantaged Workers?', p. 243; Dworkin, 'Acting Freely', p. 381. 'Acting freely' so understood is not the opposite of 'being forced' (although, Cohen says, *often* people act unfreely when they are forced).

[30] Cohen has come to embrace the explanatory account of forcings I defend. See G. A. Cohen, 'Once More into the Breach of Self-Ownership: Reply to Narveson and Brenkert', *Journal of Ethics* 2 (1998), pp. 57–96. In this article Cohen says that he has come to endorse the explanatory account of what 'being forced' means: 'one is forced to do something if and only if one does it *because* one is forced to do it' (p. 82). I think that Cohen's definition of force remains problematic. Let us refer to this claim

The attempt to criticise the libertarian thesis by arguing that capitalist wage offers are coercive is also problematic in a similar way, that is, insofar as it carries forward, rather than overcomes, some of the problems with the libertarian thesis. Reconsider the first of the two examples I mentioned at the beginning of this chapter, in which Daisy is the inhabitant of a city, located in the middle of a desert, which she is free to leave. Daisy, who would wish to leave, knows with absolute certainty that, if she leaves the city, she will not be able to survive the hardship of the desert and she will die. Her choice to remain in the city is not a voluntary one. No coercion is involved, that is, no forcing by means of threats is at stake. Daisy is not coerced, but she is nonetheless forced to remain in her city.

The point I would like to emphasise here is a point I made in the previous section, namely, that we can flesh out the conditions for voluntary choice along exactly the same lines as the conditions for non-coerced, voluntary choice are usually understood. What makes choices carried out under coercion non-voluntary is exactly what also makes other types of limited choices non-voluntary. The alternative faced by the man who hands over the money when threatened with a gun is to be killed; the alternative of a worker who sells his labour power for whatever price is to remain unemployed and suffer severe hardship. The relevant condition which undermines voluntariness in the first case is also present in the second, namely, the absence of an acceptable alternative. The options of handing over the money or of accepting a hazardous job are chosen because the alternatives – to risk being shot or to suffer severe hardship – are unacceptable. This consideration, and *not* the consideration of whether the gunman and the employer act within their rights (unlike what Robert Nozick suggests), or of how and by whom the alternative option was brought about, is what is relevant for assessing the voluntariness of the choice at issue.

---

as (EF), for 'the explanatory account of forcings'. Cohen here formulates the explanatory account by retaining his original use of 'forced', according to which to say that someone is forced to do A means 'doing A *when* one has no acceptable alternative to A' (p. 82, emphasis mine). Let us refer to this claim as (DF), for 'the descriptive account of forcings'. Strictly speaking, this formulation of the explanatory account is misleading, since, by unfolding DF as part of EF, we get the contention that 'one is forced to do something only if one does it *because* one does it when one has no acceptable alternative to it'. But this cannot be right. So, the correct version of EF is that 'one is forced to do something only if one does it *because* one has no acceptable alternative to it', where the original, non-explanatory sense of 'being forced' would then only indicate that 'one has no acceptable alternative to what one chooses'. This, however, is implausible, since claims about an agent being forced, whether of the non-explanatory or of the explanatory sort, must make reference to the agent's *acting*. The preferable formulation of the explanatory account, then, is the one that does without the descriptive notion of 'force' altogether, simply stating that a person is forced to do A if and only if she does A because she has no acceptable alternative to it.

If what I have said so far is true, then it becomes clear why the attempt to show that capitalist wage offers are coercive is unsatisfactory. In particular, it encounters two main problems. Firstly, it stretches needlessly the notion of coercion, it contributes to obscuring the distinction between coercion and other types of forcings, while at the same time it lends credibility to the (mistaken) libertarian thesis that only coercion undermines voluntariness. Secondly, this type of claim focuses on the wrong side of the coin, so to speak. Since the underlying concern is with the cogency of the libertarian thesis about the justice of capitalist wage offers, and since that thesis hinges on the claim that no one's freedom of choice, not even the worker's, is reduced, insofar as each voluntarily chooses to sell his or her labour, then it is on the voluntariness of the worker's choice that we should focus. When we ask whether capitalist wage offers can be coercive, the concern is with whether the person who is thus constrained acts voluntarily or, by contrast, is forced to act as she does. But if this is what the question asks, then it is more appropriate to pose the question in just this way, rather than to talk about coercive offers. Once again: since coercion is only one type of forcing – one which utilises threats – it is misleading to treat it as the only type of forcing.

4. VOLUNTARY CHOICE AND TWO SENSES OF RESPONSIBILITY

So far I have argued that even if we allow that the voluntariness of choice is a necessary and sufficient condition for the legitimacy of nearly all inter-ference with individuals, this does not, contrary to what libertarians claim, yield a defence of the free market. Even if we granted that the free market protects freedom and ensures that coercive interference with individuals is minimised or eliminated, it does not follow from that that the free market is just. This is because neither granting people freedom nor ensuring that they are not coerced suffices to ensure that they choose voluntarily; and voluntariness is, according to libertarians, necessary to preserve justice. By holding that the free market is just, libertarians overlook that there is a cru-cial distinction between freedom and voluntariness and unjustifiably single out coercion as if it were the only type of interference that undermines voluntariness.

At this point, however, a defender of libertarianism may reply with the following challenge. My critiques of the rights-definition definition of vol-untariness and of the claim that freedom suffices for voluntariness, it might be said, rest on tacitly assuming that, whenever individuals make choices in circumstances they do not like, they act non-voluntarily. If we accepted this assumption, the libertarian could continue, then individuals' choices will count as forced in an implausibly broad range of cases. Moreover, insofar as voluntariness is a necessary condition for responsibility, the role of responsibility in our theory of justice will be eroded. It is then more advisable to insist, as does the libertarian, that freedom (or equal freedom) is all we have to guarantee for one another as a necessary and sufficient condition for responsibility.[31]

To meet this objection, I need to show that my critique of the libertarian justification of the free market does not rely on an overly demanding notion of voluntariness, and relatedly, that it does not result in sabotaging responsibility. This is what I set out to do in this last section. I argue that we can defend an account of voluntariness that does not support an implausibly broad range of judgements of force, and I suggest that this account squares up with an attractive view of responsibility, one which does not posit unduly stringent necessary conditions for holding people responsible, such that those conditions are rarely met. As I see it, these two tasks – that of offering a defensible account of voluntariness and that of formulating an attractive view of responsibility – are intertwined. The fact that we are concerned with voluntariness as a legitimating condition for the imposition of burdens and as an important element in the attribution of personal responsibility constrains the type of voluntariness that is at issue and the sort of considerations that may be defended as relevant in deeming a choice as voluntary or forced.

Let me begin by stating what convictions a defensible account of voluntariness must accommodate, drawing on what I have said so far. Two points, in particular, must be borne in mind here. The first is that a plausible account of voluntariness must accommodate the fact that claims of voluntariness and force, being *explanatory* claims, make reference to how the nature of the options an individual faces affects her will. Secondly, and at the same time, an account of voluntariness must avoid both rendering claims of force and of voluntariness completely subjective (so that, whenever an agent finds an option unacceptable, his choice is forced) and making claims of force completely context-dependent (so that, whenever an option is worse than another, the individual's choice is forced). In line with these

---

[31] For the view that freedom is necessary, and possibly sufficient, for responsibility, which I mentioned before, see Steiner, *Essay on Rights*, p. 226. The view defended by Steiner could be either that equal freedom suffices for responsibility or that equal freedom suffices for voluntariness, which in turn suffices for responsibility.

observations, in the rest of this section I put forward some suggestions about what features of individuals' choice conditions are relevant for the voluntariness of their choices and offer an overview of the sorts of judgements the definition of voluntariness I favour would support. Throughout, it is assumed that agents do not have adaptive preferences and do not lack relevant information about the nature of the options they face.

I have suggested already that a choice is voluntary if and only if it is not made because there is no acceptable alternative to it. Conversely, a claim that a person was forced to do x means that she did x because she had no acceptable alternative to it. On this view, the voluntariness of choice is a function of *both* the individual's preferences and the acceptability or unacceptability of the options, where the criterion for the acceptability of options is an objective one. A plausible candidate here, as I mentioned earlier, is a criterion of basic needs, such that an option is unacceptable if pursuing or choosing it threatens some basic need.[32] Although an elaboration and a defence of an objective criterion of basic needs is something I do not offer here, I would like to emphasise that taking an objective standard as the criterion for the unacceptability of options is compatible with my contention that claims of force and voluntariness, being explanatory, make reference to the agents' motivations. It is possible to uphold both that, first, since claims of force and voluntariness are claims about why agents act as they do, it is agents' attitudes towards the options they face – rather than the objective nature of those options, *independently* of the agents' attitudes – that determine whether or not they act voluntarily; and second, that an option is unacceptable in accordance with an objective standard of well-being.

An account of voluntariness that adopts an objective standard of acceptability while also accommodating the subjective aspect of voluntariness and force plausibly restricts the range of cases in which individuals make forced

---

[32] We could talk of basic functionings or capabilities instead of basic needs here. For two discussions of capabilities and functionings, see A. Sen, *Inequality Reexamined* (Oxford: Clarendon Press, 1992); M. Nussbaum, *Sex and Social Justice* (Oxford University Press, 1999). Or we could adopt a more comprehensive account of needs that includes, but is not limited to, basic needs. For example, we may adopt an account of needs such as the ones defended by Harry Frankfurt or David Wiggins. See H. Frankfurt, 'Necessity and Desire', in G. Brock (ed.), *Necessary Goods* (Maryland: Rowman & Littlefield, 1998); D. Wiggins, 'Claims of Need', in his *Needs, Values, Truth* (Oxford: Blackwell, 1987). Of course, the range of judgements of force would vary depending on which of these accounts is adopted. I do not discuss here which of these views is preferable. The important point I would like to emphasise is that a defensible notion of voluntariness must invoke an objective criterion of acceptability. This, in my view, is both plausible in its own right – insofar as I think that an objective account of well-being, of which the criterion in question would be part, is more plausible than a subjective account – and is attractive as a criterion for the acceptability of options, insofar as it results in delimiting the number of judgements of force.

choices. In particular, there are three types of cases in which the account I have sketched does not, unlike what one may think at first, support the judgement that individuals are forced.

First, there are those cases in which an individual faces options that are all acceptable, according to the objective standard of acceptability, but in which the individual who faces those options *finds* them unacceptable. The fact that claims of voluntariness and force are explanatory, together with my contention that the criterion for the acceptability of options is an objective one, means that in these cases claims of force would be mistaken: that an individual *deems* an option to be unacceptable is a necessary condition for him to be motivated by the fact that it is unacceptable, and hence, for him to be forced to choose the alternative option. But it is not a sufficient condition: it does not suffice, for Audrey to be forced to do x, that *she* finds y unacceptable. To see this, consider the case of Demanding, who faces a choice between two acceptable options one of which he would, because of his preferences, never consider as worthy of his choice: it follows from my account that, to his complaint that he was forced to choose the option he chose, because the alternative was unacceptable, we could reply that he is wrong, that both options *were* acceptable and that he was not forced to choose as he did.

Second, there are those cases in which individuals face only (objectively) unacceptable alternatives to what they prefer doing, but this in no way motivates them. In these cases, their choice is not forced. That is, it is not always necessary that two acceptable options be present for a choice to be voluntary. This is because, so long as one option is acceptable and is one which the agent very much likes, the absence of an acceptable alternative may not be what motivates the agent. This claim, to the effect that a choice can be voluntary in some cases in which the agent faces only one option – namely, those cases in which the option is one the agent very much likes – may seem hard to defend. Some may believe that, for a choice to be voluntary, it is always necessary that at least two acceptable options be available. They would claim that, if only one acceptable option is available, then, no matter how attractive that option is to the person involved, the choice this person makes is not a voluntary one. The same would apply to limiting cases, that is, cases where there is only one acceptable option *and* there are no other options, acceptable or unacceptable. Some would say, of Wendy in the Wired City, whom I introduced at the beginning of this chapter, that, since she has no alternative to staying in the city – remember that Wendy is unfree to leave the city – she is forced to stay in the city. They would say that despite the fact that Wendy does not want to leave, and despite the fact that her staying in the city is in no way motivated by the fact that she is unfree to leave.

I am here disagreeing with that claim. Admittedly, cases of choosing between two acceptable alternatives are, in some way, different from cases of choosing the only acceptable alternative. For one thing, the former can be described as cases of choice as *selection*, whereas the latter are cases of choice as *election*.[33] But insofar as the voluntariness of the choice is concerned, that difference seems to me to be irrelevant. Further, even if we uphold that, strictly speaking, no *choice* is involved in these cases, it is still true that the person is not forced to do what she does. A person is forced to do something when she does that thing *because* no acceptable alternative is available. If no acceptable alternative is available, but that in no way motivates the person in doing what she does, then she is *not* forced to do what she does.

Making room for this possibility helps us to make sense of the difference between certain cases that seem to call for distinction. Take the following example. Both a worker choosing a badly paid job and a teacher who accepts a job she loves may have no acceptable alternative to taking those jobs. We can imagine that they can only either work at those occupations, or be unemployed, and neither the teacher nor the worker has enough wealth on which to live off or any means, other than by working, to make ends meet. However, on the view of voluntary choice I have sketched, it is likely that the worker is, and the teacher is not, forced to sell her labour. This is because, in the standard case, the worker accepts the badly paid job *because* she has no acceptable alternative. The teacher, by contrast, may well accept her job because she loves it, not because she has no acceptable alternative. There is a relevant difference between these two cases, and this difference is accounted for by my conception of what being forced means.

It is possible, then, for someone to choose voluntarily, even in the absence of acceptable alternatives. However, we must note that the presence of at least two acceptable options from which to choose reassures us that no adaptive preference is at stake and solves an epistemic problem: if someone has two acceptable options to choose from, then *we have more reason to be sure that*, whichever one she chooses, she chooses it voluntarily. The existence of two acceptable options, in other words, is a necessary condition for us to *know* that a choice is voluntary. This does not mean, however, that the existence of two acceptable options is a necessary condition for a choice to be voluntary; nor does it mean, therefore, that we are committed to making an implausibly large number of claims of force.

---

[33] On the distinction between choice as election and choice as selection, see M. Dan-Cohen, 'Conceptions of Choice and Conceptions of Autonomy', *Ethics* 102 (1992), pp. 221–43.

A third and final type of case which, on my account, does not count as one in which individuals are forced, is that in which individuals face options, all of which are (objectively) acceptable and one of which is much better than the others. My suggestion is that, whenever a person faces at least two acceptable options, then she is not forced to choose the option that she does choose. When at least two acceptable options are available, the fact that one of these options may be clearly superior to the other acceptable option may well make the choice a straightforward one. It may even be the case that the nature of the options the person faces is such that it would be irrational for her to make any other choice but that of the designated, and choiceworthy, acceptable option. The agent may face an offer which she really cannot refuse, in the sense that it would be irrational for her to refuse it, and no one could expect her, or any other person facing a relevantly similar option set, to refuse it. But, so long as she has an acceptable alternative, the choice is a voluntary one.

The account I defend, then, is not one on which 'people are forced to do something *whenever* the alternatives they face are considerably worse', as Nozick wants to depict the position he sets out to criticise.[34] If that were the case, then a very large number of choices would be non-voluntary, and that is indeed an implausible position to hold.[35] But that conclusion can easily be avoided. When a choice is made between two or more acceptable options, the voluntariness of that choice is not to be assessed in terms of the *comparative* attractiveness of the options one faces. The fact that, among acceptable options, some are going to be considerably worse than others, so that one option will clearly be the choiceworthy option, has no bearing on the voluntariness of the choice.[36]

These suggestions point to the fact that, by combining a concern with the objective acceptability or unacceptability of options with an interest in

[34] Nozick, *Anarchy, State, and Utopia*, p. 169.

[35] All choices made when facing choice sets that include an option which is considerably better than another option in that set would be non-voluntary, including those cases where all the options in question are acceptable. I considered Nozick's treatment of these kinds of cases in chapter 5 above.

[36] I believe that the same does not apply to choices made between unacceptable options. With such choices, I think that the difference between options may affect the voluntariness of choice. In particular, there is a difference between cases in which both options are unacceptable *and* are more or less equally unacceptable on the one hand, and, on the other, cases in which both options are unacceptable but where there is a substantial gap between them, in terms of the extent to which they negatively affect a person's well-being. In the latter case, but not in the former, a choice can be forced. The 'asymmetry of the relevance for voluntariness of the difference between options' is, it seems to me, quite plausible. When a choice between two unacceptable options is at stake, the greater the difference between the two options, the more likely it is that we choose the less bad one *because* the alternative is unacceptable. Since what is at issue in declaring a choice non-voluntary is a concern with some of the person's basic needs going unmet if an (unacceptable) option is chosen, that concern seems to warrant viewing the choice between two unacceptable options (one of which involves a much more serious threat to basic needs satisfaction than the other) as a forced choice.

the reasons and motives for which people act, it is possible to formulate an account of voluntariness that captures the fact that judgements of voluntariness and force are explanatory without rendering such judgements wholly subjective or context-sensitive. This account is not going to support an implausibly broad range of claims of force. Even if we endorse the view that voluntariness is a necessary condition for the attribution of responsibility, then, it does not seem that individuals will be excused in too large a number of cases.

So much, then, for the first part of my reply to the objection that the account of voluntariness on which I have relied to criticise the libertarian argument supports implausible conclusions, in terms of the range of judgements of force it would support, and relatedly, in terms of the extent to which it would exempt people from responsibility, given that force undermines responsibility. The second point I would like to raise in reply to this objection is as follows: even in those cases in which individuals are, indeed, forced, they are *not responsible in one sense, but responsible in another*. Recognising this fact helps us form a balanced judgement concerning the role of responsibility in conceptions of justice. To see this, we need to draw a distinction, which is often overlooked and which has been helpfully drawn by Thomas Scanlon, between two senses of responsibility, namely, responsibility as attributability (or moral responsibility) and substantive responsibility.[37] Moral responsibility is the notion invoked when we hold people morally responsible for their actions, that is, liable to moral appraisal – praise and blame – and criticism; substantive responsibility, by contrast, has to do with the obligations people have towards each other.

These two senses of responsibility differ. As Scanlon puts it, conditions for responsibility as attributability depend on the importance, for the moral appraisal of an agent, of determining whether an action reflected the agent's judgement-sensitive attitudes; conditions for substantive responsibility, by contrast, arise from the importance, for the agent, of having what happens to him depend on his choices.

When it is claimed that justice requires treating people as responsible agents, and that individuals are responsible for what happens to them as a result of their voluntary choices in a free market society, the notion we invoke is that of substantive, not moral, responsibility. Judgements of substantive responsibility include both judgements of self-responsibility, stating that the relevant individual alone should bear the consequences of his choices, thus entailing that others have no obligation towards him, and judgements about the legitimate enforceability of obligations the relevant individual may, as a result of his choices, have incurred towards others. The fact that this sense of responsibility differs from that of moral responsibility is largely overlooked, but drawing this distinction is illuminating.[38] The conditions for moral and for substantive responsibility need not – and, in my view, *are not* – the same. In particular, the account of voluntariness I have defended is one that purports to identify a condition that is necessary for substantive, not moral, responsibility.

For someone to be morally responsible – and here I am in agreement with Scanlon – it is necessary that she have certain capacities for moral agency; that the action be correctly attributable to her, so that the action is properly *hers*; and that the circumstances in which the person acts are such that the *character* of the action that can be attributed to her is not altered.[39] We could, if we wanted, refer to these conditions as adding up to the claim that there is *a sense* of 'voluntariness' or 'the voluntary' that is necessary to moral responsibility. An action is voluntary in the sense in question when it is 'intentional in the relevant respect and . . . to the extent that the agent deliberated, is the product of that deliberation'.[40] But this is a different notion of voluntariness from the one I have been talking about so far. Voluntariness, in the sense I have been referring to it, is *not*, I believe, a necessary condition for moral praise and blame. But it is, I am suggesting, a necessary condition for substantive responsibility, at least in a certain range of cases. I therefore do concede an important point to libertarians. Admittedly, the latter, as I have shown, hold that it is a necessary (and sufficient) condition in almost all cases, the only exceptions being those obligations that are correlative of individuals' libertarian rights. I do not agree with this claim. In my view, not all interference must be voluntarily chosen, and further, I am not committed to the view that voluntariness is sufficient for the legitimacy of those interferences, but only to the weaker claim that, in some cases, vitiated voluntariness renders those interferences

---

[38] See, for instance, L. Katz, 'Responsibility and Consent: The Libertarian's Problem with Freedom of Contract', *Social Philosophy and Policy* 16 (1999), pp. 94–117, where Katz's treatment of the libertarian view of responsibility conflates moral and substantive responsibility. John Roemer is one person who, following Scanlon, has drawn attention to these two senses of responsibility. See J. Roemer, *Equality of Opportunity* (Harvard University Press, 1998), pp. 16–21.

[39] Scanlon, *What We Owe to Each Other*, pp. 277–81.

[40] B. Williams, 'Voluntary Acts and Responsible Agents', *Oxford Journal of Legal Studies* 10 (1990), pp. 1–10. Williams says that, thus conceptualised, the voluntary belongs to a theory of action, not to a theory of freedom.

illegitimate. In other words, voluntariness is a necessary condition for the legitimacy of obligations only in some cases; and even in those cases, it is not a sufficient condition. These contentions certainly require greater elaboration and justification, which I cannot offer here. This, however, is not what is at issue in the present discussion. What I am pointing to here, while compatible with the view of a qualified scope for voluntariness I have just illustrated, does not presuppose it. My main claim is that the type of responsibility from which individuals who make non-voluntary choices in my sense are excused is *not* moral responsibility. The sense of 'voluntariness' which is necessary for moral responsibility and the one which is necessary for substantive responsibility, then, are *not* competing accounts of voluntariness, since they specify the conditions for two different kinds of responsibility.

It is possible, then, to hold that some choices are forced in a sense that is relevant to substantive responsibility, without this entailing that they are non-voluntary in the sense required by moral responsibility. Nor, as should now be clear, does the contention that an action is non-voluntary or forced in the sense that is relevant for substantive responsibility imply that it is unintentional or non-volitional. When we claim that someone who was forced to accept a hazardous job should not be held liable if he fails to abide by the terms of the contract he consented to, we are not suggesting that his choice cannot be attributed to him, as would be the case if his consent had been given, say, under hypnosis. As a result, this person may still be liable to praise and blame, that is, be morally responsible for what he has done.

The account of voluntariness I defend as an account of the conditions for substantive responsibility, then, although it may support more claims of force than the libertarian would wish to allow for, cannot be attacked on the grounds that it erodes the role of responsibility *tout court*. For some claims of force may still be claims in which individuals are morally responsible for their actions. So, for example, a person who intentionally and deliberately accepts a hazardous job in order to feed her starving child does act voluntarily in *one* sense – the sense that is relevant for moral responsibility – but is forced to act as she does, and hence, acts non-voluntarily, in *another* sense of voluntariness – namely, the sense that is relevant for substantive responsibility. This person may be liable to moral appraisal, and may be praised for her action, but it does not follow that the obligations she has incurred by accepting the job should be enforced, and that she has no justifiable complaint against having to comply with them. To ignore this is to overlook that the notion of responsibility is a complex one, and that judgements of responsibility are more fine-grained than is captured by a single, all-encompassing notion of responsibility.

There are at least two things, then, that can be said in reply to the libertarian's warning that moving away from a rights-definition of voluntariness, or insisting on voluntariness, as distinct from freedom, as a necessary condition for responsibility, lead us to sabotage the possibility of holding people responsible. The first is that a plausible account of voluntariness can avoid supporting too broad a range of claims of force; the second is that we should recognise that not making people pick up the costs of their forced choices is compatible with assessing them as morally responsible agents. An account of voluntariness that recognises that the latter is distinct from freedom, and that plausibly delimits the range of cases in which individuals count as forced while recognising that claims of voluntariness and force are explanatory ones, presents a viable and attractive alternative to the rights-based account that lies at the basis of the libertarian defence of the free market.

5. SUMMARY

In chapter 4 I opened my discussion of the entitlement-based argument for the free market by suggesting that we should pay more attention than has been done so far to the principle of justice in transfer favoured by libertarians, which is of crucial importance for their contention that the free market society is one where no freedom is curtailed and where all interference with individuals is voluntarily consented to. In the previous chapter I then argued that this contention relies on libertarians' use of implausible moralised definitions of harm, freedom and voluntariness. In this chapter I have taken further my critique of libertarianism and shown that a proper understanding of the relation between freedom, voluntariness and coercion reveals that some of libertarianism's main contentions should be revised. I have argued, first, that freedom and voluntariness are different notions and that freedom does not suffice for voluntariness; and second, I have suggested that coercion is only one type of forcing. This means that even if a rights-respecting free market were a realm in which people's freedom is not curtailed and transactions are not coercive, it does not follow that it would host only voluntary transactions. This critique of libertarianism, unlike others which, I have suggested, tend to make one or other of libertarianism's own mistakes, relies on an attractive account of voluntariness that does not support too wide a range of claims of force and which can provide the conditions for the attribution of responsibility.

Conclusion

A cautious defender of the market has remarked: 'we need not enter into deep philosophical territory in order to recognize that much of the time, markets help or hurt people for reasons that are unfair, in the sense that they are ill connected with any plausible conception of justice'.[1] However, as I have shown, since some philosophers seriously question what others think is an all too apparent claim, we do need to venture into deep philosophical territory to assess it. This is what I have done in this book. I have analysed in depth two main attempts at showing that a defence of the free market can occupy the moral high ground, and that there are plausible conceptions of justice on which the distributional consequences of free market choices *are* just. Defenders of desert argue that the relevant conception is a substantive one, based in desert, where the latter is interpreted as either a principle of compensation or a principle of contribution. Libertarians, by contrast, argue that the relevant conception of justice is a procedural, entitlement-based one, which holds that individuals have full ownership rights both in themselves and in external resources, and that voluntary exchange of justly acquired holdings is all that justice requires.

Despite their differences, as I have shown, both these attempts at justifying the free market invoke the importance of recognising that individuals should be treated as freely choosing and responsible agents, and that justice requires giving responsible individuals their due. Libertarians claim that this is best done by viewing individuals as self-owning persons whose voluntary choice or consent is both a necessary and sufficient condition for the legitimacy of almost all interference with them. They further argue that a free market society, one in which individuals exercise freely their full private property rights, is one in which voluntariness is respected and in which individuals are rightly held responsible for the burdens and benefits of their choices. Defenders of desert hold that giving responsible individuals

---

[1] C. R. Sunstein, *Free Markets and Social Justice* (Oxford University Press, 1997), p. 386.

their due requires giving them their just deserts, and that individuals, where economic desert is concerned, are more or less deserving than others as a result of engaging in more or less costly, or more or less productive, socially useful activities. They also claim that free market incomes adequately reflect people's deserts and that free market inequalities are therefore justified by a commitment to treating individuals as responsible agents.

However, I have argued that, when they are subjected to scrutiny, neither the entitlement-based nor the desert-based justification of the free market is successful. This is not because voluntariness, desert and responsibility are unimportant notions that should not play a role in our conception of justice. Quite the contrary. I have argued that taking these notions and their significance seriously is what supports a critique of the entitlement-based and desert-based arguments, and that libertarians and defenders of desert are not true to their underlying convictions when they set out to show that the free market is just. Their argument to this effect largely hinges on their use of unexamined and indefensible interpretations of the crucial notions they employ. Once this fact is revealed, the way is open for adopting more plausible interpretations of desert, voluntariness and responsibility, which, far from offering support to the free market, rather call for its regulation.

I have shown this clearly with the entitlement-based argument, of which I have developed an internal critique in the last three chapters. As I have now had occasion to remark several times, libertarians' commitment to the centrality of voluntariness is supposedly unequivocal. This is because voluntariness is required to preserve justice in transfer, and because, as I have suggested, a commitment to ensuring that individuals have an area in which they are not forced is what can plausibly be seen to motivate the very endorsement of self-ownership. Rights of self-ownership protect an area in which each individual is sovereign, thus allowing each person to live her life in accordance with her voluntary choices, and therefore proscribing the imposition of (nearly all) enforceable obligations an individual has not herself consented to or voluntarily undertaken. The claim that voluntariness is therefore both a necessary and a sufficient condition for the legitimacy of (nearly) all interference is a central one for the libertarian defence of the free market, but, as I have argued, the voluntariness-based argument for unbridled capitalism is unsuccessful. Once the libertarian argument that appeals to notions of freedom and of voluntariness is examined carefully, it appears to be multiply problematic. In particular, I have shown that it relies on an implausible rights-based definition of voluntariness, as well as the more familiar rights-based definition of freedom and a rights-based harm criterion; that it is based on an unexamined and incorrect understanding of the relation between freedom, voluntariness, and the related notion of coercion, which critics of libertarians have also tended to show; and that it fails to provide a defensible account of the conditions under which individuals are (substantively) responsible.

The upshot of these arguments is that the libertarian defence of the free market fails, and does so by its own standards. Nor could it succeed, since, if the analysis of voluntariness and of freedom I have offered is correct, a concern with the voluntariness of choice, be it derived from an endorsement of self-ownership or a commitment to autonomy, supports not a free market society with no redistributive measures, but a guaranteed minimum for all. Only when everyone faces a sufficient range of acceptable options can we say that individuals can live their lives in accordance with their voluntary choices, enjoy a robust rather than a formal self-ownership, and claim that individuals may justifiably be held responsible for the outcomes of their actions. This, then, is another main observation that has emerged from the analysis of the last few chapters: the adoption of voluntary choice itself provides us with the basis for supporting whatever redistributive measures may be necessary to ensure that everyone be able to make choices that are voluntary in the relevant sense, that is, so as to justify holding people responsible.

Just what sort of guaranteed social minimum can be justified by appeal to the notion of voluntariness I have defended will depend on what the defensible criterion for assessing the acceptability of options is. I have not examined that question here, but I have argued that a conception of justice that adopted an objective criterion for the acceptability of options such as a basic needs one, and that held that at least those redistributive measures that are necessary to ensure the availability of the required range of options for all, by no means threatens the role of responsibility. Two points, in particular, suggest otherwise. First, the account of voluntariness I defend is not one that supports an implausibly wide-ranging series of claims of force, as it does not conceive of voluntariness as a purely subjective or context-dependent notion. It is not the case, then, that, whenever an individual deems the options she faces as unacceptable, or whenever she faces some options that are certainly more choiceworthy than others, she is forced to act as she does and is therefore not responsible for her choices. Second, to hold that individuals should not be held responsible, or accountable, when certain conditions are not in place, is not to claim that they may not be liable to being praised or blamed. Someone who is forced to act as she does may still be liable to moral appraisal, but that appraisal need not be accompanied by a requirement to leave her to bear alone the costs of her choices.

Both judgements of voluntariness and related judgements of responsibility are more complex and fine-grained than libertarians suggest. By recognising this fact, and that some preconditions have to be satisfied for individuals to be responsible, my view by no means neglects, but rather gives expression to, the conviction that individuals are to be treated as responsible agents.

If entitlement-based arguments do not successfully establish that treating individuals as responsible agents requires that they be left to enjoy both the burdens and the benefits of their choices on a free market, desert-based arguments, I have suggested, are no more convincing in establishing that rewards generated by a free labour market are what responsible individuals are due. Desert-based defences of the free market trade on the indeterminacy of the principle of desert, selecting as they do those particular interpretations of it that are best suited for the purpose to which they are then put, without seriously engaging with the issues raised by the problem of contingency or luck. This is true of both the argument that rewards are deserved as compensation and the argument that they are deserved reward for productive contribution. Defenders of the market who appeal to desert as reward for productive contribution also present us with a false dichotomy between adopting desert and thereby accepting the inequalities due to factors that are beyond the individuals' control which that principle is taken to justify, and giving up desert and the related commitment to responsibility altogether.

This, I have argued, is unwarranted. An insistence on the requirement of responsibility that is associated with desert as a principle of justice, and on the need to neutralise the role of circumstantial luck, does not undermine desert. On the contrary, a defensible principle of desert that can justify differential rewards recognises that individuals should have a fair opportunity to deserve more or less than others. The requisite principle of desert is a principle of active desert, on which a distribution of unequal rewards is just because deserved when individuals can be held responsible for being more or less deserving than others, so that some having greater deserts than others does not reflect unfair advantage. Active desert is one interpretation of the principle of desert that meets the requirements to be eligible as a principle of justice that can justify market outcomes, and that squares up with some plausible convictions about what justice requires, including that which enjoins us to treat individuals as responsible agents. Desert as a principle of justice, then, rather than justifying the distributional consequences of free market choices, requires precisely the elimination, or at least the minimisation, of the differential brute luck that characterises the free market.

At this point, and before concluding, it is worth noting that the adoption of desert as a principle of justice seems to result in a much more demanding requirement, as far as its implications for the regulation of the market are concerned, than a commitment to voluntariness as a legitimating condition for the imposition of obligations, even when this is suitably revised so as to square up with a defensible account of voluntariness and force. Some final remarks are in order, then, about how these two principles differ and about what shape a theory of justice that accommodates both would have.

A defensible principle of desert is one which, I have observed, justifies inequalities among individuals that reflect their different choices and their comparative exercise of responsibility. Desert so understood, as a principle capable of justifying *distributions* or *patterns* of rewards across individuals, requires that choices be made by individuals, that those choices be voluntary, *and* that they not be made against differential brute luck. Only when inequalities are neither tainted by force nor the result of factors that are wholly outside of individuals' control can individuals take credit for having a *greater* or *lesser* claim than those of others and hence, to deserve more or less than them. Insofar as desert is supposed to justify a distribution of benefits and burdens across individuals, then, and insofar as, in order to do this, it is not sufficient that each person takes credit for her achievements in isolation, voluntariness is a necessary, but not sufficient, condition for desert. If inequalities result from people making non-voluntary choices, then they are not deserved; but not all inequalities that result from voluntary choices are deserved. Individuals may make choices not because they have no acceptable alternatives, but still not be able to take credit for the outcome of their choices being better or worse than those of others, and hence, not deserve to have more or less than others.

The demand that choices be voluntary, then, can be seen as *part* of an account of desert, insofar as it expresses one of the conditions for people to be differentially deserving. But whether the outcome is also one which individuals can claim to deserve depends on what other background conditions were in place before the choice was made. Consider, by way of illustration, a scenario in which Audrey and Burt live in an area that will be hit by a tornado and are warned about the danger connected with going out while the tornado is around. Endorsing voluntariness as a sufficient condition for the attribution of (substantive) responsibility commits us to the view that if, under certain conditions, Audrey goes out and is hit by the tornado, then, so long as her choice is a voluntary one, she does not have a legitimate claim against Burt, who voluntarily chose to stay at home. From this it does not follow, however, that any overall inequality that may exist between Audrey and Burt after the event is justified. If Audrey's situation, prior to exposing herself to the tornado, was worse than Burt's through no fault of her own, then Audrey may well have a claim against Burt, a claim that is independent of, and prior to, the inequality generated by their different choices. In other words, the voluntariness of choice only legitimates the outcome *relative to the pre-choice* situation, rather than *tout court*. It justifies holding people substantively responsible for the particular choice in question; but only where the overall difference between individuals is something that they can be held responsible for is the overall inequality between them deserved.

It seems clear, then, that fleshing out the conditions for voluntary choice, and, in turn, relating the voluntariness of choice to responsibility, are relevant for casting light on what desert-based justice itself requires. This is because a concern with giving individuals what they deserve, in the relevant sense, implies a commitment to ensuring that they make voluntary choices. The voluntariness of choice, however, also has moral significance that is independent of that of desert. In particular, it can play an independent role in an account of justice in the following two ways.

First, the voluntariness of choice has an independent role to play in justifying inequalities. In particular, the voluntariness of choice, rather than an endorsement of desert, is central to a justification of inequalities arising from differential option luck, where the latter is defined as a matter of how deliberate gambles turn out. Consider a case in which any existing inequality between Audrey and Burt is deserved and both face the choice of whether or not to spend some money buying a lottery ticket: so long as the choice each makes is a voluntary one, then the resulting inequality is justified, although it is not the case that that inequality is itself deserved.[2] Here

---

[2] The attempt to analyse these inequalities as putatively deserved is therefore, in my view, an unwarranted move. Where luck is involved, as with the case of the lottery ticket, trying to establish what, exactly, one (supposedly) deserves is notoriously difficult. For a discussion of what ones deserves where the supposed deserved good is affected by luck and probability, see R. Goodin, 'Negating Positive Desert Claims', *Political Theory* 13 (1985), pp. 575–98. Distinguishing between the role of voluntariness as a condition for desert and its role as an independent factor that, under certain conditions, justifies

the voluntariness of choice is what justifies an inequality which, while not sanctioned by desert itself, need not be condemned by it. An endorsement of desert may well coexist with the belief that, under certain conditions, the choice to expose oneself to luck may give rise to justifiable inequalities. Unlike the case in which choice is made against a background of differential brute luck, which I considered earlier, the case involving option luck gives rise to inequalities which the defender of a desert-based account of justice may accept by giving an independent justificatory role to the voluntariness of choice.[3]

A second way in which a commitment to ensuring that individuals make voluntary choices has force independent of any commitments to desert is the following. As I showed earlier, ensuring that individuals make voluntary choices (whether because of a commitment to desert or because of something else, such as a commitment to self-ownership or autonomy) requires guaranteeing for individuals at least some acceptable options. An account of justice that recognises the role of voluntariness as a necessary condition for holding individuals substantively responsible, then, has the resources for justifying the provision of a threshold or minimum below which individuals should not be allowed to fall. An account of this sort, then, seems capable of defusing the objection moved against so-called 'luck egalitarianism', which, in a nutshell, requires only the elimination of inequalities that are traceable to differential brute luck while allowing those inequalities which reflect people's comparative exercise of responsibility.[4] By allowing inequalities that individuals are responsible for, it has been argued, such egalitarianism allows for the abandonment and neglect of destitute and badly off individuals who are deemed to have brought their misfortune onto themselves. But by insisting on the importance of the availability of a range of acceptable options for individuals to make voluntary choices and, hence, be substantively responsible for what happens to them, an account of justice that accommodates voluntariness as informing what justice requires escapes this objection. The very fact that a defensible account of distributive justice should make room for voluntary choice and responsibility, while supporting the view that some inequalities are

---

(undeserved) inequalities is helpful. Theorists of desert, it seems to me, have often overlooked this, moving from the claim that in order to deserve something one must have made a voluntary choice to bring that something about, to the claim that, whenever a voluntary choice is made, the outcome of that choice is itself deserved.

[3] For an account that makes room for both desert and voluntariness, see M. Slote, 'Desert, Consent, and Justice', *Philosophy and Public Affairs* 2 (1973), pp. 321–47.

[4] A well-known statement of this objection is found in E. Anderson, 'What is the Point of Equality?', *Ethics* 109 (1999), pp. 287–337.

justified, also provides the basis for defending a guaranteed range of acceptable options for all.

These observations, of course, provide only a sketch of the main contours of a conception that takes voluntariness and desert to be relevant for justice. They confirm, however, that such a conception can be hospitable to notions of deservingness, as much as to notions of voluntary choice and responsibility, and that the regulated market which would realise justice thus understood, far from sacrificing these highly valued principles, is hospitable to their most plausible and attractive version.

Bibliography

Acton, H. B., *The Morals of Markets: An Ethical Explanation* (Harlow: Longman, 1971)

Adler, J., 'Luckless Desert is Different Desert', *Mind* 96 (1987), pp. 247–49

Ake, C., 'Justice as Equality', *Philosophy and Public Affairs* 4 (1975), pp. 69–89

Anderson, E., *Value in Ethics and Economics* (Harvard University Press, 1993)

Anderson, E., 'The Ethical Limitations of the Market', *Economics and Philosophy* 6 (1990), pp. 179–205

Anderson, E., 'What Is the Point of Equality?', *Ethics* 109 (1999), pp. 287–337

Arneson, R. J., 'Equality and Equality of Opportunity for Welfare', *Philosophical Studies* 55 (1989), pp. 77–93

Arneson, R. J., 'Lockean Self-Ownership: Towards a Demolition', *Political Studies* 39 (1991), pp. 36–54

Arneson, R. J., 'Property Rights in Persons', *Social Philosophy and Policy* 9 (1992), pp. 201–30

Arneson, R. J., 'Egalitarianism and the Undeserving Poor', *Journal of Political Philosophy* 5 (1997), pp. 327–50

Ball, S. W., 'Maximin Justice, Sacrifice, and the Reciprocity Argument: A Pragmatic Reassessment of the Rawls/Nozick Debate', *Utilitas* 5 (1993), pp. 157–84

Barry, B., *Political Argument* (London: Routledge & Kegan Paul, 1965)

Becker, L. C., 'The Obligation to Work', *Ethics* 91 (1980), pp. 35–49

Bedau, H. A., 'Social Justice and Social Institutions', in P. A. French *et al.* (eds.), *Midwest Studies in Philosophy* (University of Minnesota Press, 1978), vol. III, pp. 159–75

Benn, S. I., *A Theory of Freedom* (Cambridge University Press, 1989)

Berlin, I., *Four Essays on Liberty* (Oxford University Press, 1969)

Brenkert, G. G., 'Self-Ownership, Freedom, and Autonomy', *Journal of Ethics* 2 (1998), pp. 27–55

Buchanan, A., *Ethics, Efficiency, and the Market* (Oxford: Clarendon Press, 1985)

Callaghan, J. C., 'Paternalism and Voluntariness', *Canadian Journal of Philosophy* 16 (1986), pp. 199–220

Carens, J., *Equality, Moral Incentive, and the Market* (University of Chicago Press, 1981)

Carens, J., 'Compensatory Justice and Social Institutions', *Economics and Philosophy* 1 (1985), pp. 36–67

Carter, I., *A Measure of Freedom* (Oxford University Press, 1999)

Cavanagh, M., *Against Equality of Opportunity* (Oxford: Clarendon Press, 2002)

Chapman J. W. and Pennock, J. R. (eds.), *Markets and Justice. Nomos XXXI* (New York University Press, 1989)

Child, J. W., 'Can Libertarianism Sustain a Fraud Standard?', *Ethics* 104 (1994), pp. 722–38

Christman, J., *The Myth of Property: Toward an Egalitarian Theory of Ownership* (Oxford University Press, 1994)

Christman, J., 'Can Ownership be Justified by Natural Rights?', *Philosophy and Public Affairs* 15 (1986), pp. 156–77

Christman, J., 'Entrepreneurs, Profits, and Deserving Market Shares', *Social Philosophy and Policy* 6 (1988), pp. 1–16

Christman, J., 'Self-Ownership, Equality, and the Structure of Property Rights', *Political Theory* 19 (1991), pp. 28–46

Cohen, G. A., *Self-Ownership, Freedom, and Equality* (Cambridge University Press, 1995)

Cohen, G. A., *If You're an Egalitarian, How Come You're So Rich?* (Harvard University Press, 2000)

Cohen, G. A., 'Are Disadvantaged Workers who take Hazardous Jobs Forced to take Hazardous Jobs?', in *History, Labour and Freedom* (Oxford: Clarendon Press, 1988), pp. 239–54

Cohen, G. A., 'On the Currency of Egalitarian Justice', *Ethics* 99 (1989), pp. 906–44

Cohen, G. A., 'Marxism and Contemporary Political Philosophy, or: Why Nozick Exercises some Marxists more than he does any Egalitarian Liberals', *Canadian Journal of Philosophy* 16 (1990), pp. 363–87

Cohen, G. A., 'Capitalism, Freedom, and the Proletariat', in D. Miller (ed.), *Liberty* (Oxford University Press, 1991), pp. 163–82

Cohen, G. A., 'Once More into the Breach of Self-Ownership: Reply to Narveson and Brenkert', *Journal of Ethics* 2 (1998), pp. 57–96

Cowan, R., and Rizzo, M. J. (eds.), *Profits and Morality* (University of Chicago Press, 1995)

Cummiskey, D., 'Desert and Entitlement: A Rawlsian Consequentialist Account', *Analysis* 47 (1987), pp. 15–19

Cupit, G., *Justice as Fittingness* (Oxford University Press, 1996)

Dan-Cohen, M., 'Conceptions of Choice and Conceptions of Autonomy', *Ethics* 102 (1992), pp. 221–43

Daniels, N., 'Merit and Meritocracy', *Philosophy and Public Affairs* 7 (1978), pp. 206–23

Davis, L., 'Nozick's Entitlement Theory', in J. Paul (ed.), *Reading Nozick* (Oxford: Blackwell, 1982), pp. 344–54

Day, J. P., 'Threats, Offers, Law, Opinion and Liberty', *American Philosophical Quarterly* 14 (1977), pp. 257–72

Dick, J. C., 'How to Justify a Distribution of Earnings', *Philosophy and Public Affairs* 4 (1975), pp. 248–72

Dworkin, G., *The Theory and Practice of Autonomy* (Cambridge University Press, 1988)

Dworkin, R., *Taking Rights Seriously* (London: Duckworth, 1977)

Dworkin, R., *Sovereign Virtue* (Harvard University Press, 2000)

Dworkin, G., 'Acting Freely', *Nous* 4 (1970), pp. 367–83

Dworkin, G., 'Is More Choice Better Than Less?', in P. French *et al.* (eds.), *Midwest Studies in Philosophy* (University of Minnesota Press, 1982), vol. III, pp. 47–62

Dworkin, G., Bermant, G., and Brown, P. G. (eds.), *Markets and Morals* (New York: Halsted Press, 1977)

Epstein, R. A., 'Luck', *Social Philosophy and Policy* 6 (1988), pp. 17–38

Exdell, J., 'Liberty, Equality, and Capitalism', *Canadian Journal of Philosophy* 11 (1981), pp. 457–72

Feldman, F., 'Desert: Reconsideration of Some Received Wisdom', *Mind* 104 (1995), pp. 63–77

Feldman, F., 'Responsibility as a Condition for Desert', *Mind* 105 (1996), pp. 165–8

Feinberg, J., 'Causing Voluntary Actions', in J. Feinberg, *Doing and Deserving. Essays in the Theory of Responsibility* (Princeton University Press, 1970), pp. 152–86

Feinberg, J., 'Justice and Personal Desert', in J. Feinberg, *Doing and Deserving. Essays in the Theory of Responsibility* (Princeton University Press, 1970), pp. 55–94

Feinberg, J., 'Social Justice', in J. Feinberg, *Social Philosophy* (Englewood Cliffs, N.J.: Prentice-Hall, 1973), pp. 98–119

Feinberg, J., 'Noncomparative Justice', in J. Feinberg, *Rights, Justice and the Bounds of Liberty* (Princeton University Press, 1980), pp. 265–306

Frankfurt, H., 'Alternate Possibilities and Moral Responsibility', *Journal of Philosophy* 66 (1969), pp. 829–39

Frankfurt, H., 'Freedom of the Will and the Concept of the Person', *Journal of Philosophy* 68 (1971), pp. 5–20

Frankfurt, H., 'Coercion and Moral Responsibility', in T. Honderich (ed.), *Essays on Freedom of Action* (London: Routledge & Kegan Paul, 1973), pp. 65–86

Frankfurt, H., 'What We Are Morally Responsible For', in J. M. Fischer and M. Ravizza (eds.), *Perspectives on Moral Responsibility* (Cornell University Press, 1993), pp. 286–95

Frankfurt, H., 'Necessity and Desire', in G. Brock (ed.), *Necessary Goods* (Maryland: Rowman & Littlefield, 1998)

Fried, B., 'Wilt Chamberlain Revisited: Nozick's Justice in Transfer and the Problem of Market-Based Distributions', *Philosophy and Public Affairs* 24 (1995), pp. 226–45

Friedman, M., *Capitalism and Freedom* (University of Chicago Press, 1962, 1982)

Gaus, G. F., 'Property, Rights, and Freedom', *Social Philosophy and Policy* 11 (1994), pp. 209–40

Gauthier, D., *Morals by Agreement* (Oxford: Clarendon Press, 1986)

George, H., *Progress and Poverty*, ed. A. W. Madsen, Centenary Edition (London: Hogarth Press, 1979)

Gibbard, A., 'Natural Property Rights', *Nous* 10 (1976), pp. 77–86

Gibbard, A., 'What's Morally Special About Free Exchange?', in E. F. Paul, F. D. Miller and J. Paul (eds.), *Ethics and Economics* (Oxford: Blackwell, 1985), pp. 20–28

Gilbert, M., 'Agreement, Coercion, and Obligation', *Ethics* 103 (1993), pp. 679–706

Goodin, R., 'Negating Positive Desert Claims', *Political Theory* 13 (1985), pp. 575–98

Gorr, M., 'Justice, Self-Ownership, and Natural Assets', *Social Philosophy and Policy* 12 (1995), pp. 267–91

Gray, J., *The Moral Foundations of Market Institutions* (London: IEA Health and Welfare Unit, 1992)

Gray, J., 'Marxian Freedom, Individual Liberty, and the End of Alienation', *Social Philosophy and Policy* 3 (1986), pp. 161–78

Gray, T., 'Spencer, Steiner and Hart on the Equal Liberty Principle', *Journal of Applied Philosophy* 10 (1993), pp. 91–104

Griffin, J., *Well-Being: Its Meaning, Measurement and Moral Importance* (Oxford: Clarendon Press, 1986)

Hart, H. L. A., *Essays on Bentham: Studies in Jurisprudence and Political Theory* (Oxford: Clarendon Press, 1982)

Hart, H. L. A., 'Are There Any Natural Rights?', in J. Waldron (ed.), *Theories of Rights* (Oxford University Press, 1984), pp. 77–90

Hausman, D. M., 'Are Markets Morally Free Zones?', *Philosophy and Public Affairs* 18 (1989), pp. 317–33

Hausman, D. M., 'When Jack and Jill Make a Deal', *Social Philosophy and Policy* 9 (1992), pp. 95–113

Hausman, D. M., and McPherson, M. S., *Economic Analysis and Moral Philosophy* (Cambridge University Press, 1996)

Haworth, A., *Anti-Libertarianism: Market, Philosophy, and Myth* (London and New York: Routledge, 1994)

Hayek, F. A., *The Constitution of Liberty* (London: Routledge & Kegan Paul, 1960)

Hayek, F. A., *Individualism and Economic Order* (London: Routledge & Kegan Paul, 1949)

Hayek, F. A., *Law, Legislation and Liberty*, vol. II, *The Mirage of Social Justice* (London: Routledge & Kegan Paul, 1976)

Hayek, F. A., 'The Principles of a Liberal Social Order', *Politico* 31 (1966), pp. 601–17

Hohfeld's W. N., *Fundamental Legal Conceptions as Applied in Judicial Reasoning* (Westport, Conn.: Greenwood Press, 1978, first published Yale University Press, 1919)

Hospers, J., 'What Libertarianism Is', in T. Machan and D. B. Rasmussen (eds.), *Liberty for the 21st Century. Contemporary Libertarian Thought* (Maryland: Rowman & Littlefield, 1995), pp. 5–17

Hsieh, N., 'Moral Desert, Fairness and Legitimate Expectations in the Market', *Journal of Political Philosophy* 8 (2000), pp. 91–114

Hurka, T., 'Why Value Autonomy?', *Social Theory and Practice* 13 (1987), pp. 361–82

Hurka, T., 'The Common Structure of Virtue and Desert', *Ethics* 112 (2001), pp. 6–31

Hurka, T. 'Desert: Individualistic and Holistic', in S. Olsaretti (ed.), *Desert and Justice* (Oxford University Press, 2003)

Hurley, S., *Justice, Luck and Knowledge* (Harvard University Press, 2003)

Jones, P., 'Freedom and the Redistribution of Resources', *Journal of Social Policy* 11 (1982), pp. 217–38

Kagan, S., 'Equality and Desert', in L. P. Pojman and O. McLeod (eds.), *What Do We Deserve? A Reader on Justice and Desert* (Oxford University Press, 1999), pp. 298–314

Katz, L., 'Responsibility and Consent: The Libertarian's Problems with Freedom of Contract', *Social Philosophy and Policy* 16 (1999), pp. 94–117

Kernohan, 'Capitalism and Self-Ownership', *Social Philosophy and Policy* 6 (1988), pp. 60–76

Kirzner, I. M., 'Entrepreneurship, Entitlement, and Economic Justice', in J. Paul (ed.), *Reading Nozick* (Oxford: Blackwell, 1982), pp. 383–411

Kleinig, J., 'The Concept of Desert', *American Philosophical Quarterly* 8 (1971), pp. 71–8

Kramer, M., Simmonds, N., and Steiner, H., *A Debate Over Rights: Philosophical Enquiries* (Oxford University Press, 1998)

Kristjánsson, K., *Social Freedom: The Responsibility View* (Cambridge University Press, 1996)

Kristjánsson, K., 'Justice, Desert, and Virtue Revisited', *Social Theory and Practice* 29 (2003), pp. 39–63

Kymlicka, W., *Contemporary Political Philosophy. An Introduction* (Oxford: Clarendon Press, 1990)

Lamont, J., 'The Concept of Desert in Distributive Justice', *Philosophical Quarterly* 44 (1994), pp. 45–64

Lamont, J., 'Problems for Effort-Based Distribution Principles', *Journal of Applied Philosophy* 12 (1995), pp. 215–29

Lamont, J., 'Incentive Income, Deserved Income and Economic Rents', *Journal of Political Philosophy* 5 (1997), pp. 26–45

Lane, R. E., 'Market Choice and Human Choice', in J. W. Chapman and J. R. Pennock (eds.), *Markets and Justice* (New York University Press, 1989), pp. 226–49

Levine, A., 'Capitalist Persons', *Social Philosophy and Policy* 6 (1988), pp. 39–59

Levine, A., 'Rewarding Effort', *Journal of Political Philosophy* 7 (1999), pp. 404–18

Little, M. D., *A Critique of Welfare Economics* (Oxford University Press, 1960)

Locke, J., *Two Treatises of Government*, ed. Peter Laslett (Cambridge University Press, 1988)

Lomasky, L. E., *Persons, Rights, and the Moral Community* (Oxford University Press, 1987)

Macdonald, I. A., 'Rights, Rights of Enforcement, and Nozick's Critique of the "Principle of fairness"', *South African Journal of Philosophy* 3 (1984), pp. 47–53

Machan, T. R., *Individuals and their Rights* (La Salle, Ill.: Open Court, 1989)

Machan, T. R., 'The Virtue of Freedom in Capitalism', *Journal of Applied Philosophy*
    3 (1986), pp. 49–58

Machan, T. R., and Rasmussen, D. B. (eds.), *Liberty for the 21st Century. Contem-
    porary Libertarian Thought* (Maryland: Rowman & Littlefield, 1995)

Mack, E., 'Nozick on Unproductivity: The Unintended Consequences', in J. Paul
    (ed.), *Reading Nozick* (Oxford: Blackwell, 1982), pp. 169–90

Mack, E., 'How to Derive Libertarian Rights', in J. Paul (ed.), *Reading Nozick*
    (Oxford: Blackwell, 1982), pp. 286–302

Mack, E., 'Distributive Justice and the Tensions of Lockeanism', *Social Philosophy
    and Policy* 1 (1983), pp. 132–50

Mack, E., 'Dominos and the Fear of Commodification', in J. W. Chapman and
    J. R. Pennock (eds.), *Markets and Justice* (New York University Press, 1989),
    pp. 198–225

Mack, E., 'Self-Ownership and the Right of Property', *The Monist* 73 (1990),
    pp. 519–43

Mack, E., 'Personal Integrity, Practical Recognition, and Rights', *The Monist* 76
    (1993), pp. 101–18

Mack, E., 'The Self-Ownership Proviso: A New and Improved Lockean Proviso',
    Social Philosophy and Policy 12 (1995), pp. 186–218

Mack, E., 'Moral Individualism and Libertarian Theory', in T. R. Machan and
    D. B. Rasmussen (eds.), *Liberty for the 21st Century. Contemporary Libertarian
    Thought* (Maryland: Rowman & Littlefield, 1995), pp. 41–58

MacPherson, C. B., 'The Rise and Fall of Economic Justice' in C. B. MacPherson,
    The Rise and Fall of Economic Justice and Other Papers (Oxford University
    Press, 1985), pp. 1–20

Marshall, G., Swift, A., and Roberts, S., *Against the Odds? Social Class and Social
    Justice in Industrial Societies* (Oxford: Clarendon Press, 1997)

Mason, A. (ed.), *Ideals of Equality* (Oxford: Blackwell, 1998)

McLeod, O., 'Desert and Wages', *Utilitas* 8 (1996), pp. 205–21

McLeod, O., 'Desert and Institutions', in L. P. Pojman and O. McLeod (eds.),
    What Do We Deserve? A Reader on Justice and Desert (Oxford University Press,
    1999), pp. 186–95

McLeod, O., 'On the Comparative Element of Justice', in S. Olsaretti (ed.), *Desert
    and Justice* (Oxford University Press, 2003)

Miller, D., *Social Justice* (Oxford: Clarendon Press, 1976)

Miller, D., *Market, State and Community. Theoretical Foundations of Market
    Socialism* (Oxford: Clarendon Press, 1989)

Miller, D., *Principles of Social Justice* (Harvard University Press, 1999)

Miller, D. (ed.), *Liberty* (Oxford University Press, 1991)

Miller, D., 'Constraints on Freedom', *Ethics* 94 (1983), pp. 66–86

Miller, D., 'Distributive Justice: What the People Think', *Ethics* 102 (1992), pp. 555–
    93; reprinted in D. Miller, *Principles of Social Justice* (Harvard University Press,
    1999)

Miller, D., 'Equality and Justice', in A. Mason (ed.), *Ideals of Equality* (Oxford:
    Blackwell, 1998), pp. 21–36

Miller, D., 'Comparative and Non-Comparative Desert', in S. Olsaretti (ed.), *Desert and Justice* (Oxford University Press, 2003)

Milne, H., 'Desert, Effort and Equality', *Journal of Applied Philosophy* 3 (1986), pp. 235–43

Murphy, L., and Nagel, T., *The Myth of Ownership: Taxes and Justice* (Oxford University Press, 2002)

Nagel, T., *Equality and Partiality* (Oxford University Press, 1991)

Nagel, T., 'Justice and Nature', *Oxford Journal of Legal Studies* 17 (1997), pp. 303–21

Narveson, J., *The Libertarian Idea* (Philadelphia: Temple University Press, 1988)

Narveson, J., 'The Justice of the Market: Comments on Gray and Radin', in J. W. Chapman and J. R. Pennock (eds.), *Markets and Justice. Nomos xxxi* (New York University Press, 1989), pp. 250–76

Narveson, J., 'Contracting for Liberty', in T. Machan and D. B. Rasmussen (eds.), *Liberty for the 21st Century. Contemporary Libertarian Thought* (Maryland: Rowman & Littlefield, 1995), pp. 19–39

Narveson, J., 'Deserving Profits', in R. Cowan and M. J. Rizzo (eds.), *Profits and Morality* (University of Chicago Press, 1995), pp. 48–87

Narveson, J., 'Libertarianism vs. Marxism: Reflections on G. A. Cohen's *Self-Ownership, Freedom and Equality*', *Journal of Ethics* 2 (1998), pp. 1–26

Narveson, J., 'Egalitarianism: Partial, Counterproductive, and Baseless', in A. Mason (ed.), *Ideals of Equality* (Oxford: Blackwell, 1998), pp. 79–94

Nell, E., 'On Deserving Profits', *Ethics* 97 (1987), pp. 403–10

Nove, A., *The Economics of Feasible Socialism* (London: HarperCollins, 1991)

Nozick, R., *Anarchy, State, and Utopia* (Oxford: Blackwell, 1974)

Nozick, R., *The Examined Life* (New York: Touchstone, 1990)

Nozick, R., 'Coercion', in P. Laslett and W. Runciman (eds.), *Philosophy, Politics, and Society*, 4th series (Oxford: Blackwell, 1967), pp. 101–35

Nozick, R., 'Distributive Justice', *Philosophy and Public Affairs* 3 (1973), pp. 45–126

Nozick, R., 'On the Randian Argument', in J. Paul (ed.), *Reading Nozick* (Oxford: Blackwell, 1982), pp. 206–31

Nussbaum, M., *Sex and Social Justice* (Oxford University Press, 1999)

O'Neill, J., *The Market. Ethics, Knowledge, and Politics* (London and New York: Routledge, 1998)

O'Neill, O., 'Nozick's Entitlements', in J. Paul (ed.), *Reading Nozick* (Oxford: Blackwell, 1982), pp. 305–22

O'Neill, O., 'Rights to Compensation', *Social Philosophy and Policy* 5 (1987), pp. 73–87

Okun, A. M., *Equality and Efficiency: The Big Trade-Off* (Washington, DC: Brookings Institution, 1975)

Olsaretti, S. (ed.), *Desert and Justice* (Oxford University Press, 2003)

Olsaretti, S., 'Freedom, Force and Choice: Against the Rights-Based Definition of Voluntariness', *Journal of Political Philosophy* 6 (1998), pp. 53–78

Olsaretti, S., 'Debating Desert and Justice', in S. Olsaretti (ed.), *Desert and Justice* (Oxford University Press, 2003)

Oppenheim, F., 'Constraints on Freedom as a Descriptive Concept', *Ethics* 95 (1985), pp. 305–9

Otsuka, M., *Libertarianism Without Inequality* (Oxford University Press, 2003)

Paul, E. F., Miller, F. D., and Paul, J. (eds.), *Ethics and Economics* (Oxford: Blackwell, 1985)

Paul, J. (ed.), *Reading Nozick* (Oxford: Blackwell, 1982)

Perry, S., 'Libertarianism, Entitlement, and Responsibility', *Philosophy and Public Affairs* 26 (1997), pp. 351–95

Pettit, P., 'Rights, Constraints and Trumps', *Analysis* 47 (1987), pp. 8–14

Pettit, P., 'A Definition of Negative Liberty', *Ratio* 2 (1989), pp. 153–68

Pierson, C., *Socialism after Communism. The New Market Socialism* (Cambridge Polity, 1995)

Plant, R., *Equality, Markets and the State* (London: Fabian Society, 1984)

Pojman, L. P., 'Does Equality Trump Desert?', in L. P. Pojman and O. McLeod (eds.), *What Do We Deserve? A Reader on Justice and Desert* (Oxford University Press, 1999), pp. 283–97

Polany, K., *Origins of Our Time. The Great Transformation* (London: Victor Gollancz, 1945)

Pollock, L., *The Free Society* (Boulder, Colo.: Westview Press, 1996)

Rachels, J., 'What People Deserve', in J. Arthur and W. Shaw (eds.), *Justice and Economic Distribution* (Engelwood Cliffs, N.J.: Prentice-Hall, 1978), pp. 150–63

Radin, M. J., *Contested Commodities* (Harvard University Press, 1996)

Radin, M. J., 'Justice and the Market Domain', in J. W. Chapman and J. Roland Pennock (eds.), *Markets and Justice* (New York University Press, 1989), pp. 165–97

Rankowski, E., *Equal Justice* (Oxford University Press, 1991)

Rawls, J., *A Theory of Justice* (Oxford University Press, 1972; revised edn. 1999)

Raz, J., *The Morality of Freedom* (Oxford: Clarendon Press, 1986)

Reeve, A., *Property* (Atlantic Highlands, N.J.: Humanities Press International, 1986)

Reiman, J. H., 'The Fallacy of Libertarian Capitalism', *Ethics* 92 (1981), pp. 85–95

Richards, N., 'Luck and Desert', *Mind* 95 (1986), pp. 198–209

Riley, J., 'Justice under Capitalism', in J. W. Chapman and J. Roland Pennock (eds.), *Markets and Justice* (New York University Press, 1989), pp. 122–62

Ripstein, A., *Equality, Responsibility, and the Law* (Cambridge University Press, 1999)

Ripstein, A., 'Equality, Luck, and Responsibility', *Philosophy and Public Affairs* 23 (1994), pp. 3–23

Roemer, J., *Equality of Opportunity* (Harvard University Press, 1998)

Roemer, J., *A Future for Socialism* (Harvard University Press, 1994)

Roemer, J., 'A Challenge to Neo-Lockeanism', *Canadian Journal of Philosophy* 18 (1988), pp. 697–710

Rothbard, M., *For a New Liberty* (New York: Macmillan, 1973)

Ryan, A., 'Self-Ownership, Autonomy, and Property Rights', *Social Philosophy and Policy* 11 (1994), pp. 241–58

Ryan, C. C., 'Yours, Mine and Ours: Property Rights and Individual Liberty', in J. Paul (ed.), *Reading Nozick* (Oxford: Blackwell, 1982), pp. 323–43

Sadurski, W., *Giving Desert its Due. Social Justice and Legal Theory* (Dordrecht: D. Reidel, 1985)

Sampford, C., and Wood, D., 'Tax, Justice, and the Priority of Property', in W. Sadurski (ed.), *Ethical Dimensions of Legal Theory. Poznan Studies in the Philosophy of the Sciences and the Humanities* 23 (1991), pp. 181–208

Scanlon, T. M. 'Liberty, Contract, and Contribution', in G. Dworkin *et al.* (eds.), *Markets and Morals* (New York: Halsted Press, 1977), pp. 43–67

Scanlon, T. M., *What We Owe to Each Other* (Harvard University Press, 1998)

Scanlon, T. M., 'Nozick on Rights, Liberty, and Property', in J. Paul (ed.), *Reading Nozick* (Oxford: Blackwell, 1982), pp. 107–29

Scanlon, T. M., 'The Significance of Choice', in S. M. McMurrin (ed.), *The Tanner Lectures on Human Values* (Cambridge University Press, 1988), vol. VIII, pp. 149–216

Scheffler, S., 'Responsibility, Reactive Attitudes, and Liberalism in Philosophy and Politics', *Philosophy and Public Affairs* 21 (1992), pp. 299–323; reprinted in *Boundaries and Allegiances. Problems of Justice and Responsibility in Liberal Thought* (Oxford University Press, 2001)

Scheffler, S., 'Justice and Desert in Liberal Theory', *California Law Review* 88 (2000), pp. 965–90; reprinted in *Boundaries and Allegiances. Problems of Justice and Responsibility in Liberal Thought* (Oxford University Press, 2001)

Scheffler, S., 'Distributive Justice and Economic Desert', in S. Olsaretti (ed.), *Desert and Justice* (Oxford University Press, 2003)

Schmitz, D., 'Critical Notice on Hillel Steiner's *An Essay on Rights*', *Canadian Journal of Philosophy* 26 (1996), pp. 283–302

Schweickart, D., *Against Capitalism* (Cambridge University Press, 1993)

Scott Arnold, N., 'Capitalism and the Ethics of Contribution', *Canadian Journal of Philosophy* 15 (1985), pp. 89–105

Scott Arnold, N., 'Why Profits are Deserved', *Ethics* 97 (1987), pp. 387–402

Scott Arnold, N., 'Reply to Professor Nell', *Ethics* 97 (1987), pp. 411–13

Sen, A., *Inequality Reexamined* (Oxford: Clarendon Press, 1992)

Sen, A., 'The Moral Standing of the Market', in E. F. Paul, F. D. Miller and J. Paul (eds.), *Ethics and Economics* (Oxford: Blackwell, 1985), pp. 1–19

Sher, G., 'Compensation and Transworld Personal Identity', *The Monist* 62 (1979), pp. 378–91

Sher, G., *Desert* (Princeton University Press, 1987)

Sher, G., 'Effort, Ability and Personal Desert', *Philosophy and Public Affairs* 8 (1979), pp. 361–76

Shiffrin, S., 'Moral Autonomy and Agent-Centred Options', *Analysis* 51 (1991), pp. 244–54

Sidgwick, H., *The Methods of Ethics*, 7th edn (London: Macmillan, 1963)

Singer, P., 'Rights and the Market', in J. Arthur and W. H. Shaw (eds.), *Justice and Economic Distribution* (Englewood Cliffs, N.J.: Prentice-Hall, 1978), pp. 199–211

Slote, M. A., 'Desert, Consent, and Justice', *Philosophy and Public Affairs* 2 (1973), pp. 323–47

Smilansky, S., 'Responsibility and Desert: Defending the Connection', *Mind* 105 (1996), pp. 157–63

Smith, T., 'Review of Hillel Steiner's *An Essay on Rights*', *Philosophical Books* 37 (1996), pp. 66–8

Spiegelberg, H., 'An Argument for Equality from Compensatory Desert', in L. P. Pojman and O. McLeod (eds.), *What Do We Deserve? A Reader on Justice and Desert* (Oxford University Press, 1999), pp. 149–56

Steiner, H., *An Essay on Rights* (Oxford: Blackwell, 1994)

Steiner, H., 'The Natural Right to the Means of Production', *Philosophical Quarterly* 27 (1977), pp. 41–9

Steiner, H., 'Liberty and Equality', *Political Studies* 29 (1981), pp. 555–69

Steiner, H., 'Capitalism, Justice and Equal Starts', *Social Philosophy and Policy* 4 (1987), pp. 49–71

Steiner, H., 'Three Just Taxes', in P. Van Parijs (ed.), *Arguing for Basic Income* (London and New York: Verso, 1992), pp. 81–92

Steiner, H., 'Choice and Circumstance', in A. Mason (ed.), *Ideals of Equality* (Oxford: Blackwell, 1998), pp. 95–111

Steinfield, R. J., *The Invention of Free Labor* (Chapel Hill: University of North Carolina Press, 1991)

Steinfeld, R. J., and Engerman, S. L., 'Labor – Free or Coerced? A Historical Reassessment of Differences and Similarities', in T. Brass and M. van der Linden (eds.), *Free and Unfree Labour. The Debate Continues* (Bern: Peter Lang, 1997), pp. 11–42

Sterba, J. P., 'From Liberty to Welfare', *Ethics* 105 (1994), pp. 64–98

Strawson, P. F., 'Freedom and Resentment', *Proceedings of the British Academy* 48 (1962), pp. 1–25

Sumner, L. W., *The Moral Foundation of Rights* (Oxford University Press, 1987)

Sunstein, C. R., *Free Markets and Social Justice* (Oxford University Press, 1997)

Sunstein, C. R., 'Disrupting Voluntary Transactions', in J. W. Chapman and J. R. Pennock (eds.), *Markets and Justice* (New York University Press, 1989), pp. 279–302

Sverdlik, S., 'The Nature of Desert', *Southern Journal of Philosophy* 21 (1983), pp. 585–94

Tempkin, L. S., *Inequality* (Oxford University Press, 1993)

Thomson, J. J., *The Realm of Rights* (Harvard University Press, 1990)

Titmuss, R. M., *The Gift Relationship* (New York: Pantheon, 1971)

Trebilcock, M. J., *The Limits of Freedom of Contract* (Harvard University Press, 1993)

Ullman-Margalit, E., and Morgenbesser, S., 'Picking and Choosing', *Social Research* 44 (1977), pp. 757–85

Vallentyne, P., 'Self-Ownership and Equality: Brute Luck, Gifts, Universal Dominance, and Leximin', *Ethics* 107 (1997), pp. 321–44

Vallentyne, P., 'Critical Notice of G. A. Cohen's *Self-Ownership, Freedom, and Equality*', *Canadian Journal of Philosophy* 28 (1998), pp. 609–26

Vallentyne, P., 'Le Libertarisme de gauche et la justice', *Revue Economique* 50 (1999), pp. 859–78

Vallentyne, P., 'Left-Libertarian Theories of Justice' (unpublished manuscript, 1999)

Vallentyne, P., 'Brute Luck Equality and Desert', in S. Olsaretti (ed.), *Desert and Justice* (Oxford University Press, 2003)

Vallentyne, P., and Steiner, H. (eds.), *The Origins of Left-Libertarianism: An Anthology of Historical Writings* (London: Palgrave, 2000)

Vallentyne, P., and Steiner, H. (eds.), *Left-Libertarianism and its Critics: The Contemporary Debate* (London: Palgrave, 2000)

Van der Veen, R., and Van Parijs, P., 'Entitlement Theories of Justice', *Economics and Philosophy* 1 (1985), pp. 69–81

Van Parijs, P., *Real Freedom for All. What (if Anything) can Justify Capitalism?* (Oxford: Clarendon Press, 1995)

Waldron, J., *The Right to Private Property* (Oxford: Clarendon Press, 1988)

Walzer, M., *Spheres of Justice* (Oxford: Blackwell, 1983)

Wertheimer, A., *Coercion* (Princeton University Press, 1987)

Wiggins, D., 'Claims of Need', in D. Wiggins, *Needs, Values, Truth* (Oxford: Blackwell, 1987)

Williams, A., 'Cohen on Locke, Land, and Labour', *Political Studies* 40 (1992), pp. 51–66

Williams, B., 'Voluntary Acts and Responsible Agents', *Oxford Journal of Legal Studies* 10 (1990), pp. 1–10

Wolff, J., *Robert Nozick, Property, Justice and the Minimal State* (Cambridge: Polity, 1990)

Wolff, J., 'Freedom, Liberty, and Property', *Critical Review* 11 (1997), pp. 345–57

Wolff, J., 'Review of Hillel Steiner's *An Essay on Rights*', *International Journal of Philosophical Studies* 5 (1997), pp. 306–15

Wolff, J., 'The Dilemma of Desert', in S. Olsaretti (ed.), *Desert and Justice* (Oxford University Press, 2003)

Young, R., 'Egalitarianism and Personal Desert', *Ethics* 102 (1992), pp. 319–41

Zaitchick, A., 'On Deserving to Deserve', *Philosophy and Public Affairs* 6 (1977), pp. 370–88

Zimmerman, D., 'Coercive Wage Offers', *Philosophy and Public Affairs* 10 (1981), pp. 121–45

Index

n = footnote